D1615550

Studying Modern Arabic Literature

Mustafa Badawi, 1925–2012

Studying Modern Arabic Literature

Mustafa Badawi, Scholar and Critic

Edited by Roger Allen and Robin Ostle

EDINBURGH
University Press

© editorial matter and organisation, Roger Allen and Robin Ostle, 2015
© the chapters their several authors, 2015

Edinburgh University Press Ltd
The Tun – Holyrood Road
12 (2f) Jackson's Entry
Edinburgh EH8 8PJ
www.euppublishing.com

Typeset in 11/15 Adobe Garamond by
Servis Filmsetting Ltd, Stockport, Cheshire,
and printed and bound in Great Britain by
CPI Group (UK) Ltd, Croydon CR0 4YY

A CIP record for this book is available from the British Library

ISBN 978 0 7486 9662 8 (hardback)
ISBN 978 0 7486 9663 5 (webready PDF)
ISBN 978 1 4744 0349 8 (epub)

'This be the Verse' (p. 64) and 'To Write One Song' (p. 61) from *Collected Poems* by Philip Larkin,
edited by Anthony Thwaite, 1988, are reprinted by permission of Faber and Faber and Farrar,
Straus and Giroux.

The Editors are grateful to the Middle East Centre, St Antony's College, Oxford for meeting the
costs of the Index.

Contents

Part II The Academic Legacy

Figures

Introduction

Roger Allen and Robin Ostle

I t is no exaggeration to describe Mustafa Badawi as the father of the study of modern Arabic literature in the UK and the USA when one considers the impact of his career and his publications, followed by those of his energetic stable of doctoral students, most of whom are represented in this volume. His arrival in Oxford in 1964 as University Lecturer in modern Arabic literature was to transform the teaching of and research into this subject, which until that time had been treated as a marginal extension of classical Arabic and was very much taught as such. His lectures were a fresh and exciting invitation to consider Arabic as another literature of the modern world with a familiar range of genres and poetics fit to stand alongside and to interact with those areas of literary scholarship and criticism which had been long established in western universities. For the sake of Arabic, it was fortuitous that Badawi was trained in the University of Alexandria and in the UK in English literature: he published important work on Coleridge's Shakespearean criticism, and his engagement with Shakespearean studies remained constant throughout his career. When he was appointed to the Arabic post in Oxford, his passion for teaching, researching and translating English literature and criticism he simply applied to the modern literature of his native language, and thus began the transformation of its treatment in western academia. Badawi's arrival in Oxford also had a more subtle impact but one of far-reaching significance. The majority of academic posts in departments of Arabic and

Middle Eastern Studies in the West have typically been devoted to history, the various branches of Islamic studies and the study of the Arabic language, while centres of area studies of the Near and Middle East have understandably concentrated on the modern history and the social sciences relating to the region. Badawi's post in Oxford was the first of its kind in that university. It has not always been easy to maintain and enhance the profile of the discipline of literature in these programmes. While historians of the Islamic world would consider it unrealistic to have a single post holder covering the whole sweep of Islamic history, somehow the same sensitivity is not applied to the specialist in classical Arabic literature, or indeed to the counterpart in modern Arabic literature who may be expected to be knowledgeable about material produced from Morocco to Kuwait. When seeking to redress this imbalance in the representation of literature in our Departments of Near and Middle Eastern Studies, the prestige and reputation of Mustafa Badawi are a force to be reckoned with.

Something of the excitement and freshness of the Badawi approach can be gleaned from the early numbers of the *Journal of Arabic Literature* which he launched with his colleagues Pierre Cachia, Malcolm Lyons and John Mattock in 1970, the same year in which his *Anthology of Modern Arabic Verse* first appeared. This was – as it still is – the only scholarly journal devoted solely to Arabic literature, and it fulfilled a mission close to Badawi's heart. Alongside the scholarly articles, literary translations occupied a prominent place, and Badawi himself was a frequent contributor of these, especially with his skilful and sensitive versions of modern Arabic poetry. Critical debate was encouraged, Badawi leading the way with the notable example of his translation and critique of Shawqi's poem *Al-Hilal*, followed by the responses of his three other co-editors (Vol. II, pp. 127–42). Valuable bibliographies, lists of new publications and book reviews all added to the rich variety of the academic and literary material. While Badawi's own contributions related largely to the modern Arabic which was his professional specialism, this was by no means exclusively the case. Two articles which he published in the journal stand out in this respect: 'The Function of Rhetoric in Medieval Arabic Poetry: Abu Tammam's Ode on Amorium' (Vol. IX, pp. 43–56) and 'From Primary to Secondary Qasidas: Thoughts on the Development of Classical Arabic Poetry' (Vol. XI, pp. 1–31): here it is clear that Badawi's critical eye was more than capable of ranging over the whole of Arabic literature, especially in the realm of poetry. Scholars of classical Arabic such as Stefan Sperl or Julia Bray would be the first to acknowledge that his influence as teacher and critic was by no means confined to the literature of the modern period.

If there is any truth to the notion that behind and alongside every great scholar there may be a life-companion who provides and protects the environment within which he or she may read, interpret, contemplate and write, then Badawi was indeed blessed by the presence in his life of Mieke, his beloved wife, mother of his children and companion of his scholarly career. Once appointed to his position at Oxford, he was able to live and enjoy the life of an English country gentleman, serenely ensconced in the lovely cottage in Wheatley with its large garden. To this truly lovely place – where even the relatively short visitor was cautioned to lower his or her head – were invited Badawi's academic colleagues, friends and students (and, in his case, those separate categories were almost always combined into one), whether from his beloved Egypt or from the ever expanding coterie of specialists in the field of Arabic literature and especially modern Arabic literature in Britain, Europe and the United States, that being the academic field to which he was to contribute so much throughout his career. From that place and its extension through the life and career of an Oxford scholar – at the Oriental Institute on Pusey Lane and St Antony's College – there began and developed in both the anglophone context and beyond a discipline of modern Arabic literature studies, one that was firmly grounded in literary-critical principles, that, along with other non-Western cultural traditions, was to embark upon a challenge to the then Eurocentric norms of comparative literature studies and thereafter to assume the rightful place as a fully fledged participant in the broader realms of literature studies – writ large – that it occupies today.

This volume is arranged in two sections. Part I 'From Alexandria to Oxford' is largely biographical. It begins with the city which was such a key formative influence on that cosmopolitan culture characteristic of Badawi as individual and scholar. It goes on to draw extensively on materials from Badawi and his family relating to his childhood and education, and moves on to assessments of his intellectual and literary journey through his life as scholar, critic and translator. The chapters which make up Part II 'The Academic Legacy' are arranged in the appropriate chronological order of the materials treated by Badawi's doctoral students who have continued the mission which he began. This part concludes with a chapter by Elisabeth Kendall, a member of the next generation of scholars, a chapter which drives home the message that this literature and its study continue to have all the immediate human relevance and importance in which Mustafa Badawi himself believed so passionately.

La Lucha Continúa!

PART I
ALEXANDRIA TO OXFORD

I

The Cosmopolitan Alexandrian

Robin Ostle

M ustafa Badawi was born in 1925 in Alexandria,[1] the city in which he was to spend most of the first half of his life, initially as a school pupil in the 'Abbasiyya Secondary School and then as a member of the first cohort of students in the new University of Alexandria (then known as Faruq I University) which became an independent university in 1942 with Taha Husayn as its first Rector. After completing his doctorate in the University of London in 1954, Mustafa returned to his *alma mater* as a member of the Department of English, which he remained until his appointment in Oxford in 1964. During his youth and early manhood, Alexandria was still one of the great cosmopolitan port cities of the Mediterranean region, sharing many of the characteristics of its counterparts such as Beirut, Tunis and Algiers. But when the troops of Napoleon Bonaparte disembarked there in 1798, they found little more than a small crumbling seaside town of probably no more than some eight thousand inhabitants far removed from the magnificent city of the historical imagination. Yet, by the end of the nineteenth century, Alexandria was one of the most dramatic examples of that urban expansion which was characteristic of the Mediterranean port cities during this period: the number of its inhabitants has been estimated at 180,000 in 1865, and by the end of the century this figure had reached at least half a million.[2]

The vibrant oil painting by the Alexandrian artist Muhammad Nagi (1888–1956) depicts the Mahmudiyya Canal (Fig.1.1). This was a vital

Figure 1.1 Muhammad Nagi: *The Mahmudiyya Canal.* Photo Robin Ostle

feature of life in Alexandria during the youth and adolescence of Mustafa Badawi, and there are references to it in the fiction of his distinguished contemporary Edwar al-Kharrat.[3] Today within the confines of the city the canal is almost impossible to see, unusued, overgrown and its waters mainly invisible. During the childhood of Badawi and al-Kharrat its banks were pleasant promenades; it teemed with the boats, the people and the produce which went to and fro between the western port and the Delta which lay to the south and east. It was also a popular destination for pleasure trips on the water. But more significantly the Mahmudiyya Canal was the first major infrastructural project which had enabled the dramatic development and expansion of Alexandria throughout the nineteenth century from the inauspicious site discovered by the French troops in 1798.[4] Work began on the construction and dredging of the canal in 1819, and over the next twenty years some twenty thousand workers were involved in this massive project which extended all the way from the town of al-Mahmudiyya on the Rosetta branch of the Nile to the western port of Alexandria. With its tortuous winding course and relatively shallow depth (2.7 metres), the canal was a fundamental component in the development of the city: it was a source of fresh water for irrigation and human consumption; above all it was the principal conduit for commercial traffic from the Delta to the western port and vice versa. Thus the isolation from its hinterland from which Alexandria had suffered was broken, and it was established as the first port of Egypt. While the rail links which were laid down in 1851–8 between Cairo, Alexandria and Suez gave further impetus to the traffic to and from the port,[5] the Mahmudiyya Canal remained a vital artery until the Second World War, especially for agricultural produce. Both the Canal and the Port City were to become key components in the military strategy of Muhammad 'Ali (ruled 1805–48) when in the 1830s the newly established western port became the base of his naval arsenal and the city took on something of the character of a garrison town.[6]

Robert Ilbert distinguishes three phases in the development of nineteenth-century Alexandria:[7] (1) the revival of the port driven initially by the strategic priorities of Muhammad 'Ali 1820–40; (2) the growth of the city as a major commercial centre 1860–70, with the cotton boom, the opening of the Suez Canal and the increasing integration of Egypt into the colonial economies of Western Europe; (3) the rise of Alexandria as a magnet for Mediterranean cosmopolitan communities creating a city which was a credible candidate to stage the Olympic Games on the eve of the First World War and which in the 1920s and 1930s described itself as 'The Bride of the Mediterranean'.[8]

This third phase was defined by two dates in particular: 1890, the date of the foundation of the Municipality of Alexandria through which the foreign communities of the city began to accumulate rights and legal statuses not unlike those of a city state; and 1937, the date of the Montreux Convention by which the capitulations relating to such foreign communities were to be phased out.[9] It is relevant that this phase corresponds to the end of Empire (the Ottoman) and the rise of the new nation state, a period complicated as it was by the British Occupation (from 1882) and the imposition of the Protectorate during the First World War. The great cities of the Mediterranean such as Alexandria became poles of attraction, not only because of the commercial opportunities which they offered but also because they became havens from the conflicts of nineteenth-century Europe and those which accompanied the disintegration of the Ottoman Empire. Thus was created an urban tissue of Armenians, Greeks, Italians, French,

Maltese, Spanish and significant numbers of the Syro-Lebanese diaspora.[10] In Alexandria in 1907, there were fourteen non-Muslim communities; through their consulates they had access to a significant range of legal and social privileges.[11] Of course the vast majority of the city's inhabitants were Egyptian, but the character of the city was influenced profoundly by the presence of these Mediterranean communities, and, particularly at the upper levels of society, prominent Egyptians – Muslim, Coptic and Jewish – were very much part of this cosmopolitan elite, moving in the same social circles and conversing in the most common *lingua franca* – French.

The early stages of the rise of modern Arabic literature owed much to authors who were associated with Alexandria but whose roles within the historical context of that city has not hitherto been a particular preoccupation of scholars in the field.[12] In this respect one might quote names such as Adib Ishaq (1856–84), Najib al-Haddad (1867–99), one of the founders of *Al-Ahram*, Salim Taqla (1849–92), Isma'il Sabri (1854–1923), Khalil Mutran (1872–1949), 'Abd al-Rahman Shukri (1886–1958) and Ahmad Zaki Abu Shadi (1892–1955). Also prominent in the late nineteenth and early twentieth century were Alexandrian authors who wrote in French, Italian or Greek, such as Georges Zananiri (1863–1956), Michel de Zogheb (1886–1964), Enrico Pea (1881–1958), to say nothing of Constantine Cavafy (1863–1933) or Guiseppe Ungaretti (1888–1970). Most of these authors have a place in the history of their respective literatures, but until the ground-breaking work of Elena Chiti there has been no consistent attempt to situate them alongside their Arab counterparts in the common Alexandrian urban context which they shared. Interestingly, the Alexandrian authors 'Abdullah al-Nadim (1854–96) and Mahmud Bayram al-Tunisi (1893–1961), who identified with the more popular sectors of society rather than the social elites, also had their social counterparts in the Italian writers Guiseppe and Matteo Marchi (1810–90 and 1844–1918) and Pea.[13]

When Mustafa Badawi was born in 1925, Egypt was at the beginning of its turbulent period as a constitutional monarchy in which the competing interests of the Palace, the political parties and the British regularly undermined the progress of the country's 'liberal experiment'. It was inevitable that the new nation state would eventually exert increasing control over the virtual autonomies which had developed within the Municipality of Alexandria, but this was not a sudden or dramatic process. Even though the Montreux Convention signalled the end of the Capitulations, the practical impact of this was designed to spread over a twelve-year period of transition from 1937 to 1949.[14] Thus the cultural mixity of writers and artists which had flourished in Alexandria since the late nineteenth century was very much present during Badawi's youth and adolescence. For example, the Atelier of Alexandria was founded in 1934 by the painter Muhammad Nagi and the francophone author Gaston Zananiri, who was born in Alexandria in 1904.[15] The proclaimed mission of the Atelier was to bring together artists and writers of different national origins and language to practise and promote their art through readings, lectures, concerts and exhibitions. Although Badawi himself was in no sense born into the social elites of his native city, nevertheless as a culturally voracious university student he and his contemporaries of similar social origin were able to take full advantage of the bookshops, bars, theatres, cinemas, exhibitions and concerts which were so much part of the life of cosmopolitan Alexandria (see Chapter 3, p. 39 and p. 41).

One of the most influential Alexandrian personalities on the young

Figure 1.2 *The Bee Kingdom*. Abu Shadi's Villa at 60 Rue Menasce, Alexandria. Photo courtesy of Joy Garnett

Badawi was Ahmad Zaki Abu Shadi (1892–1955), who was appointed Professor of Bacteriology and Deputy Dean of the Medical Faculty in the new university in 1942. After his return from England in 1922 where he had completed his medical studies, Abu Shadi worked in a variety of hospitals in Port Sa'id, Alexandria and Cairo, but he was to make a base for himself and his family in Alexandria in the spacious villa at 60 Rue Menasce (Fig. 1.2) where as a student Badawi had the privilege of access to Abu Shadi's rich library. Distinguished scientist though he was, Abu Shadi is best known for his contribution to Arabic poetry in the Romantic period, in 1932 founding and editing *Apollo*, a journal devoted entirely to Arabic literature (especially poetry) and the arts.[16] He also set up the Apollo society, the mission of which was to promote the cause of literature and the arts and to create links between writers both within and beyond Egypt. Abu Shadi's literary criticism was notable for its judiciously balanced judgements, avoiding the acerbic and highly confrontational styles of contemporaries such as 'Abbas Mahmud al-'Aqqad or Ibrahim 'Abd al-Qadir al-Mazini. Although Badawi was to identify with those poets who, like himself, broke away from the classical conventions of rhyme and metre in Arabic poetry after 1948, he always recognised the considerable achievements of the Arab Romantics, along with some of their limitations.[17] In this he was more broad-minded than many critics and poets of his generation who tended to understate the value of Arabic poetry written before 1950.

If one leafs through the collections of poetry by Abu Shadi published in the 1920s and 1930s, as well as the numbers of the *Apollo* review itself, one is immediately struck by the Mediterranean cosmopolitanism of his cultural mission. The covers of *Apollo* depict the Greek god of the sun and the patron of poetry and music, alongside other figures drawn from Greek mythology. Other *diwans* from the period – *Al-Shafaq al-baki* (1927), *Ashi'a wa zilal* (1931), *Atyaf al-rabi'* (1933), *Al-Yanbu'* (1934) – display a wide range of iconographic material drawn from ancient Greece, the Bible, Pharaonic Egypt, the art of the European Renaissance and occasionally contemporary Egyptian art. Translations from French and English poetry are numerous, alongside reproductions of paintings by European artists. In a significant number of the illustrations, representations of the nude female figure are displayed prominently.[18] The principal characteristics which stand out from Abu Shadi's life and writings are a belief that poetry (and literature generally) is essentially a pursuit of truth over the whole range of human thought and experience, a quality which it shares with science. At the same time, the poet and his poetry must be firmly rooted in their society, and not estranged from it. As well as spanning the barriers between different areas of artistic activity such as literature, painting and music, Abu Shadi also believed in the commonalities between literature, philosophy and science.[19] This is something in the nature of a template for the subsequent intellectual development of Mustafa Badawi.

The great Alexandrian painters Mahmud Saʿid (1897–1963) and Muhammad Nagi (1888–1956) are precious sources of beguiling images of social life in the city between the two World Wars. The emancipated bathing beauties on the beach (Fig.1.3) give a sense of the life of ease and leisure available to those above a certain social level, while the good life depicted in

Figure 1.3 Mahmud Saʿid: *Women Bathing*. Photo Robin Ostle

Figure 1.4 Mahmud Saʿid: *On the Dance Floor*. Photo Robin Ostle

the canvas *On the Dance Floor* (Fig.1.4) displays aspects of human existence which were valued by Badawi throughout his own career. But it was the co-founder of the Atelier of Alexandria, Muhammad Nagi, who produced the most complete iconographic statement of the cosmopolitan nature of the city and its culture: this was his enormous mural *School of Alexandria*.[20] The finished version measures 8 by 3 metres and is displayed in the main meeting hall of the Governorate of the city. At around the same time as Taha Husayn published *Mustaqbal al-thaqafa fi Misr* (1938), a book which has much in common with the themes of this painting, Nagi began work on a number of preliminary studies, one of which in oil is reproduced here (Fig. 1.5). Throughout the next ten years the artist worked at various times on the project before the final mural was completed. The title of the work is a reference by Nagi to one of the frescos by Raphael in the Stanza della Segnatura in the Vatican, *School of Athens*. The background of the painting is dominated

Figure 1.5 Muhammad Nagi: *School of Alexandria* (Preliminary Study). Photo Robin Ostle

by the statue of Alexander the Great, the founder of the city, while the central foreground shows St Catherine of Alexandria. On one side of St Catherine, Archimedes hands the heritage of Greek civilisation on to Ibn Rushd on the other, while these figures in the centre are flanked by Egyptian and European writers, artists and intellectuals. In the completed mural in the Governorate, although not in the study displayed here, Ungaretti – with whom Nagi had attended the Swiss School in Alexandria – and Cavafy are depicted amongst the Europeans, and the Egyptian side includes Muhammad 'Abduh, the sculptor Mahmud Mukhtar, Ahmad Lutfi al-Sayyid and Taha Husayn. Even the architectural details are a mixture of the ancient and the modern, as the Pharos said to have been built by the Ptolemaic architect Sostratus towers over the waterfront of the eastern port.

This was Nagi's vision of the historical and the contemporary cultural fabric of the city in which Mustafa Badawi was born, and the nature of this vision was shared by the latter throughout his subsequent career. The young Badawi's Egyptian models were Ahmad Zaki Abu Shadi, Ibrahim Nagi (the

Romantic poet and vice-President of *Apollo*), Taha Husayn and the critic Muhammad Mandur, all of whom were to feature in his subsequent teaching and research. Theirs was an inclusive, pluralistic view of the components of Egyptian culture, which for them was an essentially Mediterranean culture. Of course Arabic and Islam are its predominant contemporary components, but in their view the Pharaohs, Greece, Rome, Judaism, Christianity and modern Europe have all contributed to the rich texture that is Egypt and the Egyptians. This broad cosmopolitan view of culture and its related activities inspired Mustafa Badawi throughout his career, and made him an inspiration to colleagues and students alike.

Notes

1. My information on the history of Alexandria in the nineteenth century is taken from the magistral work of Robert Ilbert, *Alexandrie 1830–1930*, Vols I and II, Cairo: Institut Français d'Archéologie Orientale, 1996. For the French reactions on landing in Alexandria in 1798, see pp. xxiii–xxiv.
2. Robert Ilbert, 'De Beyrouth à Alger: la fin d'un ordre urbain', *Vingtième Siècle* 32, 1991, pp. 15–24.
3. See for example, the beginning of the opening chapter of Edwar al-Kharrat's novel *Turabuha za'faran*, Beirut: Dar al-Adab, 1991.
4. Ilbert, *Alexandrie 1830–1930*, pp. 15–16.
5. Ibid., pp. 35–6.
6. Ibid., pp. 18–20.
7. Ibid., pp. 17ff.
8. Ibid., p. xxvii.
9. Elena Chiti, 'Ecrire à Alexandrie (1879–1949): capital social, appartenances, mémoire.' Doctoral Thesis, University of Aix-Marseille and Università Ca'Foscari di Venezia. December 1913, p. 45.
10. Robin Ostle, 'Alexandria: A Mediterranean Cosmopolitan Center of Cultural Production', in Leila Tarazi Fawaz and C. A. Bayly (eds), *Modernity and Culture from the Mediterranean to the Indian Ocean*, New York: Columbia University Press, 2002, pp. 314–29.
11. Ilbert, 'De Beyrouth à Alger', p. 19.
12. This was largely the case until the ground-breaking work of Elena Chiti appeared ('Ecrire à Alexandrie 1879–1930'). The particular originality of this research is that it studies Arab and non-Arab authors within the common Alexandrian

urban context which they shared. My information on the non-Arab Alexandrian authors is drawn from this source. See also the book by Hala Halim, *Alexandrian Cosmopolitanism: An Archive*, New York: Fordham University Press, 2013.

13. Chiti, 'Ecrire à Alexandrie', p. 122.

14. Ibid., p. 45.

15. Ibid., pp. 147ff.

16. Robin Ostle, 'The *Apollo* Phenomenon', *Literary Innovation in Modern Arabic Literature. Schools and Journals*, Special number of *Quaderni di Studi Arabi* 18, 2000, pp. 73–84.

17. See in particular chapter 4 of M. M. Badawi, *A Critical Introduction to Modern Arabic Poetry*, Cambridge: Cambridge University Press, 1975.

18. Some of these illustrations are reproduced in Robin Ostle, 'The *Apollo* Phenomenon', pp. 81–4.

19. Robin Ostle, 'Modern Egyptian Renaissance Man', *Bulletin of the School of Oriental and African Studies*, University of London, LVII:I (1994), p. 91.

20. For a discussion of this work, see Robin Ostle, 'Muhammad Nagi 1888–1956' in *Mediterraneans* 8/9 (Fall 1996), pp. 168–73.

2

Muhammad Mustafa Badawi in Conversation

Abdul-Nabi Isstaif

(In 1997, Abdul-Nabi Isstaif conducted an extensive interview with Mustafa Badawi which has not previously been published. We reproduce here the sections relating to Mustafa's early life and education until 1947 when he was sent to England to pursue further studies in English. Professor Isstaif, who has translated the text from the Arabic, hopes to publish the interview in full in 2015.)

ANS: May we begin with the years of your early formation in the family, the neighbourhood and your various schools in Alexandria?

MMB: I was born in the city of Alexandria in Egypt in the year 1925 in a popular quarter. We were a middle-class family, for my mother used to own a flat in the quarter with my grandmother. I grew up in that flat as the only male child among seven children: four elder sisters and two younger than me. My father had a modest education, for he was a craftsman working as a contractor (*muqawil*), and he did not have a great interest in the education of his children. However, my mother, though she herself had also had a modest education, was the opposite of my father, owing to the fact that she was descended from a family in which most men were religious scholars. So, she took care of my education and that of my sisters, enduring great financial difficulties in the process since education was not free at the time. In fact she insisted that the girls complete their studies in the School for Women Teachers in the al-Wardian quarter: this required a special uniform including a hat which led the children of the quarter to tease them about their outfits when they came back from the school. The school authorities would not allow the girls to leave on their own at the end of the school week. Hence my grandmother had to go to the school to accompany them at mid-day on Thursday of every week. She used to take me as a child to school, and among the most beautiful memories of my childhood is of that trip on the tram with my grandmother wearing the most beautiful clothes, a trip to which I used to look forward every week. My mother believed in the need to educate girls, so that they could work as teachers in order to earn their living in case of a failed marriage or lack of marriage in the first place. At that time teaching was the only respectable profession available for Egyptian women. There is no doubt that this thinking on my mother's part was progressive and ahead of its time; the reason for that may have been her own marriage, which was not as problem-free as it seemed at the time.

I was not allowed to play with the children of the quarter in the alley: my playing space was confined to the balcony of our flat on the upper floor of the house. Naturally I sometimes used to ignore the instructions of my mother and grandmother. I would go down to the alley and join the children in their games until I saw my oldest sister, who had started working as a teacher, coming back from school. Then I would return to the flat and the balcony, behaving as if I had been playing there all the time. No doubt this restricted childhood had its impact on me, for it made me introverted, always embarrassed to join in groups. However being forced to play on my own all the time led to the development of my imagination, and I used to invent whatever means were necessary to pass the time, including browsing through the coloured pictures in my sisters' books.

I grew up in Alexandria and studied in its institutes, initially in a *kuttab*, where I learned the principles of reading, writing, arithmetic and parts of the Qur'an. However, I have a rather vague memory of this period of my education. When I was seven, my mother decided that I should go to the Khedive 'Abbas elementary school, rather than the compulsory free state school. At that time, the elementary school led to qualification for secondary school and subsequently for entering university. My experience at this school had a decisive impact on my cultural future. Elementary school at the time was of great importance, for, after one had gained the elementary certificate after four years of education, society used to consider graduates of these schools as being 'cultured' individuals, and even qualified to take a government position. The ages of the pupils in school were varied, for I remember that I had with me in the fourth year, when I was only eleven years old, a pupil who was married. I excelled in all subjects, and the school had a board of honour on which each month the name of the best student would be written at the end of the month after an exam, and this would remain until the end of the year. This of course provoked some students to threaten me, and I was only saved from their bullying by my friend and competitor who was, unlike me, tall, for I was the smallest pupil in the class. After that we became friends. My literary inclination appeared at an early age. Children's literature was not available at that time, so the teacher of Arabic at the school wrote a story, printed it and distributed it among us. I read it eagerly and decided to imitate it. So I wrote a story of my own composition illustrated with pictures just like my teacher's story. I do not know what happened to this story; I do not even remember its title.

My passion for reading started then, and I read countless novels from *The Pocket Novel Series* which used to publish popular translations of novels, most of which were detective stories. I used to hide them under the school books on my desk, fearing that my older sister, the teacher, would see them. She used to supervise my education, and reading novels was not one of the things which teachers or society would encourage children to do. In the same elementary school, my passion for English also started, for the teacher of English in the final year was a truly excellent teacher, encouraging me so much that I become fond of him and started dreaming of becoming a teacher of English just like him when I grew up. One day, my father was sitting in his café as usual when a friend of his presented him with a copy of the magazine *Al-Lata'if al-musawwara*. He was surprised when he saw my photo in the magazine which had been published because I was the youngest of the talented pupils who had been awarded the elementary certificate in Egypt that year. This was the only time in my life, as far as I remember, that my father said anything related to my studies.

In 1938, I moved to al-'Abbasiyya Secondary School during its golden period. The school and its Director enjoyed a high status in Alexandria and its community. In this school I established friendships which I have maintained until now with a number of students who happened to excel later in various fields of knowledge, arts and literature. The school was in a beautiful location; it was built on a hill covered with vegetation and had a large garden with meadows and flower beds. It consisted of three large buildings, beautifully designed and decorated, containing the teaching halls, teachers' rooms and administration. My lifelong friend Edwar al-Kharrat, who was my contemporary in al-'Abbasiya School, described it in several of his writings, particularity in his story 'al-Zujaj al-Mutawahhij Naran', which was published in *al-Hilal* magazine in February 1994. In al-'Abbasiyya School I joined the Al-Tadhhibiyya Society, a religious group that advocated commitment to the teaching of Islam and upright morals. Then I joined the poetry society as I had been composing poetry since I was twelve. I read many of the Arabic heritage books in the school library and in the municipal library of Alexandria. Once, when I was thirteen years old, I found in the school library a book containing selections of English poetry entitled *The Dragon Book of English Verse*. Despite the difficulty I found in reading it because of my lack of knowledge of English at the time, the book was a window that opened on to a completely new imaginative world, since my reading of poetry until then had been confined to Arabic poetry. The poems I used to write were based on the poetry I read, poems by al-Mutanabbi and Shawqi in particular. At this same stage of my adolescence, I started reading the *Apollo* magazine and began to be influenced by the romantic poetry which it published. I also fell under the spell of Jubran Khalil Jubran. As for intellectual matters, the book by Taha Husayn *Qudat al-fikr* (by chance I found a copy of it in our house) had the greatest impact on my thinking, liberating me from traditional hidebound thought and leading me to other types of reflection and philosophy. This happened when I was a student at secondary school – a stage which determined my literary and intellectual inclinations, a time when I was to be influenced by my friendship with three colleagues of similar tendencies, namely Edwar al-Kharrat, Sami Mahmud 'Ali and Muhammad 'Abd al-Mu'ti-Qadal. They all excelled in their studies and later became distinguished in their own fields. Edwar al-Kharrat became one of our greatest and most original writers, while Sami Mahmud 'Ali became one of the most distinguished psychologists in

France and a founder of psychopathic medicine. As for ʿAbd al-Muʿti-Qadal, he excelled in both English and Arabic and, even though his native tongue was the Nubian language, he specialised in English literature, and gained a doctorate from the University of Glasgow, returning to Egypt to teach at the University of Alexandria. The three of us were in continuous discussion about various intellectual and literary issues, each of us showing the others his writing, be it poetry or prose. Each one had his own particular brand of poetic composition, either traditional poetry or what used to be called at that time 'prose poetry'. This last form, in fact, was the most favoured by Sami Mahmud ʿAli, who wrote his philosophical reflections in it as he was fascinated by philosophy. He was also, and still is, a gifted painter. We used to improvise traditional poetry and exchange what we used to call jokingly *al-shiʿr al-halamantishi*, of which Edwar al-Kharrat, may God forgive him, published a sample in one of his stories.

There is no doubt that the greatest influence on my thinking at that time were the philosophical reflections of my friend Sami, his interest in the spiritual life in the widest meaning of the term and his passion for painting and European music. My appreciation of painting and music began then, and would later strengthen and develop considerably.

We were very fortunate in our early education, for al-ʿAbbasiyya Secondary School was full of many truly excellent teachers. The teacher of Arabic in my second year there was ʿAbd al-ʿAziz Sayyid al-Ahl, a gifted traditional poet who used to encourage me to write poetry. The teacher of history in the third year, as I remember, tried to develop in his pupils the talent of research and writing. He asked a number of us to write historical papers on Alexandria, which covered several aspects of what is now called 'social history' and which he collected at the end of the academic year and published as a book, composed of our writings. As for the teacher of Arabic in the final year, he was a turbaned Azharite shaykh. Yet he was a first-class educationist, who had an infallible intuition about the psychology of every individual, as if he was well aware of the most recent theories of educational psychology. He was keen on maintaining the values of the heritage, for the Arabic language in his view was not merely an instrument or a tool for expression or mere vocabulary. Rather it represented civilisational values. He would be displeased if one of us used in a composition an expression of revolutionary aesthetic content such as 'illuminating darkness', since he considered this a type of contradiction that should be eliminated. The universe, according to his classical conventions, cannot combine these opposing notions. It is either light or darkness. The commitment of some of these teachers to their subjects, and their belief in their profession, was of the highest degree. I remember that the teacher of natural science quarrelled with me when I told him that I had decided in the following year to join the literature section, for he wanted me to study his subject, which was science. The art teacher was the painter Salah Tahir, who later became one of the most distinguished artists in Egypt. In fact, his painting class was an occasion for the discussion of what used to be considered, for us, new philosophical and intellectual questions such as Darwin's theory of evolution. Among his quotations, which he kept repeating to us, and which I would never forget, was that 'stealing in aesthetics is legitimate', a morally dangerous principle, although it had its own attractions for the young. Circumstances brought us together a quarter of a century later in the al-Ahram Building in Cairo, in the office of Najib Mahfuz or Tawfiq al-Hakim (I cannot remember exactly which one). When I reminded him of this quotation, shyness forced him to deny it. The teacher of French in the final year was the Swiss Mr Fichter, who was a distinguished figure in the cultural life of Alexandria, and the owner and editor of *Le Journal Suisse de l'Egypte*. He played a significant role in the city's social services. We developed a spiritual bond, and he made available his private library of French literature for me to borrow whatever I liked, a habit which developed my interest in French literature as far as I was able at the time. I used to consider him rather like my godfather. It is worth mentioning here that, when the University of Alexandria was established, Mr Fichter was appointed a lecturer in the Department of French, a real indication that he was fully qualified to be a university teacher.

The Second World War broke out while I was a pupil at the al-ʿAbbasiyya Secondary School. The German army led by Rommel advanced in the Western Desert and was able to threaten Alexandria, a situation which led to the migration of its inhabitants to the countryside because of the German and Italian air raids which used to occur sometimes four or five times in one night. My family left for Damanhur, and it was decided that I would go to the Damanhur Secondary School. However, when I realised that the

School had only the two sections of mathematics and science, and since I had decided to enrol in the literature section, I insisted on my decision with all the stubbornness of youth. I forced the family to go back to Alexandria despite the danger of the air raids, in order to avail myself of the opportunity to follow the specialisation I wanted. Until today I still feel some guilt at my selfishness caused by the enthusiasm of youth, but in the literature section at al-ʿAbbasiyya Secondary School, I was able to study philosophy, logic and psychology in a systematic and organised manner, in addition to literature and language.

ANS: The University of Alexandria was just beginning. Yet it was known for its openness and the participation of both Egyptian and foreign professors in teaching the small numbers of students. Could you talk about the subjects you chose to study, the courses you followed, the teachers who influenced you, the friendships you built then with fellow students and with teachers, the extra-curricular activities you had, and the beginnings of your creative and scholarly writings? In short, could you chart your cultural formation during this crucial period of your life in your beloved city?

MMB: When I finished the secondary stage of my education and the result of the national exam was announced, I realised that I had come first in Egypt, a distinction which gave me the right to study at the university with the minimum of expenses, so I joined the English Language Department in the Faculty of Letters at Alexandria University, which was then known as Faruq I University. It was established in 1942, the year in which I completed my secondary education, so I was a member of the first year to be admitted to the newly established university. It was a really curious coincidence that initially, before the University of Alexandria had its own buildings, it occupied the buildings of al-ʿAbbasiyya Secondary School, assigning each of the three buildings to one of the Faculties. The first was the Faculty of Letters; the second was the Faculty of Law; and the third was the Faculty of Science. Thus moving from the secondary stage to the university stage of my education did not mean any change in the location of my study. And my admission to the Faculty of Letters at the University limited the space for my studies to one building of the three, while I had shuttled freely among them when I was a secondary school pupil. Soon this building was transformed into something akin to a sacred place, because of the mere existence there of the teachers whom we venerated. The first Rector of the University was Taha Husayn. It was enough for me to see the Professor of Philosophy Yusuf Karam, with his 'dignified bearing' and modesty, walking lightly in the corridor of the Faculty on his way to the lecture hall to feel the respect and reverence for this institution in which a teacher like him was working.

I decided to specialise in English language in order to deepen my study of English literature so that I could see our Arabic literature in the wider context of world literature. In this way my outlook would not be confined by narrow local boundaries. I did that despite the attempt of some of the teachers of the Department of Arabic to change my mind in response to their desire for me to join their Department, for I had the highest grade in Arabic language in the Special Secondary Exam (al-tawjihiyya) in Egypt. The University at that time, despite its recent origin, or rather the Faculty of Letters, was experiencing its golden age. The number of students was extremely limited and all of them had entered the Faculty of their own free will, and not because they did not get the appropriate grades to qualify them for the Faculty of Medicine or Engineering, but because they had a genuine interest in the subject in which they intended to specialise. So my friend Sami joined the Department of Philosophy while my friend al-Qadal joined me in the Department of English. My friend Muhammad Zaki al-ʿAshmawi entered the Department of Arabic while Edwar al-Kharrat opted to join the Faculty of Law, following in the footsteps of Tawfiq al-Hakim, who had a profound influence on him at that time. The number of students in some departments was fewer than the number of teachers. In my class for example, the number of students in the English Department was six, taught by seven or eight teachers who used to divide us for tutorials into two groups. The students of philosophy in that year were three in number: Abu al-Ula ʿAfifi taught Islamic mysticism and logic, ʿAli al-Nashshar and Tawfiq al-Tawil taught Islamic philosophy, while Thabit al-Fandi and Najib Baladi taught modern European philosophy and methodology. Yusuf Karam taught ancient and medieval philosophy, and Mustafa Zuwair taught psychology. Most of them had international reputations and were among the most distinguished teachers in their subjects. In addition to the Arab teachers, a French existentialist philosopher who became prominent in the history of French philosophy, Jean Grenier, used to teach the students of French (I met recently a Professor of Philosophy at Oxford University who told me that he was writing a book on him), while John Wisdom, who later became a professor at the University of London, used to teach in the English Department. The students in those departments had to write their examinations in the courses of these two teachers in French and English. Latin was a compulsory subject, and anyone who wanted to obtain their BA or *Licence* with Honours had to take an exam in ancient Greek. This interest in Greek and Latin was due to Taha Husayn's belief in the necessity of mastering the classical foundations of European civilisation, so he made Latin compulsory in all departments of the Faculty. In the first year of study, every student at that time had to study, in addition to the subject of their specialization, the other subjects of the Faculty such as languages, history, and geography, in order to acquire a degree of general culture. This was to gain an idea about the study of these subjects at university level, a deep systematic study different from the experience of study in the secondary schools which used to depend to a large extent on learning by rote. As a result of that, the University was a genuine university, and the Faculty was a genuine faculty. Students experienced all branches of knowledge available to them at the Faculty, and each one would know the rest of their fellow students, and they would educate each other through reading and discussion. Every student had to carry out extended research on the subject of their specialisation, and we often used to read these research papers which were written by our colleagues on their various subjects in the other departments.

In my first year at university (1942) I had several experiences which had a decisive impact on my life. The first was my friendship with my female colleague, the writer Safiyya Abu Shadi, the daughter of the great poet Dr Ahmad Zaki Abu Shadi. Through her, I met her father and made use of his extensive library, which was full of books on European and English literature in particular. I used sometimes to meet his friend, the poet Dr Ibrahim Naji. I also used to meet Dr Muhammad Mandur, who was teaching at the Department of Arabic in the Faculty of Letters, and who supervised the poetry group to which I belonged. The second experience was getting to know one of the teachers in the Department of English, the novelist and critic Robert Liddell, who chose me as a member of his literary society. We used to meet in his house once a month, and one of us would present a paper on English literature. My first paper, while I was in the first year, was on the poet Shelley, of whom I was fond at that time; I knew a great deal of his poetry by heart. I owe to Professor Liddell my awareness of the existence of great poets other than the Romantics, particularly the Metaphysical poets. In this society, a deep friendship developed between me and the gifted poet Muhammad Munir Ramzi, who three years later took his life at the age of twenty as a result of a violent emotional shock. We used to exchange books, discuss what we read and what we wrote. As for the third experience it was hearing another English teacher, William Blainey, reciting for us some verses from *The Waste Land* by T. S. Eliot. This had a magical impact on me. After that, and for many years, I became a prisoner of T. S. Eliot, and, because I was not able to buy the book which included this long poem, I copied it into a notebook and learned several sections of it by heart so that some of my colleagues used to call me T. S. Badawi. I owe so much to the English teacher William Blainey; he was extremely sensitive in his reading of English poetry, and in his criticism he used to analyse texts in great depth and detail, an indication that he was influenced by the school of I. A. Richards and his followers. He used to encourage me to write poetry in English, and praised my attempts. He even once offered one of my English poems to my colleagues to be analysed and criticised. I started writing poetry in English in order to express things which at the time I imagined to be difficult or almost impossible to express in Arabic. I did not continue on this road because I realised after a while that it is not easy to produce a great deal of good poetry in a language other than one's mother tongue. On the other hand, my sense of the inability of the Arabic language to express poetically the preoccupations of modern people as a result of the dominance of its classical rhetoric and romantic style became the greatest incentive for me to attempt to change this style and even to revolutionise it, rather than to escape from the problem and resort to writing in another language. Only in this way would Arabic become qualified to express the experiences of the modern age.

In the very first year of my university education, my interest in French literature, which had started earlier in the last stage of my secondary education, developed and became more serious, particularly through the poetry of Baudelaire and the Symbolists, who influenced my poetry at this stage.

Consequently, I never thought of publishing any of my poems in any literary magazine because I was certain that the experimental tendency of my poetry would make its acceptance for publication impossible in the magazines current at the time. Also at that time I got to know two colleagues from the Department of Philosophy, who became two of my closest friends and who had a deep impact on my thinking: Mustafa Safwan, later one of the pillars of the structural school of psychoanalysis who translated into Arabic Sigmund Freud's *The Interpretation of Dreams*; and ʿAbd al-Hamid Sabra, who studied at London University with the great philosopher of science and methodology Karl Popper. After a period of teaching at Alexandria University, Sabra went to England, and then to the United States, where he was appointed to the Chair of the History of Arabic Science at Harvard University.

At that time, partly as a result of the ongoing Second World War, the students of the University were extremely fortunate in that a number of the most prominent European intellectuals and writers (mostly English and French) came to Egypt, either as visitors or temporary residents, in order to give lectures to the Allied officers and soldiers. In Cairo, a group of English poets published a literary magazine entitled *Personal Landscape*. Among the writers who lived for a while in Egypt were the two novelists Olivia Manning and Lawrence Durrell, the author of *The Alexandria Quartet*. As for the French, the most prominent among them were André Gide, and the great critic René Etiemble, who published his magazine *Valeurs*. I remember that his lectures at the Faculty of Letters in Alexandria, particularly on the writers of eighteenth-century France, were among the most important events in the cultural life of the city. Prominent English writers and professors used to come to Alexandria to give lectures at the University or at the British Council. Thus, we –the students – had the opportunity to listen to many European writers and intellectuals. Beyond the University, Alexandria was full of cultural activities, lectures, seminars and theatre performances, while concerts were organised by the French Friendship Society, and the British Council. The Cultural Circle also used to organise concerts. We learned later that it was run by the communists in Egypt, the majority of whom were foreigners. These cultural activities were not limited to European culture, for Arabic cultural life also flourished. In addition to many distinguished personalities such as Dr Abu Shadi and Dr Muhammad Mandur, there were many unofficial cultural evenings outside the university sponsored by cultural circles and held in the cafés of Alexandria. Some of these were led by the Bohemian writer Mustafa al-Nashshar, who was among the first to translate Dostoyevsky (he published *Crime and Punishment* in a popular edition in the early twentieth century). He used to be surrounded by Alexandrian poets such as ʿAbd al-Halim al-Qabbani, Mahmud al-Bashbeshi, Kamal Nashʾat and myself.

This cultural openness was the most important characteristic of Alexandria at the time, giving me the opportunity to get acquainted with most modernist European literary and intellectual movements. For example, some professors in the Department of Philosophy, both Egyptian and European, held special seminars on existentialism to which they invited students such as myself: that was in 1945–6 as far as I can remember. I got to know the work of Freud, the founder of psychoanalysis, through my friend Sami Mahmud ʿAli, and read the writing of the Egyptian surrealists such as Ramsis Yunan. I also read the novels of Albert Qusayri, written in French, which were closer to socialist realism in their depiction of Egyptian society and the proletariat than any other novels written in Arabic at that time. I was astonished when I went to England on a study mission (in 1947) to discover the extent of the ignorance of most English students of contemporary European intellectual movements such as existentialism or surrealism.

After I was awarded the *Licence* with Distinction in English literature, I was appointed as an Instructor in the Faculty. In fact, I was the first Egyptian to be appointed to the Department of English, which had until then con-sisted only of English colleagues. I taught a number of subjects, including translation, and a few months before leaving for England I got to know a member of the English Faculty, the critic, short-story writer and poet Dennis Enright, who later played an important part in English cultural life. He was then a young man, newly graduated from the University of Cambridge. During my visit to his house I saw in his library several numbers of the liter-ary criticism review *Scrutiny*, which was published in Cambridge and edited by the famous critic F. R. Leavis. Enright had published a number of his essays in it. He lent me some issues of this review, which I had not known before, and which had a deep influence on me. I remember staying up all night reading some of the essays, feeling a joy and thrill which I had never experienced before when reading literary criticism. I found in Leavis's articles a new outlook on literature to which he accorded a sublime status, considering its study and criticism an extremely serious matter that went to the heart of human civilisation.

Enright himself had registered for a doctorate in the Department of English at the University of Alexandria. When he submitted his thesis for examination, entitled, as I recall, *The Search for God in the Poetry of Some Modernist Poets*, most of whom were German such as Rilke and Stefan George, he asked me to translate the abstract of his thesis into Arabic. He had to present this in Arabic according to the regulations of the university, and this I did for him. I think he was the first to be awarded a doctorate in the Department of English at the University of Alexandria, which at the time was still known as Faruq I University.

My attitudes towards literature and criticism were defined while I was in Alexandria, and before I travelled to England. This attitude involved three essential questions: the first is the relationship between literature and politics; the second is the relationship between literature and morality; and the third is the nature of language and its function in poetry, and consequently the relationship between poetry and science, or between poetry and thought or knowledge in general. With respect to the first question, as most members of my generation in Egypt were interested in politics and social justice, it was natural that my general outlook was liberal with a leftist inclination. We all believed deeply that literature must have a message and that the writer had to be fully aware of his or her responsibility towards society which suffers from the problems of poverty, ignorance and disease. As for the nature of this responsibility, it was not as clearly defined for me as it was for some of my colleagues, who resorted to direct political activity. I felt vaguely that the writer, when resorting to political activity, is transformed from a writer whose tool is the world to a politician whose tool is action. By chance I found a book belonging to a friend and a colleague in the Faculty who was three years my senior, namely Edgar Faraj. He was the first to submit an MA thesis in the Department of English. (The subject of his thesis was the novels of Marmaduke Pickthall, who had embraced Islam and translated the Qur'an into English.) The title of the book which I found was *Life and the Poet*, published in 1942 by the English poet Steven Spender, one of the poets of the 1930s who were influenced by Marxist thought and the events of the Spanish Civil War. I borrowed this book from Edgar, read it eagerly and felt that Spender presented clearly and convincingly what I believed implicitly about the relationship between poetry and literature in general, and politics in particular. I found in it what I was searching for, and as result of my enthusiasm I translated it into Arabic in a very short time, when I was still a student, although I published this translation only a few years later after my return from England. In short, my stance was that the writer is a writer first and foremost. This does not mean a belief in the notion of art for art's sake, but, if literature has any political content, it must be fused with other elements of the literary work, so that it will be transformed into literature without remaining a flagrant call to political action. Great literature, as Spender says, contemplates the world and the human being with all his or her convictions, systems, institutions and questions. Behind every great literature lies a revolutionary motive, for it always raises questions rather than presenting easy solutions or ready forms and systems. Hence the danger of ideology dominating the thinking of the writer as writer.

As for the second question, which is the relationship between literature and morality in its widest sense, it was defined for me to some extent after the experience of my reading *Scrutiny* (1932–53) and the essays of the great critic F. R. Leavis. What attracted me most to the critical writings of Leavis was his deep belief in the importance of literature in emphasising the moral, spiritual and civilisational values of society. Literature has to be established on the foundation of a serious mature outlook on life and the universe. Literary study, therefore, has to be located at the very heart of civilisation or its centre. Leavis was against Marxism on the one hand, and against the values of commercial society and cheap popular culture on the other. Leavis used to concentrate on the literary text itself, analysing it closely rather than wasting his effort and time on general statements about the social and historical circumstances in which the text had emerged, or on a detailed study of the biography of the author in order to show the extent of his relation to the text. In this Leavis is in full agreement with his two colleagues at Cambridge University, the distinguished critic I. A. Richards (who emphasised in his book *Practical Criticism* the bankruptcy of the historical approach towards the text) and his genius of a pupil, William Empson, who showed in his analysis of texts the extent of their complexity and richness, and consequently the flow and intensity of the language of poetry.

The language of poetry is the third question through which I defined my critical stance, and which directed my graduate studies in England. A copy of Richards's book *Science and Poetry* came to me via my friend Edgar Faraj. The book had appeared in 1926 in a series which aimed to simplify thought so that it could be understood by the general reader. Since Richards was one of the giants of literary thought, his small book was a genuine addition to knowledge and a breakthrough rather than merely a summary or simplification of thought. Richards presented in that book the essential difference between the poetic use of language and the scientific or referential use. As is typical of Richards's writings, his words were so clear that they kindled my enthusiasm for the book, so I also translated it into Arabic while I was still a student in the final year of my undergraduate study, although I postponed its publication until I returned from England. This book, as well as his other work *The Philosophy of Rhetoric* (1936), showed most clearly the impact of the great English critic Samuel Taylor Coleridge, particularly on Richards's conception of the role played by words in poetry and how they invigorate each other. The writing of these critics, in addition to the critical essays of T. S. Eliot, had a deep impact on my way of reading and responding to poetical texts. These are the pillars on which I built my stance on criticism. My studies in England were a confirmation and development of this stance. It was not out of sheer coincidence that for my doctoral thesis I decided to research the writings of Coleridge, who had a deep impact on modern literary criticism, and particularly on the writings of Richards and Empson.

3

Badawi:
An Academic with a Vision.
A Personal Testimony

Sabry Hafez

This chapter is primarily a personal testimony recording my interaction with Mustafa Badawi, and his contribution to the study of literature, both Arabic and English. I did not meet Mustafa in the classroom, like most of the contributors to this volume, yet learnt a lot from him and benefited from his generosity, warmth and compassion.

By a curious coincidence, the day I returned to Oxford to take part in a colloquium commemorating his life and work was the fortieth anniversary of my arrival in Oxford for the first time in March 1973, thanks to Mustafa Badawi's insight and initiative. I was a young Egyptian critic then, who at the time thought of travelling to the West only in my dreams, and through the European novels I avidly read. I spent my late teens and early twenties, first in a small town in the Nile Delta, then in Cairo, devouring Western litera-ture, particularly Russian novels of the late nineteenth and early twentieth centuries, and living more in the fictive world they constructed than in the real world around me. During my university years, I befriended another avid reader of Russian novels, the late short-story writer Abdulla Khayrat, and we lived in the world they created and developed our own language, in which quotes from the novels took on real life such as 'I need a glass of vodka or a bowl of cabbage soup', or, when either of us was short of money, 'give me a kopek for Christ's sake'. So coming to Oxford, at the behest of Mustafa, was a fulfilment of an almost impossible, yet long-cherished dream.

I had known of Mustafa Badawi ten years before I actually met him, in fact since I started to play an active role in the Arab literary field as a young critic. The publication in 1962 of his Arabic translation of I. A. Richards's *Principles of Literary Criticism* (1924) coincided with the publication of my first article of literary criticism in *Al-Adab*.[1] Although it appeared in Arabic forty years after its publication in English, the translation of this seminal book presented a rupture with the predominant critical discourse of cliché socialist realist criticism and narrow Arabic understanding of Jean-Paul Sartre's concept of commitment. When Badawi's translation appeared, there was a growing need for fresh critical insight into literary texts that was concerned with deciphering their literariness, outlining their implied message and offering a new way of reading them. The ubiquitous fear in the cultural arena during Nasser's years led writers to develop new codes and textual strategies. The literary texts of the period, with their new and complex process of encoding, engendered a critical search for new approaches to decode them. Badawi's translation of Richards was the only book on the topic in Arabic, with a relatively fresh outlook on literature, and especially the art of textual criticism and close reading.

Previous generations of Egyptian critics who studied in the West before Badawi's generation, particularly Muhammad Mandur (1907–65) and Luwis 'Awad (1915–90), returned to Egypt in the late 1940s and early 1950s to introduce the classics of Western literary criticism to the Arabic scene. Mandur translated Gustave Lanson (1857–1934), one of the most influential students of Hippolyte Taine (1828–93), with his emphasis on social milieu, historical moment and race. Mandur's sensitivity to both the text and the socio-cultural context enabled him to mediate Lanson's concept of race into Arabic criticism as cultural specificity and ameliorate it with some individual psychological elements. Although Lanson was for years the target of Jean-Paul Sartre's ridicule, he is now seen as one of the early precursors of close reading and *explication de texte*. Mandur introduced his historical approach and his sociological insights[2] into literary works, not the new dynamics of *explication de texte*.

Luwis 'Awad, the other major critic of the generation that preceded Badawi's, returned from America to translate Horace's *Ars Poetica* into Arabic. This was ironic because, when 'Awad studied for his MA in Cambridge in the late 1940s, Richards and Leavis, who were advocating an English and more nuanced brand of close reading, dominated the critical scene there. Similarly, when he went to study for his PhD in Princeton in the early 1950s, New Criticism was the name of the critical game there, but it seems to have completely passed him by. When he returned to Egypt, he neither introduced their work nor applied any of their approaches in his own critical discourse. Apart from his brief introduction to Shelley's romanticism and his adoption of certain rudimentary Marxist notions, he used a very traditional, historical sociological approach in his criticism and did his best to avoid dealing with new literary texts of the 1960s, whose language and innovative structures demanded new critical approaches.

Both Mandur[3] and 'Awad were producing their critical work within a certain horizon of expectations in Jauss's sense of the term.[4] The Egyptian cultural scene of their youth and cultural formation, as well as the one to which they returned from their study abroad, was one concerned with the foundation of a solid base for rational liberal thinking. They had to play their role in consolidating this base, and provide the critical approaches conducive to the elucidation of the realist literature of the time. This also explains why their critical work was significant for realist literature and for the elaboration of its canon in the culture. Indeed, the change in literary sensibility towards more modernistic tendencies was still marginal at the time of their arrival on the critical scene, and none of them paid any attention to the new shoots which were emerging in narrative and painting in the late 1940s and early 1950s. Their clear neglect of these early innovative works delayed the trajectory of modernism in Egyptian literature until the arrival of the generation of the 1960s.[5]

By the time of Badawi's return from his studies abroad, the literary and cultural field in Egypt was changing. Even the dominant figures in the field, such as Haqqi, Mahfuz and Idris, were developing new forms and novel textual strategies in their work. A new group of writers, to be known later as the 1960s generation, was emerging and inventing a new language and fresh techniques of codification, effecting a cultural rupture with the dominant discourse and developing a new literary sensibility. As a result, Badawi's translation of Richards was received with enthusiasm, for it was seen as providing a response to these changes. The literary sensibility was moving towards more modernistic tendencies, and the new literary works, including those of Mahfuz and Idris, were demanding different critical approaches to decipher their sometimes puzzling and enigmatic codes. Although Richards was not the ideal reply to the emerging needs, it certainly met them half way, and introduced a fresh set of ideas into a milieu searching for new sources of inspiration. Badawi seemed to be responding to these needs, for he followed this first work with two other translations: Richards's *Science and Poetry* (1926), alas not *Practical Criticism*, and Stephen Spender's *Life and the Poet* (1942).

In order to know why Badawi was able to respond to a changing critical need, while a decade earlier both Mandur and 'Awad failed even to sense the change, let alone respond to it, one needs to delve into the context in which he was educated and culturally formed, and that to which he returned after his mission abroad. Both Mandur and 'Awad were educated in the period of national frustration that followed the failure of the 1919 revolution. Fluctuating hopes and frustration marked their university years which witnessed the international economic crisis of 1930 and its devastating impact on Egypt's economic and political life. By 1930, the most prized achievement of the 1919 revolution, namely the 1923 Constitution, was abrogated, the elected Wafdist government was dismissed and the parliament dissolved. This was replaced by the disreputable 1930 constitution and autocratic government of Isma'il Sidqi. Hence national polarisation was highly pronounced and violence and counter-violence reigned for five years. After this, the 1923 Constitution was reinstated, and a new election produced a Wafdist government in 1935. In the following year, King Fu'ad died, and his young son, King Faruq, took office, while the Wafdist government succeeded in negotiating a new independence treaty in 1936.

If Mandur and 'Awad spent their university years in the grip of the harsh and violent years of the 1930s, Badawi's cultural formation and university education took place in a radically different environment. By the end of the 1930s, the euphoria of the 1936 treaty and its promises produced the optimistic cultural vision of Taha Husayn's *Mustaqbal al-thaqafa fi Misr* (*The Future of Culture in Egypt*, 1938) on the one hand, and the decree in the same year by Muhammad Mahmud's government to establish a new university in Alexandria. Taha Husayn's vision for a new independent Egypt formulated its future culture as one of liberal rational modernity, open to and aspiring to interact with the diversity of modern European cultures around the Mediterranean. By the time the young Alexandrian Muhammad Mustafa Badawi (born on 10 June 1925) successfully finished his baccalaureate in June 1942, the new Alexandria University, with Taha Husayn as its first Rector, opened its doors to welcome its first class of students.

The rectorship of the newly established and strategically located university, on the shores of the Mediterranean, gave Taha Husayn his chance to practise what he preached in his *The Future of Culture in Egypt*. He did his best to establish a modern university based on the academic standards of the best European universities at the time. He mobilised his wide European contacts to provide him with their brightest young students to work for the new university, particularly in the Departments of English and French, to enhance the dialogue between *les deux rivages*. An indication of his success in this is the calibre of the teachers he recruited: Roland Barthes (1915–80), A. J. Greimas (1917–92) and Jean Grenier[6] (1898–1971) worked in the French Department of the University when it opened, and a number of illustrious French authors gave lectures there on a visiting basis including André Gide (1869–1951), René Etiemble (1909–2002) and Jean Cocteau (1889–1963). In the English Department there were equally important teachers, such as Robert Graves (1895–1985), John Wisdom (1904–93), Robert Liddell (1908–92), John Heath-Stubbs (1918–2006) and Dennis Enright (1920–2002).

However, the university opened in the turbulent years of the Second World War. In Alexandria foreigners feared that the war was not going well for the British, and disillusioned Egyptian masses chanted 'Forward Rommel' to save them from the occupying British. The year 1942 saw Rommel's arrival on the African Front; he advanced into the Western Desert of Egypt, and his troops were only a hundred miles from Alexandria. The economic situation was dire, with a severe shortage of basic commodities hampering the British military efforts to halt the quick advances of Rommel's forces in Egypt. His air raids on Alexandria aggravated the situation and created anger against the British, destabilising the internal front and impeding their efforts to launch a counter-offensive. Despite their dislike of the Wafd, the British felt that it was the only power capable of changing the situation and asked the King to call the Wafd to form a new government to stabilise the internal front. In the wrangle that followed, the King attempted to compromise with the British, who were in no mood for compromise; they encircled the Palace with their tanks and asked the King to abdicate. He capitulated and persuaded Mustafa Nahhas to form a Wafdist government in what is known as the '4 February 1942 incident'.[7]

Whatever the interpretation of this event, its effect on the political, social and cultural life of the country was far-reaching. At one blow the romantic dream of Egypt's independence and future evaporated, people's confidence in themselves and in their national leaders was shattered, and cracks started to appear in the Wafd Party. Yet the short-lived Wafd government (1942–4) managed to alleviate the economic crisis, make primary-school education compulsory and free, and promote Arabic as the official language in all the dealings of foreign companies. The impact of the latter was strongly felt in Alexandria, which was full of foreign companies conducting their work in English. The Wafd government also completed and opened Alexandria University and appointed Taha Husayn as its first Rector. Those last two acts were crucial for the young M. M. Badawi and his generation of Alexandrians, providing them with a university in their town to further their education without the cost of relocating to Cairo. This was vital for Badawi, since his excellent performance in the baccalaureate entitled him to free university education, but without any money for subsistence, hence he needed to stay at home to complete his education. Decreeing Arabic as the official language in all dealings of foreign companies provided the linguistically gifted of those from the lower middle class, Badawi included, with a means to finance themselves through freelance translation.

Despite the turbulent years of the war Badawi and his generation seem to have had an excellent education in Alexandria University guided by Taha Husayn and his ambitious vision. This is evident in the large number of graduates of these early classes who rose to prominence and subsequently attained distinction in the Egyptian or even international cultural field.

One cannot emphasise enough the importance of the economic independence and sense of worth the translation opportunities gave to those Alexandria University students who came from less advantaged backgrounds. Independently, and in separate conversations, not only Badawi himself but also Edwar al-Kharrat (1926–), Alfred Faraj (1926–2005) and Tawfiq Salih (1926–2013) have told me how this independent income opened vital doors for them. The income that this freelance translation provided them as young students, eager to learn, enjoy life and violate certain taboos, enabled them to achieve this, explore cultural life (such as operas, concerts and the theatre otherwise unattainable on students' pocket money) and provided them with a greater sense of independence than even their richer fellow students. Economic independence is the prerequisite for intellectual independence, and many of them felt free to embrace, sometimes on an experimental basis, radical Marxist ideologies, particularly after the patriotic party, Wafd, was discredited on 4 February 1942.

The foreign language departments of Alexandria University at the time, particularly the English Department, were full of those who came from private schools, particularly the elite Victoria College of Alexandria, such as Mahmud Manzalawi, Mustafa Safwan (1921–), Sami Ali (1926–2010), Yusuf Shahin (1926–2008), Mahmud Mursi (1923–2004) and Safiyya Abu Shadi, the daughter of the famous poet Ahmad Zaki Abu Shadi (1892–1955), the founder of the Romantic Literary Society, Apollo, and editor in chief of its influential journal, *Apollo* (1932–4). It was natural that the literary inclined among the students of her class, such as Badawi, al-Kharrat and the poet Munir Ramzi (1925–45) were attracted to her, if not for her refined literary pedigree then for her sultry romantic beauty, semi-liberal conduct and fine culture. At the time, female university students were a rarity, and the highly cultured and refined among them were even rarer. In the emotionally parched atmosphere of a relatively conservative society, the appearance in the classroom of an intelligent, cultured, relatively liberated female fired the imagination of the male students, many of whom nourished secret or overt feelings of unrequited and largely platonic love towards her, without often attempting to communicate them. In the cultural life of modern Egypt, particularly in the 1940s, there are many stories of young intellectuals falling in love with the only cultured and beautiful female students in their generation: Safiyya Abu Shadi in Alexandria and Latifa al-Zayyat (1923–96) in Cairo are among the most famous of these cases.[8]

Munir Ramzi, a close friend of Badawi, was one of those who had fallen for Safiyya, and as a romantic poet he overinterpreted every sign and suffered in silence. He nurtured his unrequited love among the 'ghosts of his pain', as one of his striking images states. In his diwan, *Bariq al-ramad* (*The Glimmering of Ashes*, 1997),[9] collected and edited posthumously, fifty-two years after his suicide, by Badawi and al-Kharrat, Badawi's introduction reads as a fresh obituary to his dearest friend, after whom he named his only son.[10] From al-Kharrat's account of the last days of Ramzi's life and his suicide, both Badawi and al-Kharrat were summoned by the public attorney investigating his suicide. The last paper he scribbled, in a mixture of Arabic and English, before shooting himself had Badawi's name repeated in it three times, as well as that of al-Kharrat.[11] It is significant that, without any prior agreement, both Badawi and Kharrat, who must have nourished similar feelings towards Safiyyah, chose to edit her and Ramzi's love for her out of their testimonies and opted to tell the public attorney nothing about his inner life. From this account we also know that Badawi was Ramzi's closest friend as was he for Badawi.

It seems that Ramzi was not only a close friend, whose loss was a personal tragedy, but also a literary model for Badawi's future poetry. If one reads Badawi's poetry, written many years after the loss of his friend, one finds echoes of Ramzi's imagery and emotions, as well as a continuation of his quest to rid Arabic poetry of romanticism, and nurture some of the embryos of modernism, nascent in Ramzi's poetry.[12] Indeed, reading it retrospectively, Ramzi's poetry seems to show a pioneering sensibility that grows out of Romantic imagination, into a gloomy vision of despair, alienation and nihilism foreshadowing future themes in Arabic poetry. This contemplative dimension in his poetry, which marries Eros with Thanatos, as well as its philosophical, almost metaphysical, undertone clearly influenced Badawi's own subsequent poetry. But Ramzi's alienation, gloom and despair, though generated by his failed love affair, were a manifestation of the general mood of Egyptian students during the war years. Badawi's formative university years were sharpened by personal loss and the turbulent events of the Second World War, many of which were taking place at the gates of Alexandria. The students were torn between the gradually discredited Wafd, and the rising polarity between communism and the Muslim Brotherhood. They were also marked in Egyptian cultural life at large by the emerging modernist sensibility, particularly in avant-garde circles and literary coteries in Cairo.

The irrationality of the situation in which Egypt found itself providing stage and support for a war that did not concern it, suffering its devastating events, and ironically helping its enemy, the British, to win the war, was strongly felt in the cultural field. The intellectuals were reading Marx, Freud, Nietzsche and Frazer, and becoming increasingly aware of modern European art and writing. In Cairo, many avant-garde groups were formed, such as Jamaʿat al-Khubz wa-l-Hurriyya (Bread and Freedom Group) and Jamaʿat al-Fann wa-l-Hurriyya (Art and Freedom Group) whose leading member Ramsis Yunan (1913–66) took over Salama Musa's editorship (1887–1958) of a monthly journal, *Al-Majalla al-jadida*, and made it the organ of new modernist sensibility. He himself was a surrealist painter, and encouraged the innovative and experimental writing of Bishr Faris (1907–63), Georges Henein (1914–73), Albert Cossery (1913–2008) and other modernists whose work was highly admired in Alexandria.[13] The pioneering works of those Cairene intellectuals were introduced to Alexandrian cultural circles through their connection with Edmond Jabès (1912–91) and the other Alexandrians whom the young Badawi and his literary contemporaries knew and greatly admired.

This other Alexandria existed in juxtaposition to the one that the Egyptian university students, and their compatriots in general, experienced, but without much interaction with it. It was a more liberal, even libertine, city that the various foreign communities inhabited, and they made it a cosmopolitan city *par excellence*. This other Alexandria, whose world can be gleaned from the pages of the *Alexandria Quartet* of Lawrence Durrell (1912–90),[14] was a culturally exciting one. It was diverse and rich, peopled with many intellectuals who went on to acquire international fame such as Constantine Cavafy (1863–1933), E. M. Forster (1879–1970), Olivia Manning (1908–80) and Edmond Jabès. It was a world of hedonism, oblivious to the world of the struggling Egyptians aspiring to develop their country and achieve independence. Some of them were citizens of the cosmopolitan Alexandria such as Cavafy and Jabès, while many others flocked to it to escape the war in Europe. Nevertheless the culturally inclined students such as Badawi often escaped to the haven of that other Alexandria. They found in it serious books, inviting bars, good theatres and cinemas, wonderful concerts and operas that nourished their souls and refined their senses.[15]

As soon as the war ended, the government asked for the evacuation of British troops and the unification of Egypt and the Sudan. This was rejected by the British. The following year, 1946, the year of Badawi's graduation, saw some of the most angry demonstrations in Egypt's modern history, culminating in the student massacre of 9 February 1946, the assassination attempt on the monarch on 11 February and the spread of irrepressible riots throughout the country. To understand the ramifications of the events of 1946, it is necessary to bear in mind the major social and cultural changes that Egypt had undergone during the Second World War, including the broadening of the middle class, the development of a rebellious intelligentsia, the growth of the working class, social polarisation in the countryside, the emergence of the communist movement and new schools of radical political thought, and the coalition between the student movement and the workers which sustained the demonstrations.[16] The succeeding years proved to be even more violent, with the reign of terror presided over by minority government and the Muslim Brotherhood's assassination of two prime ministers, Ahmad Mahir and Mahmud al-Nuqrashi.[17]

Badawi experienced some of the riots during his last year of university when he graduated in June 1946, but he escaped the worst of the violence and disillusionment of the following years. In 1947, after one year of teaching in the English Department from which he graduated, he was awarded an Egyptian government scholarship to study in England. He obtained a second Bachelor of Arts in English literature from University College, Leicester, in 1949. After graduation, his tutor in Leicester told him: 'Now you can go back to your country and teach English literature in your university, for you now know as much as I did when I started teaching'. Badawi responded that this would not be sufficient for his university, and that he must obtain a PhD. He went to Bedford College, University of London, obtaining the PhD in 1954. His thesis was published in 1973 as *Coleridge: Critic of Shakespeare*.[18] In July 1954, before returning to Egypt, he stopped briefly in Holland to marry Mieke, and returned to Egypt with his new bride in August of that year.

He now resumed his career as a teacher in the English Department of the University of Alexandria, but the Egypt to which he returned was radically different from the one he left. In his absence the turbulent political map he left behind had been replaced by an even more problematic one. Army officers seized power in 1952, forced the King to abdicate, abrogated the 1923 Constitution, disbanded all political parties, passed a concessionary land reform law, declared Egypt a republic and eased the economic situation. They harshly crushed the workers' demonstrations and, after what is known as the Crisis of March 1954,[19] there was a massive round-up of all those who challenged or even questioned the absolute power of the junta: the communists, Muslim Brotherhood, socialists, Wafdists and other independent liberals. The arrests took place a few months before Badawi's return, creating an atmosphere of fear. This continued throughout 1954 and 1955, and included fellow teachers and students from Alexandria University, posing unsettling questions to the newly returned Badawi.

The University to which he returned was enveloped in a climate of anxiety, silence and intimidation, in which he had to navigate his moves and views delicately. The inner difficulties of these early days in a radically changing Egypt can be gleaned from the poems he wrote during the period, though he did not dare publish them for more than twenty years. Unlike his colleague Mahmud Manzalawi, whose family suffered from Nasser's land reform law and who hated the new regime, Badawi's stance was much more ambivalent and complex; while he appreciated the steps towards social justice and national independence, he became increasingly aware of the absence of freedom. This was further complicated by the fact that, as a newly returned Egyptian, clearly fluent in English, and without any political record in the security apparatus, he was asked to interpret for Nasser and some of his powerful ministers several times. This pushed him to write more poems that he kept in his drawer.

For someone without Badawi's integrity and commitment to intellectual independence, this would have been a golden opportunity, opening the way for an ambitious young man, with a young family, to climb the social and political ladder. But he found himself in a quandary, approving of the newly gained sense of national dignity after Nasser's success in solving the long-standing issue of the British evacuation from Egypt, and his policies of social reform that consolidated the cultural achievement of Taha Husayn, as Minister of Education (1950–2). Husayn made secondary education free, and put in place a system for subsidising serious publication and unprofitable translation projects. But what outweighed these positive deeds was the fact that he became increasingly aware of the impact of the acute absence of freedom on his work and on academic and cultural life as a whole. One must remember that many of his colleagues in English departments were behind bars, including Luwis ʿAwad. Hence, he had to use all his diplomatic skills to extricate himself from this conundrum, dissociate himself gradually from the regime and its lure of power and influence, and devote himself to his academic career.

Like his late friend Ramzi, Badawi resorted to writing poetry in which he expressed his innermost feelings and disillusionment, without being able to publish his poems. However in 1960 he published his first collection of poetry, *Rasaʾil min London (Epistles from London)*,[20] in which he included his youthful poems, *Mukhtarat min shiʿr al-siba* (1944–6) and his poems from London (1953–4), but not the ones he wrote after his return. Those had to wait, and, when they appeared,[21] they were significantly entitled *Atlal (Ruins or Traces of a Loved Place)*, with an elegiac connotation of the Alexandria he found when he returned. They are dated (1955–7) and the date has its significance too, for 1956 was the year of the notorious Suez War, whose real truth was for many years concealed from the Egyptians, and available only to those who had access to English, and the international media. Unlike most Egyptians, who received the official version of Nasser's regime in which a devastating defeat was turned into victory, Badawi knew the truth and the scale of the defeat of the Egyptian army, how the war was misrepresented to the people, the losses and the territorial concessions concealed, and the political success very much exaggerated, and how the people were mollified by lies.[22]

This was the period in which he benefited from Taha Husayn's policy of subsidising unprofitable translation projects. After transforming his own doctorate into a book in Arabic,[23] he embarked on a number of translations. This started with *The Sense of Beauty* (1896) by George Santayana (1863–1952), which is considered to be the first major work on Aesthetics, the Arabic version of which appeared in 1958. This was followed in 1962 by the Arabic translation of I. A. Richards's *Principles of Literary Criticism*, the book which first brought Badawi's name to my attention.[24] By the time my generation found his translations and tried to look for his other work, we were told that he had left the country, but not before publishing a collection of his critical essays, *Dirasat fi al-shi'r wa'l-masrah* (*Studies in Poetry and Drama*, 1960).[25] The book did not provide the young critics of the period with what they needed, but they found some of it in his translations. Badawi's critical essays in this book, which had been published in Egyptian periodicals earlier, introduced a critical approach combining what George Watson calls 'descriptive criticism' with elements of *explication de texte*, but did not offer the fresh approach we sought, even if its embryos were in his essays waiting to be developed.

Badawi himself was aware of this, and he went on a sabbatical to England, which he elected to spend in Cambridge, the home of his two models in literary criticism, I. A. Richards and F. R. Leavis (1895–1978), in order to freshen and sharpen his critical tools. In the academic year 1962/3 he travelled with his wife and three daughters (Salma, Randa and the newly born Karima) to spend the year in Cambridge, where Leavis was a Fellow at Downing College. This sabbatical year turned out to be a decisive point in his life and a turning point in his career. Karima was diagnosed as having a very rare neurological condition that required careful handling and could not be treated in Egypt; she had to remain in Europe if she was to have any chance of a cure. Badawi had to choose between leaving his daughter with his wife's family in the Netherlands or staying with the whole family, which he was advised by Karima's doctors was the ideal option. He started to look for a job, and, fortunately, the post at Oxford, which he held from 1964 till his retirement in 1992, became available. He was appointed, and the family remained in Oxford for the benefit of his daughter who was eventually cured.

By the time the new generation of young Egyptian critics started to search for Badawi and his work, he had left the country altogether. Ten years after I first encountered Badawi's name through his translations, another coincidence brought his name into my life, this time to change it as much as the sabbatical year at Cambridge had changed his. Early in 1972 I received a telephone call from Yusuf al-Sharuni, then my boss at the Egyptian al-Majlis al-A'la li-Ri'ayat al-Funun wa-l-Adab wa-l-'Ulum al-Ijtima'iyya (something similar to the Arts Council), asking me to come to his office to meet someone from Oxford looking for me. There I met a young Saudi Arabian, 'Ali Jad, who wrote his thesis on the Egyptian novel under Badawi's supervision in the 1970s.[26] These were the years when Badawi and Derek Hopwood were building the library of the Middle East Centre, making it the best resource for modern Arabic literature in the country, and perhaps, apart from Harvard's, in the world. A few weeks later, Mustafa sent me another student, Paul Starkey, to help him get access to the elusive grand old man of Egyptian theatre, Tawfiq al-Hakim, whom he had been trying to meet for months. The day Paul Starkey phoned me to complain of his failure to meet al-Hakim, I took him to al-Hakim's office.

A few weeks later I dropped in unexpectedly on my friend Edwar al-Kharrat, and he told me that he was in the process of writing a letter to Mustafa, that 'Ali Jad would take to Oxford the following day. He asked, 'Do you need anything from him?' My answer was 'No thanks! I don't even know him to ask for anything from him. The only thing I want is to go to England.' Edwar said: 'I'll tell him that.' I thought of it all as a joke and forgot the whole thing. But Badawi took it seriously. Later I was to discover how hard he worked on this whimsical wish of mine, devising an elaborate invitation for me to stay in England for three months, so elaborate that he involved three different institutions to make it possible. SOAS paid for my ticket, as a participant in the first conference on modern Arabic literature organised by one of his first students, Robin Ostle. St Antony's put me up for the duration of my visit, and the British Council gave me some pocket money. A few months later, the invitation came in a letter delivered person-ally to me in my office in Cairo by the late Professor P. J. Vatikiotis. I realised then that the matter was serious, not only because I had an official invitation on SOAS headed paper to visit England but also because two days later I was summoned by al-Mabahith al-'Amma, the feared security agency in Nasser's Egypt at the time, and was questioned about the American spy who had vis-ited me in my office a couple of days earlier. Little did they, or even I, knew how serious this visit was for it changed my life, thanks to both Badawi and Vatikiotis, the Greek/Egyptian/American spy who came in from the cold and brought me to Oxford.

I am relating this story only to demonstrate that, while the younger gen-eration of writers and intellectuals thought that Mustafa had left Egypt for good and abandoned his role in opening new critical venues, he was avidly following the work of every emerging writer and critic there very closely. He sent 'Ali Jad to me, without ever meeting me, because he was impressed by the first bibliography of the Egyptian novel which I had published in 1969, a couple of years before Jad embarked on his thesis. From Oxford he was following the literary scene very closely, not only in Egypt but in the whole of the Arab world and was discovering every new voice and trend. After I arrived in Oxford, I discovered that he had quoted some of my articles, and discussed many of the works of writers from my generation, while writing in English on modern Arabic literature. Once in Oxford, I became familiar with the side of his work that was not known in Egypt at the time, and I was always impressed by the breadth and depth of his knowledge. When I decided to stay and pursue my own PhD, thanks to the support of Badawi and Vatikiotis who secured for me a rare SOAS bursary, I ended up being supervised by one of Badawi's early students, Robin Ostle.

In Oxford, and later in London, I discovered that Badawi had opened new venues for Arabic literary criticism and modern Arabic literature, a virtually unknown field in Western academia before his arrival on the scene. It is impossible to exaggerate the vital role he played in laying the foundations for what is now a thriving and vibrant field of study in Western academia, and helping it to flourish. He painstakingly prepared the ground for the study of its most recognised genre, poetry, compiling the first anthology of modern Arabic poetry,[27] and following it with his *Critical Introduction to Modern Arabic Poetry*,[28] which complements the anthology with critical mapping of its history and schools. He also worked with a number of his colleagues to establish an academic outlet for the new subject by launching the *Journal of Arabic Literature* (*JAL*) in 1970.

The academic contribution of Mustafa Badawi, and his role in changing the nature and direction of the study of modern Arabic literature in British academia, is multifaceted. Apart from two books on Shakespeare, his original field of study,[29] he focused his rich academic output on modern Arabic literature, providing the foundation for the serious study of two of its important genres, poetry and drama,[30] and opened venues for the study of other genres,[31] particularly the novel through the work of his early students such as Roger Allen,[32] Hilary Kilpatrick[33] and 'Ali Jad. He also encouraged me to work on the short story, for he was keen to provide comprehensive coverage of all major genres. Others of his students – David Semah (1934–97),[34] Wajih Fanus[35] and Abdul-Nabi Isstaif[36] – worked on Arabic criticism. More importantly, by devoting his whole career to the study of modern Arabic, Badawi helped to liberate the study of Arabic in general, and that of modern literature in particular, from the old 'orientalist' approach, despite being accused of orientalism by Edward Said, a subject to which I shall turn later. The inherent assumption in that old approach was that Arabic language and literature are part of a once flourishing culture that is now extinct, and no longer contributing to modern culture and thought. Before his arrival, Arabic was treated as a dead but worthy language and culture, akin to Latin. It was seen as important only for understanding the past, but not relevant to the present, let alone the future. Both in his teaching and academic research, Badawi put modern Arabic literature on the map as part of the study of modern languages in general and of culture and modern literature in particular. Many of the scholars contributing to the study of modern Arabic in British and American universities are his students, either directly or indirectly, as the contributors to this volume demonstrate.

Badawi's role in British and Western scholarship is also part of a bigger story, the story of the public intellectual who is not totally satisfied with his role as an academic. In Egypt, since the time of Taha Husayn, bright academics have aspired to play a public role in their culture, widen its knowledge and scope of vision, and change its established attitudes and conventions, and Badawi is no exception. He played this role with his early translations into Arabic before moving to Oxford. When he moved to the West, he focused on his mission to establish the discipline of modern Arabic literature as a viable field of academia. This, as well as the complicated Egyptian political scene, cut him off from both the Egyptian and the Arabic cultural scenes. By the 1970s and 1980s a new generation who had never heard of Badawi's earlier contribution was running the cultural scene. I reminded them repeatedly of Badawi's original role and persuaded them to invite him to resume it and integrate himself into the contemporary cultural scene. By the second half of the 1980s he had become a regular presence at major Arabic cultural events. He was extremely pleased when his role was recognised by the King Faisal Prize for Translation (1992), and later on by the reprinting of his early translations in Egypt.[37] The new editions of his older translations, and later of his new ones when he embarked on producing new translations of Shakespeare's major tragedies, resulted from the desire to make the Arabic cultural scene aware of Badawi's immense contribution to Arabic literature that was, for at least two decades, relatively unknown in Arabic cultural circles.

In the latter part of his career, he was keen to revisit his old territories, to participate in major cultural conferences in Cairo and other Arab capitals, and to publish, if sporadically, in Arabic when he was asked for a contribution.[38] He believed that his main focus was the establishment of modern Arabic as a major academic discipline in the West, and when I invited him to introduce my inaugural lecture at SOAS in 1993, upon the establishment of the first chair of modern Arabic at the University of London, he saw this as the zenith of his own career. Badawi was clearly aware that he was establishing a new field of study, and that this could not be done single-handedly, or through heated polemics and controversy, but had to be done calmly and collectively, through his own work, and the work of his colleagues and students.[39] Like many pioneers who open new venues and develop new disciplines, he was not willing to antagonise those who contributed even marginally to the general field, and disliked the sharp critique of old 'orientalism'. His encounter with Edward Said's work and his heated exchange with him in the early 1980s should be seen not as a battle against the new directions that Said was advocating but as rejection of his harsh method of debunking the old. However, Badawi overlooked the vital fact that the medium is the message in Said's case. In fact, later on Badawi took great pleasure and pride in some of his students who ventured into the terrain of new theories and even combative clashes with the old. For by then he was sure that the ground beneath their feet was perfectly solid and secure.

Those who are aware of the theories devoted to the study of gender, race and minorities know of the three stages a radically different discourse takes to establish its authority. First, accepting the dominant discourse, no matter how erroneous it seems, in order to gain access to its public sphere and gain recognition. Second comes the immature challenge that desires to discredit and debunk the old in its entirety and devastate it completely. Third comes the stage of elaborating difference, and celebrating its multiplicity. It is in the light of such theories that Badawi's stance vis-à-vis Said's debunking of all orientalism should be understood. Badawi was keen to establish the validity of the new discipline of modern Arabic and to gain the support of the orientalists and their recognition of the importance of the new discipline emerging in their midst. The new discipline was pulling the rug from under their feet in its uniquely subversive way. Any look at the various Arabic departments across Europe and the United States will illustrate that those who work now and worked in the last three decades on modern Arabic literature have far exceeded those who worked on classical Arabic topics and/or writers. Badawi has a lot to do with this.

Indeed, one of the many lessons I learnt from Badawi is how to appreciate the role of acting as a bridge between cultures, and more importantly that the bridge must be a two-way one working equally in both directions.[40] Badawi never neglected his other role as a scholar of English, and particularly of Shakespeare. He was keen to promote Shakespeare in Arabic as much as the study of modern Arabic literature in English. Hence he devoted the last part of his life, particularly after retiring, to the creation of new Arabic translations of the major tragedies that achieved the difficult balance between poeticality, lucidity and ease of adaptability to performance on the stage. He was extremely upset when the final product was less than perfect. Although he was aware that the standard of publication in Egypt was declining by the year, he was still keen to produce perfect editions of his new translations.

Any testimony about Mustafa cannot be complete without mention of his love of the good life, his passion for wine and appreciation of good food. When I first arrived in Oxford, Mustafa was the wine fellow of St Antony's College, a position that in those days rotated every few years. He took his task seriously and introduced me personally not only to the fine wines and gourmet food served at the high-table dinners at the College but also to the rich vocabulary of wine. When, on the occasion of his eightieth birthday, I invited him for a small tour of the vineyards in southern France, he saw the tour of the cellars of Chateauneuf du Pape as a pilgrimage, for Mustafa was one of the rare Egyptians with a strong sense of *joie de vivre*.

As I said at the beginning of this testimony, when I arrived in Oxford for the first time, Badawi was not in Oxford. He is no longer with us now, and yet his spirit and intellectual impact are very much present, and will continue to endure and influence us and our students for many years to come.

Notes

1. The monthly literary journal *Al-Adab*, edited by Suhail Idris, was the leading pan-Arab literary journal at the time, and publishing a text in it was an act of initiation into the wider Arabic cultural scene.

2. This approach was the target of I. A. Richards's attack both in his *Principles of Literary Criticism* and in its sequel, *Practical Criticism*.

3. Mandur was clearly aware of the work of the Swiss linguist Ferdinand de Saussure (1857–1913) who laid the foundation for structuralism and referred to him in his major book, *Al-Naqd al-manhaji 'ind al-'arab*, but he obviously was more aware of the needs of his culture and introduced what served those needs.

4. For details see Hans Robert Jauss, *Towards an Aesthetic of Reception*, trans. Timothy Bahti, Minneapolis: University of Minnesota Press, 1982.

5. For more details see Sabry Hafez, *The Quest for Identities: The Development of the Modern Arabic Short Story*, London: Saqi Books, 2008, pp. 260–313.

6. Grenier was the philosopher who left an indelible mark on the young Albert Camus (1913–60) when he taught him in Algeria before moving to teach in Alexandria.

7. For a detailed study of this event see Muhammad Anis, *Hadith arba'a fibrayir*, Beirut, 1970, and 'Abd al-'Azim Ramadan, *Tatawwur al-haraka al-wataniyya fi misr: 1937–1948*, Beirut, 1973, pp. 192–219.

8. These two famous cases have been immortalised in modern Arabic narrative, Safiyya's case by Edwar al-Kharrat in his novel *Raqraqat al-ahlam al-milhiyyah* (*Stirrings of Salty Dreams*, Beirut: Dar al-Adab, 1994), and Latifa's in the title story of Yusuf al-Sharuni's first short story collection, *Al-'ushshaq al-khamsa* (*Five Lovers*, Beirut, 1954). It is rather significant that the two who were distanced enough to write the stories were Copts whose different religion might have protected them from falling into the illusion of reciprocation, or made it impossible to attain success.

9. Munir Ramzi, *Bariq al-ramad*, Cairo: Dar Sharqiyyat, 1997, p. 166. I would like to thank my colleague at Qatar University, Dr Husam Jayil, for acquiring a copy of the book for me.

10. Badawi's only son Ramzi was born on 7 July 1966, more than twenty years after the death of the poet.

11. For a detailed account of this read Idwar al-Kharrat, 'Shahadah fi yawmiyyat', in Munir Ramzi, *Bariq al-ramad*, pp. 30–54.

12. See Muhammad Mustafa Badawi, *Atlal wa-rasa'il min London*, Cairo: General

Book Organisation, 1979. In this new edition of his earlier collection of poetry, *Rasaʾil min London*, Cairo: Dar al-Maʿrifa, 1960, Badawi included for the first time under the title *Atlal* his early poems of 1955–7 which show the clear influence of Ramzi.

13. For more details on these avant-garde movements and the new modernist discourse in Egypt at the time, see Sabry Hafez, *The Quest for Identities*, pp. 260–86.

14. A tetralogy of novels by Lawrence Durrell, published between 1957 and 1960. A critical and commercial success, the first three books (*Justine, Balthazar* and *Mountolive*) present three different perspectives on a single set of events and characters in Alexandria before and during the Second World War; the fourth (*Clea*) is set six years later, demonstrating change over time.

15. Many of Badawi's generation of students who later made it to prominence in cultural life (such as Kharrat, Tawfiq Salih, Alfred Faraj and others) spoke to me with yearning and nostalgia about this other Alexandria and how important it was to their cultural formation.

16. For more details see Tariq al-Bishri, *Al-Haraka al-wataniyya fi Misr*, Cairo, 1972, pp. 5–75; Jacques Berque, *Egypt: Imperialism and Revolution*, trans. Jean Stewart, London: Faber, 1972, pp. 559–615, and Rifʿat al-Saʿid, *Al-Yasar al-misri*, Beirut, 1974.

17. P. J. Vatikiotis attributes most of the assassinations to the Muslim Brotherhood in his *The Modern History of Egypt: From Muhammad Ali to Mubarak*, London: Weidenfeld and Nicolson, 1985, pp 365–8.

18. M. M. Badawi, *Coleridge Critic of Shakespeare*, Cambridge: Cambridge University Press, 1973.

19. For the details of this crisis see Vatikiotis, *Modern History of Egypt*, pp. 383–6, and Peter Mansfield, *Nasser's Egypt*, London: Penguin, 1969, pp. 50–1.

20. Muhammad Mustafa Badawi, *Rasaʾil min London*, Cairo: Dar al-Maʿrifa, 1960.

21. Those needed to wait for more than twenty years to appear in his second edition of his diwan, *Atlal wa rasaʿil min London*, Cairo: al-Hayʾa al-Misriyya al-ʿAmma liʾl-Kitab, 1979, which included, in addition to the first collection, another mini-collection, *Atlal*, which contains the poems written 1955–7.

22. I lived a similar experience when I witnessed the 1973 October War in England, and learned its real truth as another disastrous defeat, while it was and still is presented to the Egyptian masses as a great success. I experienced the difficulty of trying to quietly communicate its reality to even educated people, something that Badawi told me he experienced while in Egypt, under the Nasser regime.

23. M. M. Badawi, *Coleridge: Nawabigh al-fikr al-gharbi*, Alexandria: Dar al-Maʿarif, 1958.

24. In addition to these two major works, Badawi translated into Arabic several other works: Richards's *Science and Poetry* (1926, Arabic translation 1963), Stephen Spender, *Life and the Poet* (1942, Arabic translation 1964), George Rostrevor Hamilton, *Poetry and Contemplation: A New Preface to Poetics* (1937, Arabic translation 1958), George Watson, *Study of Literature* (1968, Arabic translation 1980) and Philip Larkin, *Selected Poems* (Arabic translation 1998). In the last years of his life after retirement from Oxford, he devoted his time to bringing out new translations of Shakespeare's major tragedies: *Hamlet, Othello, Macbeth* and *King Lear*.

25. M. M. Badawi, *Dirasat fi al-shiʿr wa-l-masrah*, Cairo: Dar al-Maʿrifa, 1960.

26. The thesis was published as Ali Jad, *Form and Technique in the Egyptian Novel, 1912–71*, London: Ithaca Press, 1983.

27. See M. M. Badawi, *Mukhtarat min al-shiʿr al-ʿarabi al-hadith*, Beirut: Dar al-Nahar, 1969.

28. M. M. Badawi, *A Critical Introduction to Modern Arabic Poetry*, Cambridge: Cambridge University Press, 1975.

29. Those are M. M. Badawi, *Coleridge Critic of Shakespeare*, Cambridge: Cambridge University Press, 1973, and *Background to Shakespeare*, London: Macmillan, 1981.

30. His two books on drama are: *Modern Arabic Drama in Egypt*, Cambridge: Cambridge University Press, 1987, and *Early Arabic Drama*, Cambridge: Cambridge University Press, 1988.

31. See also his *Modern Arabic Literature and the West*, London: Ithaca Press, 1985, *Modern Arabic Literature: The Cambridge History of Arabic Literature*, Cambridge: Cambridge University Press, 1992, and *A Short History of Modern Arabic Literature*, Oxford: Oxford University Press, 1993.

32. Roger Allen was the first student to obtain a doctoral degree in that field at Oxford, under the supervision of M. M. Badawi. The topic of the dissertation was a study (and English translation) of Muhammad al-Muwaylihi's renowned narrative, *Hadith ʿIsa ibn Hisham* (*ʿIsa Ibn Hisham's Tale*); it was later published in book form as *A Period of Time* (first [microfiche] edition, 1974; second edition, 1992).

33. This came out as Hilary Kilpatrick, *The Modern Egyptian Novel: A Study in Social Criticism*, Monographs/St Antony's College, Oxford: Middle East Centre, 1974.

34. See David Semah, *Four Egyptian Literary Critics*, Leiden: Brill, 1974.

35. Published in Arabic, see Wajih Fannus, *Dirasat fi harakiyyat al-fikr al-adabi*, Beirut, n.d.

36. Published in Arabic, see Abdul-Nabi Isstaif, *Fi l-naqd al-adabi al-hadith*, 2 vols, Damascus: Damascus University Press, 1990.

37. The National Translation Project, al-Mashruʿ al-Qawmi liʾl-Tarjama, in Egypt reprinted all his early 1965s and 1960s translations again in the 1990s.

38. These recent articles and conference papers appeared in his last book in Arabic: M. M. Badawi, *Qadiyat al-hadatha wa-masaʾil thaqafiyya ukhra fi l-naqd al-adabi*, Cairo: Dar Sharqiyyat, 1999.

39. It is worth noting that when he established *JAL* with a number of his colleagues, some of whom were classical Arabic literature scholars and others modernists, none of them was named as editor, but it was almost a collective editorship, with the role of the editor rotating each year, and the spirit of group-work reigned.

40. Although, as a translator, the bulk of his work consisted of translations from English into Arabic he also translated three works from Arabic into English: Naguib Mahfouz, *The Thief and the Dogs*; translated from the Arabic by Trevor Le Gassick and M. M. Badawi, New York: Doubleday, 1984; Yahya Haqqi, *The Saint's Lamp and Other Stories*, Leiden: Brill, 1973; and ʿAbbas Mahmud al-ʿAqqad, *Sarah*, Cairo: The Egyptian Book Organisation, 1978.

4

From the Shadow Plays of Ibn Daniyal to the Poetry of Philip Larkin: Mustafa Badawi as Editor and Translator

Derek Hopwood

This perhaps unusual title defines in a way the range of literature in which Mustafa Badawi was interested and refers in particular to two works with which he was connected. Both demonstrate his deep concern with and interest in language and with making works of literature available to the Arabic reading public. He was more concerned with the intrinsic value of each work he dealt with in the great range of world literature than with any wider popularity his own work might have. It was his calling to educate, enlighten and enhance the intellectual lives of any who might read his publications. He could not imagine a life without time for literature in all its forms. Coming from an Arabic-speaking background and living and working in an English one, he assumed the specific task of bringing to the notice of his Arabic readers examples both of their own literature that he felt to be unjustly neglected and through translation examples of English works largely unknown to that same audience in the original language – all this in addition to his comprehensive writings in English on the history of Arabic literature for an English-reading public. (It is significant that one of these works – *Early Arabic Drama* – appeared in 2013 in an Arabic translation, happily proving that a text published in 1988 in English was thought to be useful too in Arabic.)

Of the two authors mentioned in the title of this article, at one extreme there is a thirteenth-century Arabic poetic/dramatic text, at the other a translation of a modern English poet. I do not imagine that either work has attracted a very large readership but they were both produced in the greater cause of promoting literature.

Badawi and Ibn Daniyal

The story of the publication of the shadow plays of Ibn Daniyal (1248–1310) is a long and curious one. They were first noticed in Europe by the German orientalist Georg Jacob (1862–1937). He wrote about them in his *Geschichte des Schattentheaters im Morgen- und Abendlande* (1925). Jacob's friend and colleague Paul Ernst Kahle (1875–1964) developed a fascination for the texts of the plays and spent many long hours and years in editing them. He engaged a Moroccan scholar in Bonn, Taqieddin al-Hilali, to help him, and together they completed an edition of the text. Because of Nazi persecution, Kahle had to move to Oxford and spent several years working in the Bodleian Library cataloguing manuscripts. He managed to send the Arabic text of Ibn Daniyal to Cairo to be printed. One sheet had been set and a second was in hand when war broke out. After the war, Kahle was told that that there was no trace of the printed text or manuscript in Cairo – the worst nightmare of a scholar to discover years of work lost. He had to start again. His life was further disrupted by a return to Germany after the war with a large family.

But back in Oxford in 1961 he managed to reconstruct his earlier work, but not in a way suitable for publication. By then he was sadly incapable of serious work and was reduced to copying and recopying his beloved plays. I was then asked if I would help him by sorting out a critical apparatus he had compiled on the basis of comparing the four manuscripts he had used originally. This completed, I lost touch with him and he died soon after.

I thought nothing more about Ibn Daniyal for fifteen years until, on a visit to Khartoum, I was introduced to the German Ambassador, Hans Kahle, Paul's son, whom I told about my work with his father. He informed me that most of his father's unpublished work and his voluminous correspondence had been purchased by the library of the University of Turin, that there were no plans to publish Ibn Daniyal but that I was at liberty to do so. I had plenty of other work, and my mind went back to the piles of handwritten Arabic text, difficult to read in many places, the scribbled jottings, the partial translations and my own notes. My heart sank, and I knew I could not possibly prepare them on my own. I went to Turin and found the familiar material intact. It was eerily attractive.

Back in Oxford I told Mustafa Badawi about my experiences, knowing of his interest in all Arabic drama. By a strange coincidence he was just completing an article 'Medieval Arabic Drama: Ibn Daniyal',[1] without, of course, having had the benefit of a complete published text. His excitement was intense on hearing my story. 'You must continue and publish it', he said. I complained of the impossibility of my understanding all the Arabic. 'Very well' – he said – 'let's do it together.' Despite all his other commitments he was willing to devote as much time as was necessary to bring enough order to the text to have it published.

He was convinced of the essential role played by Ibn Daniyal's plays in the formation of Arabic drama and wished for the first time to place a complete text before the public and also to disprove the disparaging remarks of H. A. R. Gibb and Jacob Landau, who had both commented fairly negatively on the shadow plays, clearly without having 'first-hand knowledge of Ibn Daniyal'.[2] To Mustafa there could hardly be a worse literary critical crime than commenting on a text without having read it; to dismiss the shadow plays as stillborn Arabic drama was unforgivable. Gibb wrote that the opportunity of developing a dramatic literature was missed. 'No one who actually managed to read Ibn Daniyal's plays would make this summary judgement that Arabic drama was stillborn.'[3] On the contrary, wrote Badawi, the shadow plays are as important in the universal dramatic tradition as are the medieval morality plays in Europe or the French *sottie* plays. You can feel very strongly his irritation with the two orientalists who did not have a proper grounding in Arabic or, for that matter, European drama. They were belittling to the mind of the uninformed reader the literary and dramatic value of Ibn Daniyal. Badawi does quote with approval, however, the German orientalist Georg Jacob, who had studied the texts and had called Ibn Daniyal 'the most witty and amusing poet in the Arabic language'. Arabic drama was not stillborn, wrote Badawi. On the contrary 'in Ibn Daniyal we are presented with sophisticated art with conventions and rules capable of earning the respect of literary critics. It behoves us to treat [the plays] with the necessary critical respect they deserve.' 'Both in dramatic technique and in spirit they come very close to medieval European drama.'[4] Perhaps Badawi was overstating his case a little here, but he was striving to establish a serious (non-orientalist) tradition of literary criticism. To do this he was willing to spend hours of effort in preparing another's work for publication. Only the smallest corrections of obvious miscopying errors were made. Even on occasions mistakes were left in the text when the correct version was given in the footnotes.[5]

In his wide-ranging article with its many erudite references to European literature Badawi analyses in some detail the three shadow plays – *Tayf al-khayal*, *'Ajib wa-gharib* and *al-Mutayyam wa'l-yutayyim* – which offer a vivid picture of medieval Cairo society, its life, its trades, professions, low life and crime. The author gives importance to every human act and through laughter creates an atmosphere in which nothing is taboo. The plays are aimed at a sophisticated audience in a language that must have been generally understood, despite its jargon and esoteric references. This language abounds in curses, oaths, sexually suggestive puns and insolent references and what Badawi calls 'intolerable obscenities'. It is interesting that a scholar of medieval literature should consider the obscenities intolerable. In what sense intolerable? Were they acceptable to a medieval audience? Can we imagine a mixed audience in Cairo enjoying them? A certain Islamic sensitivity must be at work here. Surely they are not really intolerable in context (on which, see Larkin later), yet Badawi explains (away) the obscene and stresses a clear religious side to the plays and an eventual redemption. The immoral leading character (Amir al-Wisal) in repentance finally makes the pilgrimage to Mecca.

So there we had Kahle's text with my attempt to gather together the notes. Badawi felt it must be published. Only a 1963 published text by Ibrahim Hamada existed – woefully inadequate, with defective scholarship and with a ruthless omission of (what Hamada too regarded as) obscenities.[6] We decided that unfortunately we could not publish a translation (Kahle had written out a partial German, and then English translation, with many blanks or latinisms for the 'obscene' parts), as it would have taken too long and, because neither of us was a professional pornographer, we would have found it too perplexing to translate all the 'technical' material in order to produce an 'un-bowdlerised' text.

For Mustafa, all this work was an act of selflessness and a demonstration of his devotion to the subject. Others had done the really hard work, and he was willing to facilitate the publication so that yet others could work on it. There was a very clear *isnad* in the publishing of these shadow plays.

Badawi and Philip Larkin

From Shakespeare to Coleridge, to I. A. Richards, from al-ʿAqqad to Mahfouz, and with histories of Arabic poetry and drama, Mustafa Badawi tirelessly worked at his self-imposed task of spreading a knowledge of literature. His last works were translations from English into Arabic, Shakespeare and the modern British poet Philip Larkin. One would not normally mention Ibn Daniyal and Philip Larkin in the same breath, but it is possible to see that, if as a scholar you have the aim of furthering the cause of literature for both English- and Arabic-speaking audiences, the two authors are both embraced as part of one academic mindset, of one academic aim – to spread a delight in literature.

Badawi's interest in Larkin stemmed from his early days in England (he had published a volume of his own poetry in 1956 – *Rasaʾil min London – Letters from London*) and his interest in the poetry of T. S. Eliot, W. H. Auden and others. Larkin fits into that tradition. Eliot in particular had a 'strangely powerful influence'[7] on the minds of certain young Arab literary scholars. Mustafa obviously thought it worth the effort of translating a selection of Larkin's works for an Arabic reading public. Translating poetry is a notoriously difficult undertaking, as, in addition to the perhaps obvious meaning of a poem, there are often allusions, colloquialisms and humour appreciated perhaps only by the native reader. Badawi himself recognised this. He wrote that 'many readers, who are not acquainted with the language of the original, inevitably, poetry being what it is, get only a much watered down version of poems in other languages'.[8] And the very Englishness of Larkin is a striking feature of his poetry. Badawi published his translation of Larkin – *Mukhtarat*[9] (*Selections*) – in Cairo in 1998. The *Collected Poems*[10] of Larkin contains 245 items; Badawi has selected sixty to translate. I cannot see anywhere that he justifies his choice of poems. I imagine he chose those that would have a more direct appeal to the Arabic reading public. In an intriguing introduction he discusses influences on Philip Larkin, the works of poets such as W. B. Yeats, T. S. Eliot and W. H. Auden, and analyses how he fitted into the literary scene of his time. He also analyses one or two individual poems to underline his interpretation of Larkin's approach.

Larkin, he says, is a poet hardly anyone has heard of in the Arab world, even though he is the most widely read and appreciated English poet of his generation. Arab poets had not really caught up with him. They had turned to the poetry of T. S. Eliot 'when it was already beginning to look old-fashioned, having in the meantime been succeeded by the work of the generations of Auden and Philip Larkin'.[11] Larkin was thus worth translating although Badawi recognises that he has that particular Englishness which makes it difficult to do so. It is a 'pessimistic observation of emotions, places, relationships and diminished expectations'. But it is not all gloom, and he can enjoy other sides of English life – irony, sarcasm, mockery and humour, which are difficult to translate into another language that has a dissimilar culture. But much of his poetry transcends a narrow localism to embrace wider horizons of humanity and a universal openness.

Larkin was a modern man who had suffered the fate of one who had lost his faith and rid himself of all illusions. Yet in his freedom he had not found a meaning to his life or to life in general, either in his freedom from religion or his freedom in sex. He continued to search for certainty while suspecting there was none. 'The secret of his personality is that it enabled him to put all this into masterful poetry which unites sympathy with technical discipline and simplicity and a mockery that are free from falseness and deliberate obscurity.'[12] This admiration for technical skill (as evinced as well for Ibn Daniyal) combined with sympathy for the state of humanity is at the root of Mustafa's approach to literature.

Despite the difficulties of translation, Larkin for Badawi was an ideal poet to present to the Arabs.[13] Other English-language poets had been known to the Arabs, but by the 1970s Larkin seemed to stand alone. He was a post-Romantic who brought to his own works a certain detachment and direct engagement with everyday experiences. His language is colloquial and ironic, far from what one might usually consider poetic. Although influenced by Romanticism, Larkin, even in his first poems, was not entirely seduced by it and was aware of its shortcomings. To illustrate this point, Badawi takes the poem 'To write one song, I said',[14] in which the poet confronts the difference between what his Romantic imagination and knowledge might have led him to expect in a certain situation and what he finds in the real world.

To write one song, I said,
As sad as the sad wind
That winds around my bed,
Having one simple fall
As a candle-flame swells, and is thinned,
As a curtain stirs by the wall
– For this I must visit the dead.
Headstone and wet cross,
Paths where the mourners tread,
A solitary bird,
These call up the shade of loss,
Shape word to word.

That stones would shine like gold
Above each sodden grave,
This, I had not foretold,
Nor the birds' clamour, nor
The image morning gave
Of more and ever more,
As some vast seven-piled wave,
Mane-flinging, manifold,
Streams at an endless shore.

(*The North Ship*, 1943–4)

قلت لكي أكتب أغنية حزينة

قلت لكي أكتب أغنية حزينة
مثل الرياح الحزينة
التي تَطُوف حول فراشي
أغنية ذاتَ إيقاع بسيطٍ يتهاوي
مثل اللهب في شَمعة ينبهج ثم يصير هزيلا
مثل ستارٍ يهتزُّ قُربَ الحائط
يلزمني أن أزور الموتى
فشوَاهدُ القبور والصلبانُ النديّة
والطرقُ التي ضربت فيها الجنازات
وطائرٌ وحيدٌ

هذه يستثيرُ شبحَ الفقدان
وتصوغُ الألفاظَ الملائمة.

ولكني ما تنبُّأت
بأن الحجارة ستلمع مثل الذهب
فوق كل قبر غارقٍ في الماء
ولا تنبُّأت بجَلَبَة الطيور
ولا بما أتى به الصباحُ
من صُوَرِ الكَثرة الكثيرة
مثل موجةٍ هائلة من سبع طبقات
متعددةِ الأشكالِ تزُجُّ برَأسها
وتندفعُ نحو شاطئٍ لا نهاية له.

Larkin's title has become in Arabic 'Qultu li-kay aktuba ughniyatan hazina' – with *hazina* added to the title (as emphasis) and to the first line rather than as in Larkin twice in the second line. Larkin says he intends – in the manner of a Romantic – to write one song which will be sad as the wind, sadness (longing, regret), writes Badawi, being one of the basic foundations of Romanticism. His sad song is like the wind that walks round his bed and has one simple fall (*iqaʿ*) as a candle flares and gutters. To write this kind of song the poet finds it necessary to prepare the right kind of atmosphere. He must visit a cemetery where there are mourners and damp gravestones, where one solitary bird helps to call up the shade of loss. All these could help to build up a Romantic atmosphere.

But Romanticism has moved on, and things do not work out the way he expected. Larkin continues that to his surprise the gravestones are not wet but shining; there are many birds that make a loud clamour, and the morning brings great activity. The poet is taken aback. 'This, I had not foretold,' he says. What he had expected from Romanticism was not there; instead of death, loss, deprivation, silence and rain, the poet discovers before him life, plenty, voices and light. The sea beats against an endless shore, manifold and 'mane-flinging' – translated as 'flinging its head – *tazujju bi-ra'siha*' which blurs the image of horses surging from the sea.

Badawi clearly felt it necessary to emphasise the element of surprise in the poet's reaction and moved 'This I had not foretold' to the first line of the second verse so that the words '*Walakinni ma tananabba'tu / Bi-an . . .*' ('But I had not predicted / That . . .') stand out rather more than in the original. He also repeats the words in the fourth line. In this poem, noted Badawi, Larkin's criticism and even mockery of the Romantic position are clear.

The Arabic version of 'To write one song' shows us the problems of translating Larkin and the way Badawi has attempted to surmount them. He makes no attempt to imitate the rhythm or rhyme of the original and uses a straightforward language and, if thought necessary, transposes or adds words in the search for clarity. The translation should best be read together with his analysis in the introduction.

Another poem – 'Vers de Société' – demonstrates difficulties of a different order for the translator. Larkin, the rather lugubrious observer of modern society, commented on commonplace experiences in a colloquial style – 'a plain style in modern times' – that involved a certain crudity of language, using words previously taboo. In face of criticism he wrote that the forbidden was a source of inspiration to him as, he said rather improbably, daffodils were to Wordsworth. In 'Vers de Société' Larkin set out to shock in his description of an evening drinks party by using vulgar language. Badawi does not follow suit in his translation and thereby loses some of the point of the poem which is to show just how boringly pretentious such parties can be. (The French title is surely ironic.)

> My wife and I have asked a crowd of craps
> To come and waste their time and ours: perhaps
> Perhaps you'd care to join us? In a pig's arse friend.

In translation 'craps' becomes *asdiqa'* – friends – a neutral word hardly implying that the people you have invited are unbearable; 'pig's arse' becomes *lahm khanzir* – pig's flesh, pork – thus losing the impact of the original. Larkin mocks the drinks served at parties as 'washing sherry', therefore the cheapest of booze. That becomes 'a glass of wine' (*ka's nabidh*) and the 'bitch' who is talking drivel at the party is merely *imra'a* in Arabic – a woman. In the English she reads only the consumers' magazine *Which?*, something that shows a narrow interest in material things. In Arabic it has become 'a certain magazine' (*majalla min al-majallat*) which cannot in the same way mock the ordinariness of her reading. It is all this rather jejune language that makes Larkin such a challenge to translate.

Similar difficulties of language occur in the final poem to be mentioned, 'This Be the Verse'. It is the best known of Larkin's works both because of its use of strong language and of its message.

> They fuck you up your mum and dad.
> They may not mean to, but they do.
> They fill you with the faults they had
> And add some extra just for you.
>
> But they were fucked up in their turn
> By fools in old-style hats and coats,
> Who half the time were soppy-stern
> And half at one another's throats.
>
> Man hands on misery to man.
> It deepens like a coastal shelf.
> Get out as early as you can,
> And don't have any kids yourself.
>
> (*High Windows*, April? 1971)

لتكن هذه الأبيات

يعقّدك أبوك وأمك
ربما عن غير قصد منهما , إلا أنهما يعقّدانك
يملآنك بما فيهما من عيوب
ويضيفان إليها عيوبا أخرى لأجلك أنت.

ولكنهما بدورهما عقّدهما حمقى آخرون
يرتدون قبعات ومعاطف من طراز عتيق
يمضون نصف وقتهم في خليط من الحنان للفرط والصرامة
والنصف الآخر ممسكين بخناق بعضهم البعض.

بتناقل الإنسانُ البؤسَ أباً عن جد
ويتفاقم البؤس كالرفِّ الصخريِّ قرب سطح الماء
فلتخرُج منها في أقرب وقت
ولا تنجب أنت أيِّ أولاد.

Larkin claimed, as we have noted, that the 'forbidden' was a source of inspiration to him. In this poem he is saying what was previously unsayable by making use of a common swear word well known to all schoolboys and soldiers but not commonly used in poetry. In the context, use of the word 'fuck' was new but it enabled the poet to get his meaning across in a totally unexpected way. The word at the time (1971) was taboo in polite society. Its use had caused a furore in D. H. Lawrence's *Lady Chatterley's Lover* (1928) which came into the public domain only in 1960 after a court case. The critic Kenneth Tynan had first used it on television in 1965, hoping, he said, that it would not be diabolical, revolting or totally forbidden. It has by now become a common swear word with little sexual connotation whose meaning has been expanded by adding 'up' to denote 'to mess up'. The shock of this poem is the claim that parents 'fuck up' their children. It is no surprise post-Freud to know that parents influence their children. It was a shock to learn that they 'fuck you up'. Badawi again dodged the challenge of English usage – although he admitted that the poem was well known for its use of obscene language – and translated 'fuck up' as *yuʿaqqidu* – from the root meaning 'knot'. The second form means 'to tangle or knot up' – therefore, your parents complicate your life for you.

While the meaning is clear, the shock is lost. The poem adds that your parents in turn had been 'fucked up' by other 'fools' from an older generation. Finally, Larkin observes gloomily that 'Man hands on misery to man – Get out as early as you can', which Badawi translates as 'get out from it as soon as possible' without specifying what *it* is.

Badawi ends his commentary on this poem and its final line 'And don't have any kids yourself' by noting that this pessimistic philosophy is not unlike that of the blind Arab poet from the eleventh century, Abu'l-ʿAlaʾ al-Maʿarri (973–1058), who also expressed his worldview in the recommendation that, as life was too painful, parents should bring no more children into this world. The mention of al-Maʿarri brings us back to medieval poetry and reminds us again of Ibn Daniyal. Mustafa Badawi's long journey through literature is completed.

Notes

1. *Three Shadow Plays by Muhammad Ibn Daniyal*, ed. by P. Kahle. Cambridge: E. J. W. Gibb Memorial, 1992, p. 6.
2. Ibid., p. 10.
3. Ibid.
4. Ibid.
5. Once the text was published it encouraged the appearance of several Ibn Daniyal studies and criticisms. While scholars were ready to criticise and correct Kahle's text (something we hoped would happen), nobody has yet produced a better version. A seminar was held in California University to discuss the text and one scholar wrote that 'The appearance at last of this long awaited volume is an event of considerable significance to students of medieval Arabic literature'. Li Guo published in 2012 his *The Performing Arts in Medieval Islam. Shadow Play and Popular Poetry in Ibn Daniyal's Mamluk Cairo*, Leiden: Brill, 2012. However, more excitingly, a partial English version was performed for the first time in New York in 2013. Perhaps it was translated from Kahle's text. I think that would have pleased him enormously.
6. See Badawi, *Three Shadow Plays*, p. 11.
7. M. M. Badawi, *Modern Arabic Literature and the West*, London: Ithaca Press, 1985, p. 121.
8. Ibid., p. 99.
9. Philip Larkin, *Mukhtarat (Selections)*, translated by M. M. Badawi, Cairo, 1998.
10. Philip Larkin, *Collected Poems*, London: Faber and Faber, 1988, ed. by Anthony Thwaite, p. 180.
11. Badawi, *Modern Arabic Literature*, p. 124.
12. All these words can be found on the rear cover of *Mukhtarat*.
13. The ideas summarised here are all from the introduction to *Mukhtarat*.
14. Larkin, *Collected Poems*, p. 291.

PART II
THE ACADEMIC LEGACY

5

Beginning and End:
Exploring the Qur'anic 'Grand Story'

Mohamed Mahmoud

S cholars have spoken about different dimensions of religion, one of which is that of myth or narrative.[1] Though religions are usually treated primarily as belief-systems, it may be argued that the narrative dimension is the basic and overarching element that defines the system, holds it together and gives it its ultimate meaning. Religion has always had to contend with the big and perennial questions of beginnings and ends and ultimate meanings. In contrast to philosophy (and science), religion has tended to address these issues through the device of myths and narratives.

This narrative element operates in the Qur'an on several levels: beginnings, biblical past, non-biblical past, present and eschatological future. The totality of these levels constitutes what may be described as the Qur'anic 'grand story'. By 'grand story' I refer to the underlying, basic conceptual scheme that informs Qur'anic stories and bestows meaning and coherence on them. This basic conceptual scheme is predicated on a relationship between humankind and God that leads to either salvation or damnation. In expressing this relationship, the Qur'anic narrative form turns God into a person with a dramatic presence and human attributes. The focus in this chapter will be on the beginnings as expressed by the creation story and on the eschatological future.

Some key elements of this grand story are succinctly summed up in 16: 112–13 which reads:

69

God has struck a similitude: a city that was secure, at rest, its provision coming to it easefully from every place, then it was unthankful for the blessings of God; so God let it taste the garment of hunger and of fear, for the things that they were working. There came indeed to them a Messenger from amongst them, but they cried him lies; so they were seized by the chastisement while they were evildoers.

At the centre of the story we come across the three dramatic elements of God, God's messenger and the people of the city. Furthermore, there is a cluster of three elements that are in operation: the ingratitude (*kufr*) of the people of the city, the message of the messenger and the chastisement (*'adhab*) sent by God. Though the first and third elements in this cluster are indicated explicitly, the second element is implicitly suggested in the phrase, 'There came indeed to them a Messenger from amongst them'. These elements present us in fact with the commonest primary blocks of Qur'anic narratives that are reworked and redeveloped throughout the Qur'an.

As a story that serves the function of representing some of the key elements of the grand story, the story of 16: 112–13 is of an abstract nature. The people to whom God's message is addressed are figuratively referred to as a 'city' (*qarya*), the city itself is anonymous, and the messenger is nameless (the only thing we know about him is that he belongs to the people of the city). No mention is made of the time when the events of the story unfold, and no details of the manner of the people's punishment are provided.

Evidently the function of this skeletal and abstract story ties in with the overall Qur'anic scheme of pointing out the way to salvation. What the Qur'an offered its seventh-century Arabian audience was a fresh chance of salvation. When this audience was exposed to the story of these verses and heard the phrase 'a Messenger from amongst them', they would most likely have immediately inferred the implied link between this nameless messenger and their own messenger. We may also reasonably assume that they were not puzzled by the silence of the Qur'an on the nature of the messenger's message, for they would most likely have concluded that it was a message similar to what the messenger in their midst preached. Furthermore, it would have been unlikely that they would have missed the veiled Qur'anic threat to them when the verses recounted how the people of the city ended up being seized by divine chastisement.

The seed of the Qur'anic grand story is what may be described as the cosmic beginning. This beginning is narrated in 41: 9–12. After stating that God created the earth in two days and ordained its provisions in four days, the narrative passage progresses to tell us:

> Then He lifted Himself to heaven when it was smoke, and said to it and to the earth, 'Come willingly, or unwillingly!' They said, 'We come willingly.' So He determined them as seven heavens in two days, and revealed its commandment in every heaven. And We adorned the lower heaven with lamps, and to preserve; that is the ordaining of the All-mighty, the All-knowing. (11–12)

This beginning is to all intents and purposes a preparation of the physical stage for the climactic moment of the human beginning when God creates Adam.

The dramatic tension we witness in 41: 9–12 is absent in 7: 54 which recaptures the cosmic beginning by re-filtering the traditional Biblical narrative and giving it a Qur'anic slant. Hence we read:

> Surely your Lord is God, who created the heavens and the earth in six days – then sat Himself upon the Throne, covering the day with the night it pursues urgently – and the sun, and the moon, and the stars subservient, by His command.

Since the Biblical account of God resting on the seventh day after six days of working on creation was incompatible with the Qur'anic notion of a perfect and omnipotent God, it was replaced with a Qur'anic account according to which God sits on the throne on the seventh day.[2]

The dramatic tension of 41: 9–12 is transposed to the Qur'anic account of the creation of Adam. Unlike the Genesis account, the Qur'anic account starts at an earlier point when Adam is still a mere idea in the mind of God that has not yet been conceived and so we read:

> And when thy Lord said to the angels, 'I am setting in the earth a viceroy'. They said, 'What, wilt Thou set therein one who will do corruption there,

and shed blood, while we proclaim Thy praise and call Thee Holy?' He said, 'Assuredly I know that you know not.' (2: 30)

This disagreement and tension between God and the angels over the would-be humans and what they could potentially be and do places Adam, even before his appearance on the scene, right at the centre of the drama of creation.[3] God's brief and cryptic reference that He knows what the angels do not know is not meant to be a statement that reveals to the angels something that they do not already know (for, undoubtedly, the angels are fully aware that God is all-knowing). Rather, God's reference is of a dramatic significance that is to be revealed in the light of the 'naming' event. Soon after God's creation of Adam, he teaches him 'the names, all of them'. When the angels fail God's test to tell the names and Adam tells them the names, He says to them, 'Did I not tell you I know the unseen things of the heavens and earth? And I know what things you reveal, and what you were hiding' (2: 33).

The version of Chapter 2 of the creation and disobedience story proceeds briskly and we read:

And when We said to the angels, 'Bow yourselves to Adam'; so they bowed themselves, save Iblis; he refused, and waxed proud, and so he became one of the unbelievers. And We said, 'Adam, dwell thou, and thy wife, in the Garden, and eat thereof easefully where you desire; but draw not nigh this tree, lest you be evildoers.' (2: 34–5)

What we note about the account is not only that it is anthropocentric but also that it is, more specifically, androcentric – it is Adam, the male element, who is the object of the celebratory bowing; Eve appears on the scene after this decisive event. As in the Genesis account, the creation of Qur'anic Adam precedes that of the female. However, in contrast to Genesis, the Qur'an does not mention the name of Eve – she is referred to only as Adam's 'wife'. Though God addresses only Adam in verse 2: 35, He addresses both of them in verse 2: 36 when he banishes them from Paradise and we read: 'and We said, "Get you all down, each of you an enemy of each; and in the earth a sojourn shall be yours, and enjoyment for a time"'.[4] However, verse 2: 37 which declares God's forgiveness and mercy, reverts to the androcentric mode, as it is only Adam who is at the centre of the divine act.

The Qur'an presents us with a more fully developed portrayal of the Devil (*al-shaytan*, *Iblis*)[5] than Genesis. Iblis is given a Qur'anic voice and the chance to present his case. When he refuses to bow to Adam (in defiance of God's command), he says that he is better than Adam by virtue of being created of fire whereas Adam is created of clay. After being granted a respite till the day of the Last Judgement, he sets out his plan to lead people astray and declares:

> Now, for Thy perverting me, I shall surely sit in ambush for them on Thy straight path; then I shall come on them from before them and from behind them, from their right hands and their left hands; Thou wilt not find most of them thankful. (7: 16–17)[6]

From this moment on, the human becomes the field of a constant showdown between God and Satan, and it is this dramatic situation that provides the grand story with its dramatic substance. When we examine the situation that subsequently culminates in the creation of Adam and the disobedience of Satan, we find that the real centre of the grand story is in fact Adam, without whose creation Iblis would not have acquired his identity as Satan or the Adversary of God[7] and God Himself would not have acquired a dramatic presence and significance as part of a grand story.

If the disobedience of Satan and his refusal to bow to Adam is the first major blow to God's authority, a further blow soon follows when Adam and his wife disobey Him and taste the forbidden tree. The forbidden tree has the crucial dramatic function of serving as a silent, beckoning agent leading to the fall of Adam and Eve. The first mention of the tree in 2: 35 is in the context of a summarily stated divine command not to draw near it. Whereas in the Biblical account we encounter two trees, a tree of life and a tree of the knowledge of good and evil, and we hear God put forth the reason for His prohibition, we come in the Qur'anic account across one tree and we do not hear God give the reason for His command. The giving of this reason is assigned in the Qur'anic account to Satan. In 7: 20, Satan says to Adam and Eve: 'Your Lord has only prohibited you from this tree lest you become angels, or lest you become immortals' and we read in verse 20: 120, 'Adam, shall I point thee to the Tree of Eternity, and a Kingdom that decays not?'[8] Is Satan communicating to them a truth about the nature of the tree or is he deceiving them? This is an issue about which the Qur'anic account is silent. Instead, the Qur'anic narrative voice shifts the focus to Satan's real motive which is 'to reveal to them that which was hidden from them of their shameful parts' – and that is exactly what happens when they eat from the tree. Hence the Qur'anic reconstruction of the Biblical story focuses on the one tree that is dramatically significant, namely the tree of the knowledge of good and evil, and pushes the tree of eternity into the mist of Satanic whisper.

But how does the creation story and the specificity of the 'Adamic beginning' relate to the grand story? In addressing this question, the Qur'an responds in two ways. On the one hand, it makes a clear identification between Adam and the rest of humankind at the very moment of the 'Adamic beginning' and so we read: 'We created you, then We shaped you,[9] then We said to the angels: "Bow yourselves to Adam" . . .' (7: 11). On the other hand, the Qur'an constructs a narrative of a very special covenant: 7: 172 reads:

> And when thy Lord took from the Children of Adam, from their loins, their
> seed, and made them testify touching themselves, 'Am I not your Lord?'
> They said, 'Yes, we testify' – lest you should say on the Day of Resurrection,
> 'As for us, we were heedless of this'.

According to the exegetical material, this covenant took place on earth when God drew forth all the offspring of Adam from his loins and made them testify.[10] It is because of this testimony that each and every single human being is drawn into the 'Adamic beginning', not just by virtue of Adamic descent but also on account of having entered into a primordial, binding covenant with God. When the Qur'an asserts that humans cannot plead heedlessness of their covenant on the Day of Judgement it immediately establishes the affinity between the primeval beginning and the eschatological end.

Eschatology is a key theme in the Qur'an; it is presented chiefly through an omniscient narrative voice. The scenes of the Last Judgement and the final reward of believers with Paradise and the punishment of unbelievers with their consignment to Hell are among the most vivid and stirring dramatic scenes in the Qur'an.

The Qur'an clearly indicates that the seed of what will happen at the end of time is sown at the very beginning. When Satan expounds his plan as to how he will misguide humans, God reacts by expelling him and saying, 'Go thou forth from it, despised and banished. Those of them that follow thee – I shall assuredly fill Gehenna with all of you' (7: 18). This verse of the version of Chapter 7 of the story is followed by the verse in which we read, 'O Adam, inherit, thou and thy wife, the Garden . . .' What we note here is that though we are not aware of any spatial dimension within which the creation event and the disobedience of Satan and his disputation with God take place, we come across two specific place references, namely Gehenna (*jahannam*) and the Garden (*al-janna*). In this narrative passage the mention of Hell precedes that of Paradise, but there is what may be described as an 'existential disparity' between them at the particular time of the dispute – Paradise exists (and it is a place into which Adam and Eve can move), whereas Hell does not yet exist.

The Qur'anic narrative of eschatology is linear, with a beginning, middle and end. Just as the beginning of creation is cosmic, so is the beginning of the eschatological event heralding the Day of Judgement. The coming of the Hour is described in terms of a cataclysmic rending of the universe and so we read:

> When the sun shall be darkened, when the stars shall be thrown down, when the mountains shall be set moving . . . when the seas shall be set boiling . . . when heaven shall be stripped off . . .' (81: 1–3)

and

> Upon the day when Heaven shall be as molten copper and the mountains shall be as plucked wool-tufts . . . (70: 8–9)

These apocalyptic images reach their climax in the image of complete annihilation described in 89: 21, which says, 'No indeed! When the earth is ground to powder'. Immediately after this, God makes His entrance in His full majesty and splendour and the reckoning of humans starts:

> and thy Lord comes, and the angels rank on rank, and Gehenna is brought out, upon that day man will remember; and how shall the Reminder be for him? (89: 22)

Though verses like 'The day that men shall be like scattered moths, and the mountains shall be like plucked wool-tufts' (101: 4–5) present an image that subsumes humans within the order of the complete annihilation of things, this proves only temporary in their case – for, after all, it is the human who is the centre of the Judgement event. The notion of the Day of Judgement (*yawm al-din*) is effectively a subset of the notion of the Day of Resurrection (*yawm al-qiyama*) (which occurs far more frequently). Naturally, the vast number of humans will be subject to the resurrection event (captured through images such as 'abasing their eyes, they shall come forth from the tombs as if they were scattered grasshoppers, running with outstretched necks to the Caller' (54: 7)). The hapless who will actually be alive when the 'earthquake of the Hour' (*zalzalat al-sa'a* (22: 1)) takes place are described in images such as

> on the day when you behold it, every suckling woman shall neglect the child she has suckled, and every pregnant woman shall deposit her burden, and thou shalt see mankind drunk, yet they are not drunk. (22: 2)

The highly dramatic scenes of this reckoning and questioning constitute the middle of the eschatological narrative. Though the object of this reckoning is the individual in the first place ('We shall inherit from him that he says, and he shall come to Us alone' (19: 80)), an entire community (*umma*) can also be its object:

> (And thou shalt see every nation hobbling on their knees, every nation being summoned unto its Book: 'Today you shall be recompensed for that you were doing. This is Our Book, that speaks against you the truth; We have been registering all that you were doing.') (45: 28)

The notion of collective accountability is made the more dramatic through the image of a 'witness': 'And the day We shall raise up from every nation a witness against them from amongst them, and We shall bring thee as a witness against those' (16: 84).[11] The witness idea operates likewise on the individual level as described in the grim and solemn scene of verse 50: 21: 'And every soul shall come, and with it a driver and a witness'. Though the previous verse speaks about the individual as a disembodied soul (*nafs*), the basic Qur'anic concept of the individual subject to divine reckoning is of a corporeal being. It is by virtue of this corporeality that the individual is made to face the ultimate testificatory predicament described in 24: 24:

and there awaits them a mighty chastisement on the day when their tongues, their hands and their feet shall testify against them.[12]

This seemingly cacophonous scene is contrasted by another muted and noiseless scene describing the state of being in the presence of God:

On that day they will follow the Summoner in whom is no crookedness; voices will be hushed to the All-merciful, so that thou hearest naught but a murmuring. (20: 108)

Judgement leads to either salvation or damnation. These are not abstract concepts but rather existential states that are vividly dramatised through the images of Paradise and Hell. Among the sacred scriptures, the Qur'an is indubitably the scripture with the most intense and graphic descriptions of paradisiacal pleasures and infernal torments. As existential states, Paradise and Hell are predicated on the corporeal condition referred to above: humans do not enter these places and experience them as souls but as physical beings capable of bodily enjoyment or suffering. Though the jinn are accorded a status parallel to that of humans in God's creation scheme (as attested by 51: 56, which affirms: 'I have not created jinn and mankind except to serve Me), they are completely absent from the descriptions of paradisiacal pleasures and infernal torments.[13]

Besides Paradise and Hell, the Qura'nic imagination had touched on the idea of what functions as a Purgatory in the passage 7: 46–9. This intermediate space (described in the Qur'an as a 'veil' (*hijab*)) is inhabited by the men of 'the Ramparts' (*al-A'raf*) who are torn between a thirsting hope of entering Paradise and a gnawing fear of being consigned to Hell.[14] However, their story ends well and they are eventually allowed into Paradise (though with a lowly status according to some exegetes). The concept, however, remained underdeveloped, and the Qur'an did not deal with it beyond this passage. Hence, what the Qur'an presents us with is essentially a vision of an irreducible dualistic order where the Paradise/Hell opposition serves as a logical extension and an eschatological resolution of the God/Satan and the believer/ unbeliever oppositions.

The Qur'anic accounts of paradisiacal pleasures and infernal torments are without scene or plot. To be sure, these accounts have a narrative function but their structure is not typically narrative in the sense of having a dramatic progression. Though a verse such as 54: 55 in the passage, 'the godfearing shall dwell amid gardens and a river in a sure abode, in the presence of a King Omnipotent' (54: 54–5) can be read as an expression of an ultimate experience akin to the Christian notion of a beatific vision, the Qur'anic accounts of Paradise do predominantly stress states of sensual pleasures. These states of everlasting pleasure and joy are summed up in 44: 51–5, which affirm, 'Surely the godfearing shall be in a station secure among gardens and fountains, robed in silk and brocade, set face to face. Even so; and We shall espouse them to wide-eyed houris, therein calling for every fruit, secure'.

The bleakness of Hell is described in scenes that recur throughout the Qur'an. A general scene of enveloping agony is depicted in 4: 56, which proclaims:

> Surely those who disbelieve in Our signs – We shall certainly roast them
> at a Fire; as often as their skins are wholly burned, We shall give them in
> exchange other skins, that they may taste the chastisement . . .

An important aspect of torment that receives particular attention is what the inhabitants of Hell eat and drink. One variety of their food is the Tree of al-Zaqqum, whose eating is 'like molten copper, bubbling in the belly as boiling water bubbles' (44: 44–5). When it comes to drink, the evildoer 'is given to drink of oozing pus, the which he gulps, and can scarce swallow' (14: 16–17). The evildoer is eternally locked in an eternal state with no exit and constantly lives and relives the harrowing experience of finding himself in a plight where 'death comes upon him from every side, yet he cannot die' (14: 17).[15] This image may be read as the answer to the unbeliever's wish expressed in verse 78: 40, where we read, 'upon the day when a man shall behold what his hands have forwarded, and the unbeliever shall say, "O would that I were dust!"' This was clearly a narrative possibility that could have been pursued, closing the grand story with the happy and simple end of a return of righteous humankind to Paradise and consigning unrighteous humankind (and jinn-kind) to extinction. This end was, however, consciously dropped in favour of a complex end that retains Hell and denies the unbelievers any final release.

The Qur'anic grand story is meant to involve every single human being in the past, the present and the future. The present is perceived as only a transitional stage that bridges a primordial beginning and an eschatological end – and in that sense it is meaningless without these dimensions. In assessing the Qur'anic grand story we can say that it is a grand tragedy in which what the angels fear in verse 2: 30 turns out to be true and in which God's plan goes awry from the very start when Satan challenges His authority. God's preconceived plan of having a 'viceroy' is not fully realised in that He ends up with disobedient and wayward humans, the majority of whom are sent to Hell. The Qur'anic grand story does not present us with an end of perfect unity and harmony but rather one in which division and discord have become a permanent feature of existence. Unlike the simple, innocent, and unified existence of the beginning, the existence of the end is stained, torn and fractured.

This, however, leaves us with an intrinsic paradox. On the one hand, the end may be read as a vindication of God's ways and a victory of His will. But, on the other hand, the end may plausibly be read as a confirmation of Satan's vision and a victory of his great rebellion. If God can point out to Paradise as the ultimate symbol of His triumph, Satan may likewise point out to Hell as his indelible and eternal mark on existence. Such a state of affairs is the more paradoxical because both God and Satan are ultimately pointing out to the same entity: the human.

Notes

1. See Ninian Smart, *Dimensions of the Sacred: An Anatomy of the World's Beliefs*, Berkeley and Los Angeles: University of California Press, 1996, pp. 130–65.
2. It is important to note that though the statement 'then sat Himself upon the throne' is meant to contrast and refute the biblical resting account, it is not conclusive and it is open to the interpretative possibility that the 'sitting on the throne' can still be seen as tantamount to resting. It might be the case that this possible counter-reading gave rise to verse 50: 33, which pointedly asserts: 'We created the heavens and the earth, and what between them is, in six days, and no weariness touched Us'.
3. Exegetes struggled to explain how the angels made their statement about God's intended creation while they are not in a position to know the Unseen (*ghayb*) and their nature does not allow them to utter unfounded belief. To solve this conundrum, the exegetes constructed a 'prehistory' that involved the creation on earth of a species of jinn who did corruption and shed blood and recounted

how God sent Iblis to them to rid earth of their misdeeds. This prehistory hence provided the angels with a foundation for their belief. See Muhammad b. Jarir al-Tabari, *Tafsir al-Tabari*, Beirut: Dar al-Kutub al-'Ilmiyya, 1992, Vol. I, pp. 238–40.

4. The imperative *(i)hbitu* (rendered as 'Get you all down') is plural and so the exegetes were inclined to read it as addressed to a plural audience of more than two (since Arabic has a dual form). This audience, according to many an authority, includes, besides Adam and Eve, Satan and the serpent (which plays the crucial role of helping Satan slip into Paradise) (see al-Tabari, *Tafsir*, Vol. I, pp. 277–8).

5. The name Iblis occurs ten times in the Qur'an. In eight instances it occurs in the context of Iblis's refusal to bow to Adam. As such, the name is a dramatic element that serves as a proper name without necessarily carrying any negative association. In contrast, the name al-Shaitan occurs far more frequently and has a decidedly negative denotation. Hence, when the Qur'an describes the moment of Adam's and Eve's seduction (2: 36; 7: 20; 20: 120) we note that Iblis assumes the name of al-Shaitan.

6. Iblis's statement, 'Thou wilt not find most of them thankful' implies that some humans will be thankful. This implication is brought to the fore in another reworking of the scene where Iblis says, 'My Lord, for Thy perverting me I shall deck all fair to them in the earth, and I shall pervert them, all together, excepting those Thy servants among them that are devoted' (15: 39–40).

7. Exegetes were keen to construct a prehistory for Satan before his disobedience. According to Ibn 'Abbas, 'Before committing his disobedience, Iblis was an angel called 'Azazil. He used to live on earth and was one of the most conscientious and learned of angels and this made him predisposed to pride.' Al-Tabari, *Tafsir*, Vol. I, p. 262. The Qur'an, however, is not consistent about Satan's identity. 2: 34 reads, 'And when We said to the angels, "Bow yourselves to Adam"; so they bowed themselves, save Iblis . . .' This verse clearly indicates that Iblis belongs to the angels. By contrast, 18: 50 reads, 'And when We said to the angels, "Bow yourselves to Adam"; so they bowed themselves, save Iblis; he was one of the jinn . . .' This verse makes the point of affirming that Iblis belongs to the jinn. This affirmation makes sense in the light of the orthodox Islamic belief that angels are incapable of disobeying God. The jinn, by contrast, are like humans in that they are capable of obedience and disobedience. Exegetes strove hard to reconcile the inconsistency by claiming for instance according to a tradition attributed to some companions of Muhammad that 'Iblis was given the

sovereignty of the heaven of the earthly world and he belonged to a tribe of the angels called the jinn. They were called the jinn because they were the guardians of the janna (Paradise). Besides being a sovereign, Iblis was a guardian.' Ibid., Vol. I, p. 262. Another similarly forced interpretation is given by Qatada, who adopts a linguistic strategy. Going to one of the root meanings of the verb *janna* in the sense of 'to conceal', he maintains that the jinn designation of Iblis pertains to the fact that he '*janna* of the obedience of God (*janna 'an ta'ati rabbihi*)' in the sense of having been concealed or blocked or deprived of the obedience of God. Ibid., Vol. I, p. 263.

8. With a slight vocalic change, the word 'angels' ('*malakain*', more accurately 'two angels') can be read as *malikain* which means '(two) kings'. This reading makes better sense than the canonical reading of 'angels' in the light of what Satan says in 20: 120 about 'a Kingdom that decays not'. It is unlikely that Adam would have been impressed by the angels after excelling them in the naming test. This variant reading was in fact suggested by some earlier authorities (see al-Tabari, *Tafsir*, Vol. 5, p. 450).

9. Both pronouns here are in the plural.

10. See for instance al-Tabari's treatment in *Tafsir*, Vol. 6, pp. 110–17.

11. From the point of view of the central belief that God is omniscient and the Qur'anic explicit assertion that 'God is witness over everything' (4: 33) it may seem that the witness image in connection with the Last Judgement is redundant. It may, however, be argued that the function of the image is dramatic in the first place as the witness of prophets does not only vindicate their work but also heightens the dramatic intensity of the scene.

12. The same idea is reiterated in verse 36: 65, which says, 'Today We set a seal on their mouths, and their hands speak to Us, and their feet bear witness as to what they have been earning'. However, in this verse the unbelievers' tongues are silenced and the tongues hence do not play the witness role they play in 24: 24. This anomaly was, of course, bound to exercise the exegetes. Al-Tabari, for instance, tries to explain the difficulty away by maintaining that the verb '*tash-had*' in this context is not in the sense of 'to bear witness' or 'testify' but rather in the sense of 'witness' or 'see' – a seeing, evidently, that does not lead to speaking as their tongues are sealed. See al-Tabari, *Tafsir*, Vol. 9, p. 292.

13. 7: 38 and 179 speak about the jinn as among the inhabitants of Hell. Curiously, the Qur'an does not mention the jinn in connection with Paradise.

14. The exegetes had to contend with the peculiar problem as to why all the inhabitants of the Ramparts are exclusively men. A tradition attributed to Muhammad

provides the answer: they are men who fought in the cause of God without securing the permission of their parents; God exempts them from hellfire on account of their fighting for Him but does not allow them into Paradise on account of their disobedience to their parents. Al-Tabari, *Tafsir*, Vol. 5, p. 501.

15. Though the language of the Qur'an tends to use the masculine form, it is, of course, understood that the torment accounts include both men and women. In fact, according to the hadith material, women constitute the majority of the inhabitants of Hell (see al-Bukhari, *Sahih al-Bukhari*, ed. Qasim al-Shamma'i al-Rufa'i, Beirut: Dar al-Qalam, 1987, Vol. 1, p. 77).

6

Modern Arabic Literature as Seen in the Late Nineteenth Century:
Jurji Murqus's Contribution to Korsh and Kirpichnikov's *Vseobshchaya Istoriya Literatury**

Hilary Kilpatrick

Mustafa Badawi's contribution to the study of modern Arabic literature has been immense, indeed one can hardly imagine what the field would have looked like without it, at least in the English-speaking world. His teaching and writing in Oxford over some thirty years stimulated interest in what in the 1960s was a little-known and undervalued subject and it laid the foundations for much subsequent research. His scholarly achievements were even more influential because they were combined with a gift for friendship and with commitment and great generosity toward his students.

It was not academic considerations that brought Mustafa to Oxford, however, nor was he the first scholar of literature from the Arab world to move to Europe for personal reasons. Among earlier academic migrants was the Syrian Jurji Ibrahim Murqus (1846–1912);[1] his account of modern Arabic literature is the subject of this chapter. The son of a Greek Orthodox priest, Jurji Murqus left Damascus in 1860. After secondary education in Constantinople he studied at the Faculty of Oriental Languages of the University of St Petersburg, being awarded a silver medal for his dissertation on the speeches, letters and sayings ascribed to the Caliph ʿAli, and was then appointed to teach Arabic at the Lazarev Institute of Oriental Languages in Moscow.[2] There he worked until 1900, when he retired with the rank of general.[3] In 1906 poor health caused him to return to Syria, and he spent the last years of his life in Zahle.

Krachkovskii characterises Murqus as conscientious but not outstanding either as a teacher or as a scholar; nor was he very familiar with the contemporary state of scholarship. The disparate subjects he published on include the situation of the Oriental Christians, carrier pigeons in the East[4] and the *Muʿallaqa* of Imruʾ al-Qays, which he translated into Russian. He performed an important public service with his articles supporting the (Arab) Greek Orthodox Christians of Syria in their struggle for their national rights over against the Greek higher clergy, which were based on his knowledge of both the Arab and the Greek Orthodox worlds.[5] So wide was the response to these texts in Syria, Greece and the Balkans that the Tsarist government felt compelled to ban further articles by Murqus on these subjects.[6] Murqus's greatest contribution, however, lies in his annotated Russian translation of Bulus Ibn al-Zaʿim's (Paul of Aleppo's) famous account of the journey he and his father, Patriarch Makarios III Ibn al-Zaʿim, made to Constantinople, the Romanian principalities, Ukraine and Muscovy from 1652 to 1659, the *Safrat* (or *Rihlat*) *al-batriyark Makariyus.*[7] This major travel account had previously been known only in a faulty English translation whose author was not well informed about the Balkans, Russia or Orthodox Christianity; Russian translations of this English rendering also existed. Murqus, with his knowledge of Russian, literary Arabic and Syrian dialect, was excellently placed to produce a far more reliable version translated directly from Arabic.[8]

The text presented here is, according to Krachkovskii, the most important of Murqus's short articles.[9] It is an account of modern Arabic literature which was appended to the chapter on Arabic literature contributed by I. N. Kholmogorov to the *Vseobshchaya Istoriya literatury* (*Universal History of Literature*) edited by V. F. Korsh and A. I. Kirpichnikov, in which Kholmogorov covered the Arabic language and Arabic literature of the pre-Islamic and Islamic periods.[10] Writing in 1928, Krachkovskii judged Murqus's text to be completely out of date; elsewhere, however, he considered it valuable as a contemporary testimony.[11] Krymskii, in his history of modern Arabic literature left unfinished at his death in 1942, characterises it as cursory,[12] while referring to it several times.

Here is a slightly abridged rendering of Murqus's text.

From the end of the Arab caliphate intellectual activity among the Arabs ceased, and literature consisted in imitating models of the classical period. Only in the present century since Muḥammad ʿAli's conquest of Egypt has a new intellectual movement begun, engaged in chiefly by Christians, while Muslims have continued to follow the old models. Under the influence of European missionaries who have taught and produced textbooks on elementary subjects, Christians have developed a national literary movement. They have learned European languages, especially French, and come to know European ideas and culture. American missionaries who have entirely mastered Arabic have produced manuals on all kinds of subjects, not only religious.

Corresponding to this dual trend in writing, the Arabic literary productions in this century fall into two categories, Muslim and Christian, with a conservative and a European spirit and tendency respectively. Muslim writers continue to imitate the old models, hardly adding anything to them in their multi-volumed works on syntax, etymology and lexicography. Although poets are numerous, the only ones to have achieved anything remarkable are Ahmad Efendi al-Jindi[13] and al-Kasti,[14] the authors of many of the widely known songs. Although the Muslim legal scholars have an excellent knowledge of the language, they very seldom write anything and are entirely occupied with interpreting classical Islamic authors. The best of them are attached to al-Azhar mosque in Cairo.

Perfecting the Arabic language among Arab Christians in the present century started with the Maronite Metropolitan Germanos Farhat,[15] who began his education under the guidance of a shaykh and then entered a monastery in Lebanon where a French monk taught him French and Latin. He read Sylvestre de Sacy's *Grammaire arabe* and in imitation of it wrote his first book, *Al-Dalil fi l-sarf*, and then *Bahth al-matalib*. Although extant copies of Farhat's books are full of copyists' mistakes, his own command of Arabic is beyond suspicion. His lexicon testifies to this; although it follows the old model of al-Firuzabadi,[16] it is free of rarely used words and turns of phrase and is consequently much used by Christians. Among subsequent writers, Shaykh Nasif al-Yaziji,[17] despite being a Christian, belongs to the conservative school by education. After working as a secretary of Emir Bashir he moved to Beirut. His first book on grammar, *Fasl al-khitab*, follows the model of Farhat's *Bahth al-matalib*. He subsequently wrote many books on grammar, most notably an exposition of syntax in verse in imitation of Ibn Malik[18] to which he added a commentary along the lines of that of Ibn ʿAqil,[19] entitled *Kitab nar al-qira fi sharh jawf al-fara* (*Fire to Cook Refreshments: Commentary on the Belly of the Wild Ass*).[20] This work of 1,400 verses, based on al-Zamakhshari's[21] *Kashshaf* and al-Sabban,[22] stands out for its accuracy and its second hemistichs being free from padding, a fault often encountered in the texts of the age of decline. Another of his books is *Majmuʿ al-adab fi lisan al-ʿarab* (*Collected Rules of Usage in the Arabic Language*) in which he followed al-Taftazani's *Miftah*.[23] As a poet he is famous for his collection of *maqamat* entitled *Majmaʿ al-bahrayn*, modelled on those of al-Hariri, in which he included fine maxims and verses of the Qurʾan. He also left three *diwan*s of poetry. Characteristic of the poetry of the period is his panegyric of Sultan ʿAbd al-ʿAziz, in which the numerical value of the letters of each line add up to the year of the Sultan's accession, the initial letters of each verse combined make up a couplet which includes the year of his accession twenty-eight times, all the separate distichs begin alternatively with a pointed (*muʿjam*) or unpointed (*muhmal*) letter, letters of each hemistich make up the year of his accession, {the pointed letters of each hemistich together with each of the other three hemistichs produce the same year, the pointed and unpointed letters in the same sequence form the same thing}.[24] Yet despite these constrictions this panegyric has nothing forced, like all al-Yaziji's poetry. Having addressed here chiefly what may be called educational writings on Arabic grammar, we cannot ignore al-Bustani's excellent recent dictionary *Muhit al-muhit*, in which he introduced the European method of tracing words.[25] To conclude, we may mention the unfinished but interesting linguistic work of Faris al-Shidyaq,[26] *Sirr al-layal fi l-qalb wa-l-ibdal* on the transmutation of letters, which shows related meanings of words with similar sounds principally of the roots.

As already mentioned, scientific literature first appeared in Egypt, after Muhammad ʿAli had sent young men to France to study the sciences and arts. They translated textbooks on mathematics, geography, chemistry, medicine and astronomy. These translations are fairly successful, except for some problems of terminology, but they suffer from a complete absence of plans and illustrations, even in books on natural history and anatomy. When scientific knowledge spread in Syria with the help of the American missionaries, many textbooks with an incomparably better appearance were published. Some were written by local Christians who had studied with the American missionaries, but others were written by the Americans themselves, some of whom had a superlative command of Arabic.

The accounts of journeys to Europe by Faris al-Shidyaq, Salim Bustrus[27] and especially Shaykh Rifaʿa[28] are interesting.[29] They include accurate observations of aspects of the Europeans which from an Arab point of view are amusing and numerous original remarks about European life. Here one may also refer to the extremely interesting account of Patriarch Makarios's journey to the court of Tsar Alexei Mikhailovich, which has been translated into English and of which manuscripts exist in the Archives of the Ministry of Foreign Affairs and the library of the Asiatic Department in St Petersburg.[30]

The fictional literature which has arisen since the penetration of new European trends consists almost entirely of translations of tales and stories, although in this generation attempts have been made to create original works with subjects drawn from contemporary and older Arab life. For the artistic quality of his style and his skill in conveying European notions in an Arab form, the translations and articles of Professor S. I. Nawfal[31] are especially remarkable. We may also mention as a particularly interesting and more or less independent work a recent comedy in imitation of Molière's *L'avare*; it is almost an original composition. It was authored by Mr Naqqash in Beirut and according to the *Journal des Débats* it was the subject shortly afterwards of an article in the *Journal Asiatique*. For the Russian reader it is not uninteresting to mention the adaptation of the epic of ʿAntar made by Mr ʿAtaya and very successfully performed by the students of the Lazarevsky Institute at the Sekretarev Theatre in Moscow.[32]

As for Christian religious literature, it goes back long before Muhammad and numbers a whole series of writers in the pre-Islamic and early Islamic period.[33] In later times, apart from the many editions of the Bible published by the American missionaries and other religious societies, and also books on liturgy, spirituality and ethics, it is almost all polemical and of little interest. A very significant religious writer is the priest Yusuf

Muhanna Haddad, who died a martyr's death in the massacre of 1860 in Damascus. He made new translations of religious books from Greek and revised existing translations. Two other Damascenes, the priest Spiridon Sarruf and his son Theodore, were similarly active.[34] Equally memorable is Mikha'il Mishaqa, the former American consul in Damascus, who successfully introduced colloquial Arabic into literature.[35] We may also mention the Catechism in Arabic by Sophronios, Patriarch of Jerusalem, and his *Ethics*, translated from Greek.[36] Especially important are the works of Anthimos, Patriarch of Jerusalem, who died in 1808. His most noteworthy books are the *Commentary on the Psalms* and the *Kitab al-hidaya* (*The Book of Guidance*). The latter was printed in Vienna in 1792; a Western scholar wrote of it: 'This work deserves the highest praise for its many-sided learning and the purity of its Arabic language'.[37] Anthimos wrote it in Greek but then translated it himself into Arabic. Even now these books are extremely important for Arab Christians in the East, and the *Kitab al-hidaya* is read in church on Sundays during Lent. Anthimos's learning and profound knowledge of Greek, Arabic and Persian are shown by the fact that a British academy sent two scholars to ask his advice about how to translate the Old Testament into Persian.[38] Moreover, there exist some diwans, collections of religious poetry and many translated books on spiritual subjects mostly made from Latin or Greek. An example of contemporary ecclesiastical language is the superb translation of Metropolitan Innokentii of Moscow's *Guide to Attaining the Kingdom of Heaven* by Gerasimos Yarid, the present rector of the religious seminary of Pskov.[39]

To complete our sketch of recent Arabic literature we may mention the literary societies now appearing in Syria. The Syrian Society, founded in Beirut in 1852, aimed to spread the love of scientific knowledge and seek means to draw closer to Europe quickly, as the publications by its members show. It had only forty members drawn from the American missionaries and the most educated sections of the population. The best thing it did was to set up the first public library, which still exists today. To make clearer what the activities of this society were, we quote the titles of some articles written by its members and read at its meetings: 'On the Profit and Pleasure of Scientific Learning'; 'The Intellectual Movement in Syria in Rrecent Times', 'The Link between Syria and Europe', 'The Advantage of

Education for Public Servants'; 'On the Advantage of Educating Women'; 'The Sciences of the Ancient Arabs', 'The Bases of the Natural Sciences'. This is all callow and immature, of course, and the society itself existed only for five years.[40] A second society, the Syrian Learned Society, was founded in 1867 and developed further. Although it numbered up to 210 members, however, it lasted only two years.[41] At present there are two societies in Beirut and in Tripoli. Judging by the activities it has recently started, one of the Beirut societies, which is called Zahrat al-Adab, promises to become very useful and interesting.[42] This society has fixed increasing the number of schools as a goal and it has set up a printing press. Independently of these societies nearly all the Christian communities in Beirut and the other Syrian cities have established various fraternities with charitable and philanthropic aims. Their work in spreading literacy is of the same nature.

The first Arabic printing press in the East appeared in Aleppo at the beginning of the eighteenth century and then transferred to the Monastery of St John the Baptist at Shuwayr in Kisrawan. Later on presses were set up in Egypt, Constantinople, Beirut, Jerusalem and other cities. At present there are as many as nine presses in Beirut alone, and thirteen newspapers and periodicals are published there. This is apart from Egypt, which is in any case the centre of modern Arabic literary activity. Most of these papers are published by missionary societies, and the rest by local Christians. The oldest of them is *Hadiqat al-akhbar*, which was launched in 1857[43] and is published in two languages, Arabic and French.[44]

It will not have escaped the reader that Murqus is not always accurate in his information. An obvious instance of this is his renaming Shaykh Amin al-Jundi as Ahmad Efendi al-Jindi. Another example is his account of Germanos Farhat's early career. There is a glaring anachronism in the statement that Germanos Farhat (1670–1732) took Sylvestre de Sacy's Arabic grammar as his model; de Sacy (1758–1838) published it in 1810. And Farhat was educated in Aleppo, not Lebanon.[45] As a result of Murqus's mistake in chronology he appears in this text as a contemporary of Muhammad ʿAli. The account which Murqus gives of Nasif al-Yaziji's virtuoso panegyric of Sultan ʿAbd al-ʿAziz is only partly correct, and one wonders if he was simply relying on what he had heard about it. If he had verified the statements about pointed and unpointed letters, he would have seen that they do not correspond to reality – at least not in this poem. The dates which he gives for the founding of various societies are inaccurate, though this could be simply due to the difficulty of keeping up to date in Moscow with cultural life in Syria. But he is well informed on some other recent events. He knows of the third of Nasif al-Yaziji's diwans, which was published posthumously in Beirut in 1884, and also of al-Shidyaq's *Sirr al-layal fi l-qalb wa-l-ibdal* (*The Secrets of the Night: On Metathesis and Substitution*) which came out the same year in Constantinople. He does not use al-Shidyaq's Muslim name, however, although the writer had converted to Islam in 1860.

Leaving aside these factual aspects, one may turn to some fundamental questions: when does modern Arabic literature start? What are its main trends? Who are major authors and by whom have they been influenced? Murqus's text is too brief to discuss these issues in depth, but it suggests some answers. In his view Muhammad 'Ali's policies set off the new intellectual movement of the period through the translation of textbooks. He was closely seconded in this by the American missionaries, whose work Murqus greatly admires.[46] Napoleon, whose expedition to Egypt so often opens accounts of modern Arabic literature, does not rate a mention.[47] Besides Muhammad 'Ali, Germanos Farhat stands at the start of modern Arabic literature with his writings on the Arabic language, followed by Nasif al-Yaziji – who would have been almost Farhat's contemporary if Murqus's chronology were correct.

Murqus, however, also takes earlier writers into consideration; he does not see modern Arabic literature as completely divorced from the literary activity of the preceding period. Shaykh Amin al-Jundi and the two patriarchs of Jerusalem, Sophronios and Anthimos, are late eighteenth-century writers and Bulus Ibn al-Za'im, author of the account of Patriarch Makarios's journey to Russia, lived in the seventeenth century. It could be argued that Murqus's inclusion of this last author is to be explained by his personal interest in the *Safrat al-batriyark Makariyus* rather than serious historical considerations, but Jurji Zaydan also had a high opinion of it. Makarios Ibn al-Za'im is the first author he mentions in the fourth volume of his *Ta'rikh adab al-lugha al-'arabiyya*, and he qualifies his son Bulus's travel account as unparalleled in that period, remarking that the Arabic original deserves to be published.[48]

Murqus draws a distinction between Muslim and Christian writers, seeing the former as conservative and the latter as taking part in the new intellectual movements under European influence. This may partly be explained by his coming from Syria and being better informed about Syrian cultural life, where Christians were prominent, whereas Muslims pioneered the *nahda* in Egypt. Moreover the first half of the nineteenth century saw few Muslims active in the field of linguistic reform to which he accords much importance. But the division between Muslims and Christians is not hard and fast. On the one hand Nasif al-Yaziji, despite being a Greek Catholic, belongs to the conservatives, on the other the Muslim Rifa'a Rafi' al-Tahtawi appears alongside (Ahmad) Faris al-Shidyaq and Salim Bustrus as one of the authors of travel accounts – and a memorable one at that. And Murqus admires the Azhar shaykhs' command of Arabic. Towards Christians Murqus's approach is ecumenical: the Protestant al-Bustani rubs shoulders with the Maronite Germanos Farhat, the Greek Catholic Nasif al-Yaziji and the Greek Orthodox Salim Bustrus.

Murqus's presentation of the most recent Arabic literature concentrates on the evolution of the Arabic language, on prose writers and on translators. His opinion of modern (in his terms) poets in general is not high. The poets he mentions are authors of popular lyrics – in other words accessible to a wide public – and the only poem about which he gives any details, Nasif al-Yaziji's panegyric of Sultan 'Abd al-'Aziz, belongs in the general presentation of this writer's oeuvre and focuses on its linguistic brilliance. He starts with the Arabic language, noting that the philological writings – dictionaries, grammars, books on rhetoric and morphology – by Germanos Farhat, Nasif al-Yaziji, Butrus al-Bustani and Faris al-Shidyaq have enabled the Christians of nineteenth-century Syria and Lebanon to master the literary language thoroughly. These major authors' linguistic work is rooted in the Arabic philological tradition, as he makes clear with his naming of their sources, but they have complemented it with methods acquired through their contacts with Europeans or Americans.[49]

Of the four authors listed above, the one to whom Murqus devotes most attention is Nasif al-Yaziji.[50] Al-Yaziji is an educator, rendering the works of earlier authorities on Arabic accessible to his contemporaries and to the next generation. He is also a poet in rhymed prose as well as poetry, combining a superb command of the language with a natural style and making apt use of proverbs and maxims, a standard ingredient of Arabic poetry since the beginning. When Murqus describes the linguistic fireworks in his panegyric of Sultan 'Abd al-'Aziz and then observes that his style there as in all his poems is unforced, twenty-first-century readers may suspect a joke or at least some irony until they consult the text, but what Murqus says is true. He evidently expresses the judgement of contemporaries about al-Yaziji's oeuvre, and this is a useful indication of how very different the literary sensibilities of mid-nineteenth-century Arab writers and readers were from those of their successors. Already by Jurji Zaydan's time, however, al-Yaziji's works were becoming less well known, and Louis Cheikho, despite his overall admiration for him, found his emulations of Mamluk and Ottoman poets forced.

Where prose genres are concerned, Murqus recognises the significance of travel writing and mentions the most important authors, Rifa'a Rafi' al-Tahtawi and Ahmad Faris al-Shidyaq. His inclusion of Salim Bustrus in the list may seem surprising. This young Beiruti merchant's account of his six-month journey to Europe hardly appears in later scholarship,[51] and a comparison of it with the two other texts has not been undertaken. At the time, however, it was widely read in Syria because of its treatment of subjects of contemporary interest, and Murqus was reflecting this general enthusiasm.[52] Apart from the intrinsic value the text might have, another reason to include it was that Salim Bustrus's family had close ties to Russia and Salim himself was decorated twice by the Tsar.[53] He was probably the only secular writer in Murqus's account who was likely to be known to Russian non-orientalist readers. Another surprising aspect of this passage is Murqus's singling out the wit and entertainment value of these travel accounts. Whereas *Al-saq 'ala' l-saq* is justly famed for its wit and irony and read partly as a parody, humour is not a characteristic generally associated with *Takhlis al-ibriz fi talkhis Bariz*.[54] Modern research has concentrated on al-Tahtawi's representation of French life and culture and his contrasting it with that of Egypt in his time, but Murqus's remark suggests that some readers of *Takhlis al-ibriz* took a more detached view of it and the message it was intended to convey.

Murqus considered translation in itself significant, as is clear from his references to textbooks, especially those produced in Lebanon. But either he was not very interested in translations of fiction from Western European

languages or else he did not know much about them. At all events, he refers
to them without mentioning any names. Likewise, he indicates that original works of fiction are starting to appear in Arabic without specifying any
authors. He is, however, aware of the first stirrings of modern theatre in
Arabic, possibly because his colleague Mikha'il 'Ataya took an active interest
in it.

The final section of Murqus's presentation of modern Arabic literature
is perhaps the most unexpected to the twenty-first-century reader, since it
focuses on Christian religious writings. Dismissing polemics, a flourishing
genre in the Ottoman period,[55] Murqus concentrates on translations especially of works of spirituality. Apart from Mikha'il Mishaqa he mentions
only Orthodox writers, no doubt because they were the ones he knew and
also because they would interest his Russian readers. Mikha'il Mishaqa's
appearance in their company is unexpected, for he was a Greek Catholic
convert to Protestantism who did engage in polemics. He is, however, better
known for his treatise on Arabic music and for his history of Mount Lebanon
in the nineteenth century, *Al-jawab 'ala iqtirah al-ahbab.* When Murqus
observes that he introduced colloquial Arabic into literature he presumably
has this text in mind. Interestingly, Murqus's admiration for Nasif al-Yaziji's
linguistic prowess did not prevent him also appreciating Mikha'il Mishaqa's
innovative use of unpretentious language.[56]

Murqus relegates information about literary societies and printing presses
to the end of his survey, unlike Zaydan and Cheikho, who put these topics
at the beginning of their histories of modern Arabic literature. Given that he
has concentrated throughout on developments in Bilad al-Sham, the reader
is not prepared for his passing remark that Egypt is the current centre of literary activity. The absence of any explanation for this may have to do with one
important reason for it, 'Abd al-Hamid's censorship which drove so many
Syrian and Lebanese writers to Egypt. Censorship, after all, was in force
in the Russian Empire too when Murqus was writing, and he himself had
suffered from it earlier in his career.

The red thread running through Murqus's account of modern Arabic
literature is the Arabic language. Farhat's educational writings and those of
the nineteenth-century philologists; Nasif al-Yaziji's poetry and prose demonstrating his superlative command of literary Arabic; Mikha'il Mishaqa's

history in a more colloquial style; the translations into Arabic by Patriarch Anthimos and Gerasimos Yarid; the unnamed Azhar shaykhs' mastery of Arabic: all these are evidence of a sensitivity to language whatever the subject treated and whoever the author. Even in the case of the nineteenth-century translations of textbooks imparting modern knowledge, the significance of whose contents Murqus recognises, a linguistic criterion plays a part.

Murqus does not see a radical break in the Arabic language's development occurring some time in the early nineteenth century but rather a continuous evolution, with the medieval and post-medieval linguists and grammarians still providing indispensable points of reference for writers up to his day.[57] His view is a corrective to those who are inclined to regard the *nahda* chiefly in terms of *iqtibas*, the introduction and adaptation of new genres and modes of expression. And now that research has begun to study seriously the texts of what for long was known as the *'Asr al-inhitat*, the Age of Decline, his sense of the continuity of nineteenth-century writing with that of earlier centuries may be taken more seriously.

Another aspect of Murqus's account which adds to the conventional picture of nineteenth-century Arabic literature concerns the role of translations. Translations by Christians in Aleppo from the early eighteenth century on and then by Muhammad 'Ali's civil servants in Egypt, American missionaries in Lebanon and later reformers are recognised as having played an essential part in the process of acquiring modern knowledge, developing the Arabic language and modifying literary sensibility. Murqus's references to eighteenth- and nineteenth-century (Arab) Greek Orthodox translations are a reminder that there was another strand in the translation movement which is rarely, if ever, mentioned. The Greek Orthodox of Bilad al-Sham had already begun to translate liturgical texts into Arabic in the Middle Ages, and Meletios Karma, Archbishop of Aleppo from 1612 to 1634, undertook a revision of these disparate translations to produce unified texts faithful to the Greek originals.[58] He also envisaged an ecumenical Arabic translation of the Bible, taking account of existing versions in different languages.[59] The travelling Patriarch of Antioch Makarios Ibn al-Za'im and one of his successors, Athanasios Dabbas (1647–1724),[60] translated texts of Byzantine and post-Byzantine religious culture and history and encouraged others to do so too. The late eighteenth-century Patriarchs of Jerusalem Murqus mentions were continuing a tradition, with Russian as a source language being added in the nineteenth century. The literary importance of the translations of liturgical texts in particular is that they gave the Orthodox and Catholic Christians of the Byzantine tradition in Bilad al-Sham, who make up the majority of its Arabic-speaking Christians, access to Byzantine liturgical poetry with its wealth of metaphors, images and Biblical allusions.

Mustafa Badawi would have disputed some of Jurji Murqus's statements on sound scholarly grounds. As a man of the twentieth century and with a very different background and intellectual development from Murqus, he would also have taken issue with many of his judgements on modern Arab writers. But he would certainly have been delighted to see modern Arabic literature given a place so early in a universal history of literature. After all, bringing Arabic literature into the wider arena and 'allowing it to make its effect on the outside world'[61] was something to which he was passionately committed.

Notes

* I thank Mr Andrea Cantinotti (Bibliothèque cantonale et universitaire, Lausanne) for his advice on some Russian expressions, Dr Carsten Walbiner (Bonn/Bir Zeit) for important references and corrections and Dr Andreea Dunaeva (Bucharest) for some additional information.

1. For Murqus's biography see Louis Cheikho [Luwis Shaykhu], *Tarikh al-adab al-'arabiyya fi l-rub' al-awwal min al-qarn al-'ishrin*, Beirut: Matba'at al-Aba' al-Yasu'iyyin, 1926 (henceforth referred to as Cheikho, *Tarikh 1900–1925*), p. 87; Adham al-Jundi, *A'lam al-adab wa-l-fann*, Damascus: Matba'at Sawt Suriyya, 1954, pp. 222–3; I. Yu. Krachkovskii, *Arabistika v Rossii* (*Arabic Studies in Russia*) in Tom' V of Krachkovskii, *Izbrannye Sochineniya* (*Collected Works*), Moscow: Izdatel'stvo Akademii Nauk SSSR, 1958, pp. 113–15, 138–9; Andreea Dunaeva, 'L'arabisant russe Georges Abramovič Mourqos, spécialiste de l'œuvre de Paul d'Alep', in Ioana Feodorov (ed.), *Relations entre les peuples de l'Europe Orientale et les chrétiens arabes au XVIIe siècle. Macaire III Ibn al-Za'im et Paul d'Alep*. Actes du Ier Colloque international le 16 septembre 2011, Bucarest, Bucharest: Editura Academiei Române, 2012, pp. 59–68.

2. The Lazarev Institute, established in 1814, taught the languages of the Near East and the Caucasus. From 1871 it offered an advanced course with a practical orientation to train mainly dragomans and consular officials (David

Schimmelpenninck van der Oye, *Russian Orientalism. Asia in the Russian Mind from Peter the Great to the Emigration*, New Haven: Yale University Press, 2010, p. 176).

3. Krymskii, *Istoriya*, pp. 306–7.

4. Ibid., pp. 210–11. His translation of Mikha'il Sabbagh's *Musabaqat al-barq wa-l-ghamam fi su'at al-hamam* was occasioned by a discussion in Russian military circles after the Russo-Turkish war of 1877–8 about the military use of carrier pigeons.

5. Cheikho, *Tarikh 1900–1925*, p. 87.

6. Dunaeva, 'L'arabisant russe', pp. 60–1.

7. Makariyus Ibn al-Za'im (c. 1600–1672), Patriarch of Antioch, transmitter of the Byzantine heritage and historian; Bulus Ibn al-Za'im (Paul of Aleppo) (1627–69), historian, traveller and translator. For basic information about these and most other authors mentioned here I have relied on the following works: Louis Cheikho [Luwis Shaykhu], *Tarikh al-adab al-'arabiyya fi l-qarn al-tasi' 'ashar. Al-juz' al-awwal. 1800–1870*, second ed., Beirut: Matba'at al-Aba' al-Yasu'iyyin, 1924; Cheikho, *Tarikh al-adab al-'arabiyya fi l-qarn al-tasi' 'ashar. Al-juz' al-thani. 1870–1900*, Beirut: Matba'at al-Aba' al-Yasu'iyyin, 1910; Georg Graf, *Geschichte de christlichen arabischen Literatur (GCAL)*, Vols III and IV, Vatican City: Biblioteca apostolica vaticana, 1951–2; 'Umar Rida Kahhala, *Mu'jam al-mu'allifin*, Beirut: Dar ihya' al-turath al-'arabi, 1957; Joseph E. Lowry and Devin J. Stewart (eds), *Essays in Arabic Literary Biography 1350–1850*, Wiesbaden: Harrassowitz Verlag, 2009; Julie Scott Meisami and Paul Starkey (eds), *Encyclopedia of Arabic Literature* (henceforward *EAL*), London and New York: Routledge, 1998; Joseph Nasrallah, *Histoire du mouvement littéraire dans l'Eglise melchite du Ve au XXe siècle (HMLEM)*, Vol. IV – *Epoque ottomane 1516–1900. Tome 2: 1724–1800*, Louvain: Peeters, 1989; Jurji Zaydan, *Mashahir al-sharq fi l-qarn al-tasi' 'ashar*, Vol. II: *Fi rijal al-'ilm wa-l-adab wa-l-shi'r*, Cairo: Matba'at al-Hilal, 1903; Zaydan, *Ta'rikh adab al-lugha al-'arabiyya*, Vol. IV, reprint, Cairo: Dar al-Hilal, n.d. Lack of space has prevented me giving the precise references for individual authors.

8. On the previous translations and scholarly evaluation of Murqus's translation see Duneeva, 'L'arabisant russe', pp. 63–7.

9. Krachkovskii, *Arabistika v Rossii*, p. 114.

10. G. A. Murkos, 'Noveishaya literatura arabov', in V. F. Korsh and A. I. Kirpichnikov (eds), *Vseobshchaya Istoriya literatury*. Tom' II: *Istoriya sredneve-kovoi literatury (The History of Medieval Literature)*, St Petersburg: Izdanie Karla

Rikkera, 1885, pp. 374–80. It follows I. N. Kholmogorov's 'Arabskii yazik i do-musul'manskaya literatura' (The Arabic Language and Pre-Islamic Literature) and 'Mugammedanskii period' arabskoi literatury' (The Muhammadan Period of Arabic Literature) (pp. 269–373). Strictly speaking, *noveishaya* means 'most recent' or 'latest' and the precise translation is 'The most recent literature of the Arabs'.

11. Krachkovskii, *Izbrannye Sochineniya*, Tom' III, Moscow: Izdatel'stvo Akademii Nauk SSSR, 1956, p. 51, n. 1, in the preface to K. V. Ode-Vasil'eva, *Obraztsy novoarabskoi literatury (1880–1925)* (*Samples of Modern Arabic Literature 1880–1925*), published in 1928; Krachkovskii, *Arabistika v Rossii*, p. 114.

12. Krymskii, *Istoriya*, p. 265 and index.

13. Murqus is presumably referring to Shaykh Amin al-Jundi (1764–1837), a composer of Sufi *ghazal* poetry using the metres of traditional popular songs (al-Jundi, *A'lam al-adab wa-l-fann*, pp. 27–30). John A. Haywood describes him as 'the Syrian "pop" idol of his time' (*Modern Arabic Literature 1800–1970*, London: Lund Humphries, 1971, p. 42). Many of his *muwashshahat* and *qudud* are still performed today in traditional Aleppine musical circles.

14. Abu l-Hasan Qasim ibn Muhammad al-Kasti (1840–1910), Beirut man of letters, poet and author of two diwans.

15. A study on Farhat which supplements the above reference works is Nuhad Razzuq, *Jirmanus Farhat – hayatuh wa-atharuh*, Kaslik: Manshurat ma'had al-tarikh fi Jami'at al-Ruh al-Quddus, 1998.

16. D. 1415, author of *Al-Qamus al-muhit*, 'the single most influential dictionary [of Arabic] in both the Arab world and the West' (M. Carter).

17. Nasif al-Yaziji (1800–71), leading Lebanese man of letters.

18. I.e. *Al-khulasa al-alfiyya* of the famous grammarian Muhammad ibn Malik (d. 1274).

19. 'Abdallah ibn 'Abd al-Rahman ibn 'Aqil (d. 1367), Shafi'i jurisconsult and grammarian. His commentary on the *Alfiyya* is a classic.

20. The book is a commentary on al-Yaziji's *urjuza* on syntax entitled *Jawf al-fara*. Murqus adds a footnote to explain the sense of the title, which alludes to an Arabic proverb, '*Kullu l-saydi fi jawfi l-fara*' meaning roughly 'No dish can compare with the *plat de résistance*'. A translation such as 'The cooking fire to roast the *plat de résistance*' gives an idea of the word-play, though not of the rhyme.

21. Abu l-Qasim Mahmud al-Zamakhshari (d. 1144), philologist, theologian and Qur'an commentator. His *Kashshaf 'an haqa'iq ghawamid al-tanzil* is one of the most highly appreciated commentaries on the Qur'an.

22. Abu l-ʿIrfan Muhammad b. ʿAli al-Sabban (d. 1792), Egyptian scholar, littérateur and author of works on language, rhetoric, logic, hadith and other subjects.

23. Saʿd al-Din Masʿud ibn ʿUmar al-Taftazani (d. 1390), noted for his commentaries on earlier works of logic, rhetoric, theology and jurisprudence, and author of two commentaries on al-Khatib al-Qazwini's (d. 1338) *Talkhis al-miftah*, itself a summary of the section on rhetoric in al-Sakkaki's (d. 1229) *Miftah al-ʿulum*. Murqus must be referring to one of his two commentaries.

24. {–} This passage is not entirely clear in Russian, and it is not supported by the text of the poem. The *qasida* is to be found in *Diwan al-shaykh Nasif al-Yaziji* (Beirut: Dar Marun ʿAbbud, repr. 1983), pp. 332–7. The first letters are clearly marked and the couplet they form is printed above the *qasida*. As the introductory note points out, the numerical value of the letters of the couplet amounts to eight times the Sultan's year of accession, 1283 (1861); '28' could be a misprint. It adds that in the *qasida* proper each half-verse contains a chronogram of the same year, as Murqus says.

25. On al-Bustani and his dictionary see Dagmar Glaß, 'Butrus al-Bustani (1819–1883) als Enzyklopädiker der arabischen Renaissance', in Otto Jastrow, Shabo Talay and Herta Hafenrichter (eds), *Studien zur Semitik und Arabistik: Festschrift für Hartmut Bobzin zur 60. Geburtstag* (Wiesbaden: Harrassowitz, 2008, pp. 107–39, especially pp. 111–12) and the references there. Al-Bustani lists the entries under the first radical of the root instead of under the last, as is done in older Arabic dictionaries.

26. Ahmad Faris al-Shidyaq (1804–87), highly controversial, original and provocative Lebanese man of letters, translator and journalist.

27. Salim Bustrus (1839–83), wealthy Beiruti merchant and man of letters. See Axel Havemann, 'A View of the "other": Berlin in 1855 through the Eyes of Salim Bustrus', in Bernard Heyberger and Carsten Walbiner (eds), *Les Européens vus par les Libanais à l'époque ottomane*. Beirut: In Kommission bei Ergon Verlag Würzburg, 2002, pp. 111–19).

28. Rifaʿa Badawi Rafiʿ al-Tahtawi (1801–73), Egyptian reformer, educator, journalist and translator.

29. For a comparison of nineteenth-century travel accounts by these three authors and their contemporaries see Ibrahim Abu-Lughod, *Arab Rediscovery of Europe: A Study in Cultural Encounters*, Princeton: Princeton University Press, 1963, chs IV–VI.

30. See notes 7 and 8.

31. Salim Irinei Nawfal (1828–1902), professor of Islamic law and Arabic language

at the Educational Department of the Russian Ministry of Foreign Affairs and author of scholarly articles in French.

32. Marun al-Naqqash (1817–55), Lebanese dramatist. Mikhail Yusuf 'Ataya (1852–1924) teacher of Arabic at the Lazarevsky Institute for some fifty years.

33. In a lengthy footnote, Murqus enumerates poets and other pre- and early Islamic personalities who were, or are thought to have been, Christians.

34. Spiridon Sarruf (d. 1858), author of sermons and a catechism; Theodore (Wahbat Allah) Sarruf (1839–1913), translator, reviser and author of a pastoral handbook.

35. Mikha'il Mishaqa (1800–88), doctor, musicologist, historian and polymath. Krymskii, however, states that Mishaqa wrote clearly and elegantly for ordinary people (*Istoriya*, p. 425).

36. Sophronios al-Killizli (c. 1710–80), Patriarch of Jerusalem and later Constantinople, translator and author of polemical and educational works.

37. Anthimos, Patriarch of Jerusalem from 1788, translator and author. On the Psalter see Geoffrey Roper, 'The Vienna Arabic Psalter of 1792 and the Role of Typography in European–Arab Relations in the 18th Century and Earlier', in Johannes Frimmel and Michael Wörgelbauer (eds), *Kommunikation und Information im 18. Jahrhundert: Das Beispiel der Habsburgermonarchie*. Wiesbaden: Harrassowitz, 2009, pp. 77–89. The 'Western scholar' was the Austrian diplomat and orientalist Bernard de Jenisch.

38. Might this be a garbled reference to a visit to the Patriarch by members of one of the British missionary societies engaged in translating the Bible into various languages? The Society for the Propagation of the Gospel in Foreign Parts was founded in 1701 and the British and Foreign Bible Society in 1804.

39. Gerasimos Yarid (1840–99), later bishop of Saydnaya, Ma'lula and Zahleh. His translation, *Al-Dalil al-sarih 'ala mulk al-masih*, was printed in Jerusalem in 1886.

40. Al-Jam'iyya al-Suriyya's full name was Al-Jam'iyya al-Suriyya li-ktisab al-'Ulum wa-l-Funun (The Syrian Society for Sciences and Arts). It was founded in 1842 by American missionaries together with local Christians. Butrus al-Bustani published some of its papers in 1852, the last year of its existence, under the title *A'mal al-Jam'iyya al-Suriyya*, and Murqus apparently had a copy of the book. See Fruma Zachs, *The Making of a Syrian Identity: Intellectuals and Merchants in 19th Century Beirut*, Leiden: Brill, 2005, pp. 138–9 and pp. 141–5).

41. Al-Jam'iyya al-Suriyya was apparently a refoundation of the Majma' al-Tahdhib (The Educational Academy) set up by Butrus al-Bustani in 1845.

42. Jamʿiyyat Zahrat al-Adab was founded in 1873 under the auspices of the Ottoman governor of Beirut. See for details Zaydan, *Ta'rikh adab al-lugha al-ʿarabiyyaf* (henceforth *Ta'rikh*), pp. 70–1.

43. Khalil al-Khuri set up a printing press, al-Matbaʿa al-Suriyya, in 1857 (Zaydan, *Ta'rikh*, pp. 46, 53–4). His *Hadiqat al-akhbar*, founded in 1858, continued for over fifty years (Zachs, *The Making of a Syrian Identity*, pp. 88, 100, 163–73).

44. A curious feature of Murqus's contribution is the existence of three pages ('Noveishaya literatura arabov', pp. 377 a, b, v) which are partly replaced by the pages 377–80. They contain a detailed biography of Cornelius van Dyck, an account of Salim Shahada and his geographical and historical encyclopedia, and a description of an amazing celestial chandelier developed in Beirut.

45. Razzuq, *Jirmanus Farhat*, pp. 29–36; Brustad, 'Jirmanus Jibril Farhat', pp. 243–6. Krymskii had already pointed out the anachronism (*Istoriya*, p. 137).

46. This emerges most clearly from the biography of Cornelius van Dyck on pp. 377a–b. The absence of any reference to the role of Catholic missionaries is not surprising, given that the Université de St Joseph, founded as a French-speaking institution in 1875, opened its Faculté orientale only in 1902.

47. Cf. Paul Starkey, *Modern Arabic Literature*, Edinburgh: Edinburgh University Press, 2006, pp. 22–3, for a discussion of Napoleon's importance in modern Arabic literature.

48. Zaydan, *Ta'rikh*, pp. 8–9.

49. Cf. Kadhim Jihad Hassan's characterisation of the philological activities of the Christians and the motivation for them in 'La *nahda* par l'*ihya*", in Boutros Hallaq and Heidi Toelle (eds), *Histoire de la littérature arabe moderne. Tome I: 1800–1945*, Arles: Actes Sud/Sindbad, 2007, pp. 116–17.

50. For the evaluation of al-Yaziji in particular and modern Arabic literature in general in nineteenth-century Western Europe, see Paola Pizzo, 'Nasif al-Yaziji, Syrian Scholar and Intellectual: His Fortunes in East and West at the Beginning of the *Nahdah*', paper delivered at 'The Christian Contribution to the Arab Renaissance', 37th International Conference of ARAM Society for Syro-Mesopotamian Studies, Oxford, 15–17 July 2013, pp. 2–6. Murqus knew al-Yaziji personally (Krymskii, *Istoriya*, p. 374).

51. Havemann's article (see note 27) is the only study exclusively dedicated to it with which I am familiar.

52. Krymskii, *Istoriya*, p. 444. Murqus maintained close contact with Syrian intellectual circles throughout his life (ibid., p. 314).

53. Zaydan, *Mashahir al-sharq*, pp. 122–3.

54. Cf. the discussion of the two works by Hamarneh in Allen, *Essays 1850–1950*, pp. 321–4 and 341–4.

55. Information on them can be found in the works of Graf and Nasrallah mentioned in note 7.

56. Judging from the published passages of the text, *Muntakhabat min 'Al-jawab 'ala iqtirah al-ahbab' li-l-duktur Mikha'il Mishaqa* (selected and prefaced by Asad Rustum and Subhi Abu Shaqra, Beirut and Jounieh: Manshurat al-maktaba al-bulusiyya, second ed 1985), the language has few typically colloquial traits. But they were enough for Cheikho to criticise Mishaqa's weak style – though ideological considerations seem to have played a part in his judgement too.

57. In the following generation Jurji Zaydan established a reading programme of medieval Arabic poetry and prose texts for himself which reflected the same attitude to the language, and he also recommended it to his son Emile (Anne-Laure Dupont, *Gurgi Zaydan 1861–1914: Ecrivain réformiste et témoin de la renaissance arabe*, Damascus: Institut français du Proche-Orient, 2006, pp. 139–43).

58. *GCAL*, I, pp. 625–31. Karma's work is set out in *HMLEM*, Vol. IV (1) *Période ottomane, 1516–1724* (Louvain: Peeters, 1979), pp. 70–6.

59. Hilary Kilpatrick, 'Meletius Karmah's Specimen Translation of Genesis 1–5', in Sara Binay and Stefan Leder (eds), *Translating the Bible into Arabic: Historical, Text-critical and Literary Aspects*, Beirut: In Kommission bei Ergon Verlag Würzburg, 2012, pp. 63–73.

60. For his life and work see *HMLEM*, Vol. IV (1), pp. 132–46.

61. *Journal of Arabic Literature* I (1970), p. 1 (Editors' introduction).

7

The 'Second Journey' (*Al-Rihla al-thaniya*) of Muhammad al-Muwaylihi's *Hadith* '*Isa Ibn Hisham* Revisited

Roger Allen

In the late 1980s, when Mo Badawi was contemplating his retirement, he wrote to me with the suggestion that I prepare my Oxford DPhil thesis of 1968, a translation and commentary on Muhammad al-Muwaylihi's famous narrative *Hadith 'Isa ibn Hisham*, for publication in book form.[1] It duly appeared in 1992 as *A Period of Time*.[2] Later in the 1990s another Egyptian scholar, Gaber Asfour, requested that I prepare for publication the complete works of both al-Muwaylihis, Muhammad the son (1858–1930) and Ibrahim the father (1843–1906). Those also appeared in Cairo in 2002 and 2007 respectively.[3] All these projects took me back to a much earlier period in my career, indeed to its incipient phases when the impact of Mo Badawi's arrival in Oxford in 1963 was immense, in my own case and that of several generations of scholars aspiring to specialise in modern Arabic literature who followed. I had started reading Muhammad al-Muwaylihi's already renowned text for the 'special paper' on modern Arabic literature for finals. Such was my interest in the work – much stimulated by Mo's tutorials – that it was to become the focus of my postgraduate studies and eventual DPhil thesis. That process included a period of nine months in Cairo (1966–7), during the course of which a perusal of the entire run of the al-Muwaylihi newspaper, *Misbah al-sharq*, and of other newspapers of the 1890s and 1900s (in the Dar al-Kutub collection then housed in the Citadel) showed me that the subsequently published texts of both al-Muwaylihis, all of which had appeared initially in newspaper-article form, were in need of much further investigation, not only for their initial political and social context but also because of the often substantial changes that both writers made to the original texts before their republication in book form. Thus began a lengthy period of interest in the al-Muwaylihi family and its writings, a project to which I have occasionally returned in recent decades.[4] And, in this tribute to the mentor who originally dispatched me along this path, I now come back full-circle, as it were, by discussing the second part of *Hadith 'Isa ibn Hisham*, the 'second journey' (*Al-Rihla al-thaniya*), which was included only in the fourth edition of the text (1927) after it had been selected as a school textbook by the Egyptian Ministry of Education.[5] A feature of the discussion that now follows will be one that has been part of my investigations from the outset many years ago, namely that most versions of the text currently available (apart from my recent edition of the complete works) do not include the complete original text.[6]

Al-Muwaylihi's 'first journey' in *Hadith 'Isa ibn Hisham* takes the narrator, 'Isa ibn Hisham, and a Pasha resurrected from the era of Muhammad 'Ali, on visits to a variety of Cairene venues at the turn of the century, later accompanied by an Egyptian 'Friend' (*Sadiq*).[7] The 'second journey', which we will be discussing here, takes the same group of 'characters' to visit Europe, and more specifically Paris, in order to visit the Exhibition (Exposition universelle) of 1900. While such detailed focus on the Exhibition itself may be somewhat unique, al-Muwaylihi's account of a visit to Europe is by no means the first by Egyptians and other Arab intellectuals. Indeed it has numerous precedents in nineteenth-century writing: most famous is Rifaʿa Rafiʿ al-Tahtawi's (1801–73) *Takhlis al-ibriz fi talkhis Bariz* (*Gold Refined in Summarising Paris*, 1834), but equally significant in their different ways are Ahmad Faris al-Shidyaq's (1804–87) *Al-Saq 'ala al-saq fi-ma huwa al-Far-yaq* (*One Leg Over Another / The Pigeon on the Tree-Branch / Concerning the Personage of Far[is al-Shid]yaq*, 1855), 'Ali Mubarak's (1823–93) *'Alam al-din* (1882), and Ahmad Zaki's (1866–1934) *Al-Safar ila al-muʿtamar* (*The Journey to the Conference*, 1894). Of this selection of travel narratives, it is al-Shidyaq's that most closely approaches al-Muwaylihi's compositional method, in that al-Shidyaq creates the 'personae' of 'Faryaq' and his wife as means for describing and discussing the phenomena that they encounter during the course of their travels. However, al-Muwaylihi's fictionalised account of his own visit to the Paris Exhibition replicates the techniques used in the Cairene segment of his own *Hadith 'Isa ibn Hisham*, in that, as we will hope to illustrate in what follows, the narrator, 'Isa ibn Hisham, is able to describe the reactions of the very mixed group of his companions to Paris of 1900 and the Exhibition itself, ranging from those of the amazed and curious Pasha from a past era, to the hyper-critical Egyptian 'Friend' who warns his colleagues about the dangers of excessive imitation of everything Western, and to the French philosopher (*hakim*, or, in the earlier episodes, *shaykh faransawi*) who provides his Egyptian visitors with all kinds of information and at the same time offers judicious comments on the virtues and faults of Western civilisation and its exportation to other cultures. We thus see repeated in this description of a visit to Paris al-Muwaylihi's previous attempt in the Egyptian context at achieving a balanced approach to the assessment of the confrontation between West and East, the so-called traditional and modern, such social and cultural tensions being reflected in the Cairene portion of his famous narrative as being between the turban and the tarbush.

Almost immediately following the publication of the final episode of *Fatra min al-zaman*, Muhammad al-Muwaylihi's series of newspaper articles devoted to Egypt, he left his homeland in June 1900, initially in order to report to the newspaper on the Khedive's visit to England but thereafter to move on to Paris in order to visit the Exhibition.[8] His report from London duly appeared on 13 July 1900. It concludes with a paragraph that may not be lost on a British readership:

> To Almighty God is the complaint about London weather! The sun has vanished and the moon is nowhere to be seen. Do you have any information to share with me about the sun or news of the moon? It has been such a long time, and I can only hope that God will compensate me for London weather with better in Paris. Farewell.

As a second part of *Hadith 'Isa ibn Hisham* in book form, *Al-Rihla al-thaniya*, al-Muwaylihi's account of his visit to Paris, includes nine episodes of *Fatra min al-zaman* that were first published in *Misbah al-sharq* between August and December 1900; the number and order are replicated in the nine chapters added to the text of the fourth edition of *Hadith 'Isa ibn Hisham*, each with a newly assigned title.[9] The first episode of this 'second journey' is prefaced with an introductory paragraph:

> This is the first episode of *Hadith 'Isa ibn Hisham* concerning the visit to the Paris Exhibition. It has been sent to us by Muhammad al-Muwaylihi following his previous report on the visit of the Khedive of Egypt to Her Majesty the Queen of England.[10]

This series of episodes follows the pattern established by the previous series set in Cairo in two significant ways. Firstly they are all entitled *Fatra min al-zaman* (*A Period of Time*) which was the title found at the beginning of each of the original Cairene episodes. The title of the later book version, *Hadith 'Isa ibn Hisham* (first book edition, 1907) by which the work has subsequently become so famous, was added to the text only when the book was published, although it had been used before then in columns of the newspaper, *Misbah al-sharq*, in notices referring to forthcoming episodes.[11] The titles which now accompany each 'chapter' of the complete text (i.e. both first and second journeys) were added to the third edition (1923) for the Cairene segment, and the fourth (1927) for the Parisian. Secondly, each *original* episode begins or, in the book version, most chapters begin, with a passage of *saj'*, the traditional form of rhyming and cadenced prose first encountered in the pronouncements of pre-Islamic preachers, and then replicated in the Qur'an and, still later, in the renowned narrative genre, the *maqama*.[12] Once that passage of elaborate discourse (most commonly involving descriptions of place and the movements of the 'characters') is completed, the remainder of the episode in question is in the elevated prose style typical of the writings of both al-Muwaylihis.

The first episode, later entitled 'Paris', sets the scene, with the three Egyptians wandering in amazement through the crowded streets of Paris (which provide plenty of fodder for al-Muwaylihi's descriptive powers in *saj'*):

> They all seemed as scared as sparrows, looking anxiously around like sandgrouse in the desert. One false glance, and they would be dead; one slip of the foot, and blood would flow; a single disdainful stare, and perdition would soon ensue. They all stuck to the two sides of the street, like a

drowning man clutching the shore. On either side the shops were loaded down with incredible wares, costly goods, things that would lead the most fervent ascetic astray and make him desire them, that would tempt the stingiest of misers into buying them. They were all full of customers and crowds of people sitting down; everyone had a glass of wine in one hand and the evening newspaper in the other. In this kind of situation we were so shocked and befuddled that we almost lost our minds; such was the anxiety we felt that we hardly knew where to turn

> In a square where even Luqman the wise,
> were he there, would no longer be so wise.[13]

The three Egyptians take refuge from the crush of people in a café-bar, where 'Isa ibn Hisham proceeds to respond to an inquiry from the Pasha – that being, of course, a regular narrative device in *Hadith 'Isa ibn Hisham* for opening a discussion on a particular topic – by extolling the achievements of Western civilisation. Their 'Friend' objects to 'Isa's laudatory characterisation of the French and the West in general, and, as part of his objection, proceeds to offer a categorised listing of different types of Egyptian visitors to Europe – students, tourists and government officials, all of whom fail to offer a balanced picture of the positives and negatives of the society that they are encountering. When the Pasha again suggests that they need to find a French person to advise them, the group go to a restaurant where they overhear an argument between three Frenchmen: a writer, a businessman and a philosopher. The first two are both eager to export the benefits of Western civilisation – words with the first, products with the second – to the non-Western world. The philosopher, on the other hand (later described as an 'orientalist scholar') points to the fact that not only does a civilisation such as that of China have different cultural bases but that it is considerably older than that of the West – and, with those expressed ideas in mind, it is interesting to note firstly that the major segment of his response is omitted from the text of the fourth edition of *Hadith 'Isa ibn Hisham* in book form and secondly that the argument in the original episode is expressed in the voice of a would-be Chinese respondent:

> You have Western civilisation, and we have our own Eastern civilization established by one generation after another, from father to son. It is a well

known fact that the passage of time serves like a sieve, ridding culture of what is bad while preserving what is good. Nothing remains unless it is proved to have strong bases and firm roots. If you were to record that your own culture dates back some seven thousand years, ours can be dated back hundreds of thousands. If your civilisation is one hundred years old, then ours goes back dozens of eras and represents the experience of many, many centuries – retained by us in its purest form as refined by the hand of time and the passage of ages. One of the characteristics of genuine civilisation is that people should live in peace and security, not crave what does not belong to them, and not trample on a right that belongs to others.[14]

The French philosopher goes even further in his dispute with his French colleagues by citing the Boxer Rebellion in China (1898–1901) as an example of the negative consequences of the combination of Western imperialism and Christian evangelism (a passage that is again excluded from the fourth edition):

Christian missionaries deliberately set out to challenge the very bases of Chinese faith. They took over cemeteries, scattered the bones of the dead, and proceeded to construct churches and monasteries on top of their shrines and temples, overtopping the royal palace itself. So please tell me, by God, would any of these missionaries be daring to insult the religion of a major country with over four hundred million inhabitants if there were no ambassador with his own Christian background – he himself being duly supported by guns and weaponry?

Encouraged by what they have overheard of the French philosopher's apparently balanced approach to debates over trans-cultural values, the Egyptians strike up a conversation with him. When they request his aid as a guide, he accepts.

Thus are established the discussion parameters for the visit to the Exhibition itself. 'Isa ibn Hisham is to serve as the scene-setter and orchestrator of the sequence of events, while the Pasha, his companion on their previous adventures in turn-of-the century Cairo, is to continue his role as poser of questions and negative responder to phenomena that offend his traditionalist values. Their Egyptian 'Friend' meanwhile is to express the opinions and reactions of an intellectual from a younger Egyptian generation, one that is still deeply sceptical about the benefits of the unguarded and limitless acceptance of 'modernity' as represented by the Western values and systems that are being imported into his homeland with increased intensity following the British occupation of Egypt in 1882. And where better, one might suggest, to debate the value of such principles, institutions and products than through a visit by three Egyptians to an exhibition in Paris put on by representatives of that modern Western 'civilisation', an exhibition that is specifically designed to show off its achievements and benefits to their best advantage?

It is into this triangle of variegated Egyptian opinion and reaction that the French 'philosopher' is to insert his information concerning French society and the Exhibition itself. After the initial episode/chapter, 'Paris', discussed above, the next four – 'The Exhibition', 'The Grand Palais', 'Trees and Flowers' and 'Views and Vistas' – describe the three Egyptians and their French guide entering the Exhibition grounds and visiting a number of its buildings: among others, the art and sculpture exhibits in the Petit Palais and Grand Palais, the lavish gardens, the labyrinth of mirrors, and the pavilion devoted to dance from different world cultures. As part of their discussions, the philosopher provides the Egyptians with brief histories of Western art, of labyrinths (including the legend of the Cretan minotaur), and of dance. In answers to specific inquiries, he informs the Egyptian visitors about the costs of the entire Exhibition project, its entrepreneurial bases and the losses that are being incurred by its sponsors. The displays in several of the pavilions and exhibits provoke both positive and negative responses from the Egyptian visitors, the most negative coming especially from the Pasha. A gallery of paintings in the Grand Palais illustrating concepts such as nature and virtue in the form of naked women leads to a discussion of the use of female models in creating such art. The Pasha's reaction is immediate and anticipatable:

PASHA: What is this [disgusting debauchery] scandalous conduct you're describing to me?
PHILOSOPHER: In our culture there's nothing scandalous or debauched about it. Women suffer no shame for doing such things. As far as they are concerned, it's one of the respectable professions, and there's nothing wrong with practising it; it has no effect on their reputation.[15]

With this reaction of the Pasha in mind, it is not surprising that he is similarly offended by demonstrations of the cancan and ballet that they witness during their visit to the dance pavilion.[16] However, if the Egyptians' reactions to the various pavilions in the Exhibition are mixed, there is complete unanimity when they visit the so-called Egyptian exhibit, which, we learn from the French philosopher, is not sponsored by the Egyptian government but rather by non-Egyptian entrepreneurs living in Cairo. The title of the episode/chapter in which it is described, *Al-Iftira' 'ala al-watan* (*Slandering the Homeland*), warns the reader what to expect.[17] Attracted by the sound of drums, they arrive at the entrance, to be greeted by a man offering to write for them a passage from the Qur'an on a piece of paper; he turns out to be a Syrian Christian trying to earn a living wage. Once inside, the three Egyptians are horrified to find their country represented at the Exhibition by displays of belly-dancing and by a replica of a *kuttab* (Qur'an school), complete with a set of students gathered around a teacher who periodically swats them with a palm-branch. Hurrying to escape from such an embarrassing display, they emerge into the public space but only to encounter a so-say typical Egyptian wedding procession on the street. An obliging participant in the display explains to them that the women taking part in this public display are actually not Egyptian but rather Syrian. They too have been brought to Paris by the need to earn a living, and the procession itself has taken to the streets because the sponsors of the Egyptian exhibit are desperately trying to attract paying visitors; like the sponsors of the Turkish and Algerian exhibits, the backers of the Egyptian exhibition have incurred huge losses because of a lack of public interest. As the three Egyptians and their French host hurry away, they find some comfort in the parting words of their informant:

> The big losers are the shareholders. Current estimates put the losses to date at eighty-thousand francs. One can only hope that this loss will serve as an object lesson and corrective so that they won't try again to embark on such a project which runs the risk of not only their own loss but also the denigration of Egyptians.

The two remaining chapters devoted to the Exhibition – 'The Bread of Civilisation', and 'The Eighth Wonder' – take the group underground and above ground. In the first they go down into a simulated coal-mine, the gruesome description of which leads one to suspect that al-Muwaylihi may have read Zola's famous 1885 novel on the same subject, *Germinal*. In the original episode this vivid description is prefaced by a description of the German pavilion and the increasing degree of militarism that it displays at France's expense in the immediate wake of the Franco-Prussian War (1870–1); but yet again the bulk of it was omitted from the text of *Hadith 'Isa ibn Hisham*. What appears to have been the final Parisian episode describes the view from the second level of the newly constructed Eiffel Tower. When the French philosopher dubs it the eighth wonder of the world, the Pasha duly performs his usual narrative function by asking what are the previous seven. Leaving aside the Pyramids, the philosopher gives a lengthy account of the other six.[18]

It is at this point that the history of the episodes entitled *Fatra min al-zaman* takes an interesting turn. The episode describing the Eiffel Tower ends with the usual 'to be continued' and the two *mim*s to indicate the author's name, but nothing in the series was to follow for a period of fourteen months. It was not until February 1902, long after al-Muwaylihi's return to Cairo, that three more episodes were published under the same title, '*Fatra min al-zaman*'.[19] Without any further explanation, the first of these new episodes commences as follows:

> 'Isa ibn Hisham said: Our coverage of the visit we paid to the mother of all European capitals and our stay in the hub of civilisation finished with a description of the Great Exhibition, the different people we met there, the variety of exotic items, the precious and creative objects of every conceivable kind of craft that were on display, the night-clubs and music-halls scattered across the grounds, the splendid views it afforded visitors and the undesirable subtext out of sight. The Pasha, our Friend and I had emerged from it with mixed feelings: praise, criticism and outright condemnation. We were still in the company of the French philosopher with his whitened temples, who was still willing to share his knowledge with us.[20]

In the context of the clearly rigorous editorial process that al-Muwaylihi was to undertake in preparing his work for its fourth edition published many years later in 1927, two things about this later set of three episodes are of particular interest: firstly, a large segment of the first episode was extracted and used to create a final chapter for the earlier Parisian set, under the title *Min al-gharb ila al-sharq* (*From West to East*)[21] and is thus now part of the text of *Hadith 'Isa ibn Hisham* as a book; and secondly, that no other part of these three episodes was included in the book text.

In fact these later episodes differ from their predecessors in that all three appear to constitute a continuum; only the first of them starts with one of al-Muwaylihi's virtuoso exercises in *saj'*, and the other two simply continue with the same topic and in the same style as the remaining part of the first. The cue that the narrative provides for these episodes is yet again a request from the Pasha, namely that the philosopher describe the French Republican system. That he duly does, including a lengthy analysis of the Presidency, the Chamber of Deputies, the Senate and the entire electoral process. The detailed information presented in these episodes is clearly a reflection of both Muhammad al-Muwaylihi's considerable knowledge of French and European culture and society gleaned from many years of exile (including at one point in the second episode an extract from an essay by Herbert Spencer on the virtues of the parliamentary system)[22] and his desire to share that knowledge with the readership of *Misbah al-sharq*, the family newspaper, the editorship of which he had now taken over from his father. And yet, one must assume that, as he considered what to include and exclude as part of the editorial process for the new 1927 edition of his by now famous work, he realised that these later adjuncts to his 'second journey' (*Al-Rihla al-thaniya*) no longer suited the trans-cultural context of both 'journeys' that he had converted into a book two decades earlier, namely *Hadith 'Isa ibn Hisham*, a work that was about to achieve almost canonical status as a school text, a kind of 'modern classic'.[23]

A further interesting feature of these three later episodes is that al-Muwaylihi seems to have decided to make explicit the goals of his narrative strategy, the outlines of which were analysed above in discussing the relative roles of each 'character'. The second of the episodes opens with an interesting exchange between the Egyptian 'Friend' and the French philosopher concerning the latter's attitude to his function as guide. The Friend thanks the philosopher for providing them with a great deal of information, but requests that the Frenchman also give them more of his own personal opinions concerning the things they are seeing and the cultural principles that are being put forward. The French philosopher responds:

I don't think it is necessary for me to express a personal opinion while I am giving you information about various aspects of the system, both the more and less obvious. That is not the way I have been dealing with you. My preferred method is to lay things out clearly for you and discuss current conditions so that I can assess the impact that my commentary has on you and the disagreements that may arise. In that way I myself can benefit from my own previous verdicts on things, whether it is to support or oppose them.[24]

The use of the word 'information' here points, I would suggest, to a significant difference between al-Muwaylihi's two sets of episodes, one depicting Cairo and the other Paris; a difference that is evident enough from a comparative reading of the relevant chapters in *Hadith 'Isa ibn Hisham* as a book, but even more noticeable when the book version is compared with the original episodes. For, while the identity of the 'characters' in both locations may be the same, the social and cultural context for the Cairene episodes was presumably familiar to the readers of the al-Muwaylihi newspaper and later of *Hadith 'Isa ibn Hisham* in its book form. There is thus a minimal need for the kind of 'information' with which the Parisian episodes are filled, only part of which makes its way into the later text of *Hadith 'Isa ibn Hisham*. Al-Muwaylihi here may thus be seen as presenting readers of his family's newspaper and, to a somewhat lesser extent, of his book with a updated picture of French society and Paris that is more nuanced and critical than that of his illustrious forebear, al-Tahtawi.

At the conclusion of the third of these later episodes, the French philosopher suggests to the Egyptians that the best way of seeing the principles of the French Republic in action is to visit the Chamber of Deputies and watch a session. The idea is warmly accepted by the Egyptians, and the episode finishes – yet again – with a final note 'to be continued'. And yet again, nothing follows; the entire series of *Fatra min al-zaman* comes to an end with no further comment. In my discussion in *A Period of Time* of the series of episodes as a whole starting in 1898, I noted that Muhammad al-Muwaylihi's assumption of the primary editorial role at the newspaper *Misbah al-sharq* at some undefined point in 1902 was accompanied by a gradual but increased reliance for articles on translated material rather than the pungent social and political comment and criticism penned by both father and son that had been such a prominent feature of their newspaper's earlier years.[25] Not only that, but in late 1902 Muhammad al-Muwaylihi found himself at the centre of a social scandal involving an apparent insult to a young nobleman which resulted in his being slapped on the face in public.[26] The ever-shy author, whose chronic stammer made him acutely self-conscious in public, was mortified by the incident and gradually retired from public life altogether.[27] The newspaper continued for a few more months but eventually closed for ever in August 1903.

As part of the just mentioned study of the publication history of *Hadith 'Isa ibn Hisham*, I also noted that, in the context of the earlier Egyptian episodes of *Fatra min al-zaman*, some of the most pointed criticisms found in the first three editions of the book – 1907, 1912 and 1923 – were omitted from the fourth.[28] In addition some episodes were placed in a different order, and others were combined into lengthy chapters such as the one describing a wedding.[29] From this analysis of the contents of the Parisian episodes of *Al-Rihla al-thaniya* in both their original episodic form and as an addition to the book text in 1927, it becomes even clearer that the preparation for this fourth edition was used by the author to undertake a substantial revision that involved decisions regarding not only the original episodes published over a four-year span but also the first three editions of the work in book form. In that context, the dating of editions of the book is interesting: the second edition, unaltered from the first, seems to reflect immediate demand for the book, in that it appeared in 1912, only five years after the publication of the first edition. On the other hand, the publication of the third edition (1923), to which the author adds chapter titles for the first time, precedes the all-important fourth edition by only four years. Even from a self-imposed internal exile, it would appear, al-Muwaylihi continued to be involved in ensuring the continuing availability and popularity of his famous work.

With regard to differences in the content of the various episodes of *Fatra min al-zaman* and editions of *Hadith 'Isa ibn Hisham* that resulted from the publication of the fourth edition in 1927, one can only speculate as to what balance of criteria for inclusion and exclusion al-Muwaylihi may have used in the context of the demands for a text that was to be used in secondary education. Insulting anecdotes about Muhammad 'Ali and highly sarcastic accounts of al-Azhar shaykhs discussing commercial profits and debating the validity of geography would presumably have been ready candidates for exclusion, and perhaps lengthy disquisitions on French government structures, German militarism and European imperialism in Asia may also have seemed less than relevant for young Egyptian readers in the late 1920s. Whatever the case may be, what is clear is that the fourth edition of *Hadith 'Isa ibn Hisham* and subsequent editions that were based on it presented their readers with a text which was significantly different from that of its predecessors in book form and, above all, the original texts that al-Muwaylihi published in *Misbah al-sharq* between 1898 and 1902. One might suggest that, from a critical perspective that wished to regard al-Muwaylihi's work as a transitional phase in the development of modern Arabic fiction and thus to identify some kind of narrative sequence and cohesion, the substantial revisions undertaken for the fourth edition do offer many of the features that would support such a quest. On the other hand, the availability of the complete works edition now allows readers to experience to the full the lively and contentious social and political context within which the work first appeared and to note the many topics covered in the episodes that are no longer to be found in the book text. Beyond that, they also make it possible to trace its development from a series of highly literate newspaper articles to an important early monument of modern Arabic narrative.

Notes

1. It had originally been the first DPhil thesis that Mo Badawi supervised at Oxford (1968) and was subsequently published in microfiche form in 1974 (Albany: State University of New York Press).
2. Roger Allen, *A Period of Time: A Study and Translation of* Hadith 'Isa ibn Hisham *by Muhammad al-Muwaylihi*, Reading: Ithaca Press, 1992. I should note here that I am currently (2014) preparing a new parallel-text version of the original set of newspaper articles entitled *Fatra min al-zaman*, which were, in heavily edited form, to be the basis of the book *Hadith 'Isa ibn Hisham*, first published in 1907. The text is to appear in the Library of Arabic Literature series, edited by Philip Kennedy and published by New York University Press.
3. Muhammad al-Muwaylihi, *Al-Mu'allafat al-kamila*, 2 vols, Cairo: Al-Maglis al-A'la li-al-Thaqafa, 2002; and Ibrahim al-Muwaylihi, *Al-Mu'allafat al-kamila*, Cairo: Al-Maglis al-A'la li-al-Thaqafa, 2007.

4. On Ibrahim al-Muwaylihi: *Spies, Scandals and Sultans: Istanbul in the Twilight of the Ottoman Empire* (a translation and commentary on *Ma hunalik* [1896]), Lanham: Rowman and Littlefield Publishers, 2008; Roger Allen, 'The Works of Ibrahim al-Muwaylihi (1843?–1906)', *Middle Eastern Literatures* 13:2 (August 2010), pp. 131–9; and Roger Allen, 'Ibrahim al-Muwaylihi's *Mir'at al-'alam*: Introduction and Translation', *Middle Eastern Literatures* 15:3 (December 2012), pp. 318–36; and 16:3 (December 2013), pp. 1–17. On Muhammad al-Muwaylihi: Roger Allen, '*Hadith 'Isa ibn Hisham* by al-Muwaylihi; Thirty Years Later', in *Arab and Islamic Studies in Honor of Marsden Jones*, Cairo: American University in Cairo Press, 1997, pp. 117–24; and Roger Allen, 'Muhammad al-Muwaylihi's Coterie: The Context of *Hadith 'Isa ibn Hisham*', *Literary Innovation in Modern Arabic Literature: Schools and Journals* (special issue of *Quaderni di studi arabi* 18 (2000)), pp. 51–60.
5. Details concerning the many and various editions of the work are included in *A Period of Time*, pp. 32–48.
6. The second part of *Hadith 'Isa ibn Hisham, Al-Rihla al-thaniya*, has been the subject of some recent studies: see, for example, Kamran Rastegar, *Literary Modernity Between the Middle East and Europe*, London: Routledge, 2007, pp. 88–100; and Yves Gonzalez-Quijano, 'Reading Muhammad al-Muwaylihi's Description of Paris: A Modern Egyptian Chapter of the West at the Beginning of the 20th Century', *Middle Eastern Literatures* 13:2 (August 2010), pp. 183–9. On page 184 of the last article, Gonzalez-Quijano terms *Al-Rihla al-thaniya* 'undervalued'.
7. The phrase 'first journey' is used by al-Muwaylihi himself in the final lines of the first three editions of *Hadith 'Isa ibn Hisham* (1907, 1912 and 1923); in other words, before the addition of *Al-Rihla al-thaniya* to the fourth edition.
8. Muhammad al-Muwaylihi's departure is duly noted in a small announcement in *Misbah al-sharq* 107, (8 June 1900): "Isa ibn Hisham: Muhammad al-Muway-lihi is travelling to Paris this coming Sunday to visit the Paris Exhibition, and our newspaper will be publishing details of 'Isa ibn Hisham's comments and opinions on the remarkable things that he will be seeing there.'
9. The Arabic titles of the chapters are: *Baris, Al-Ma'rad, Al-Qasr al-kabir, Al-Ashjar wa-al-azhar, Al-Mara'i wa-al-mashahid, Al-Iftira' 'ala al-watan, Khubz al-madaniyya, Al-Mu'jiza al-thamina* and *Min al-gharb ila al-sharq*.
10. *Misbah al-sharq* 116 (17 August 1900).
11. See, for example, *Misbah al-sharq* 30 (5 January 1899).
12. The exception here is when a number of original episodes are combined into

a single chapter, such as *Al-'Urs* (*The Wedding*) in the Egyptian section of the work, where a number of original episodes are combined. The passages of *saj'* with which the original episodes began thus occur in the middle of the combined chapter.

13. The translations included in this study will be included in the parallel-text version of the text mentioned above in note 2. The passage itself is in Muhammad al-Muwayhlihi, *Al-Mu'allafat al-kamila*, Vol. 1, p. 398.

14. See *Fatra min al-zaman*, *Misbah al-sharq* 116 (17 August 1900).

15. *Misbah al-sharq* 118 (31 August 1900); *Al-Mu'allafat al-kamila* Vol. 1, p. 422. The words in brackets occur in the original episode, replaced, it would appear, by something a little less vitriolic in the fourth edition text.

16. *Misbah al-sharq* 123 (5 October 1900); *Al-Mu'allafat al-kamila*, Vol. 1, p. 432.

17. *Misbah al-sharq* 126 (26 October 1900); *Al-Mu'allafat al-kamila*, Vol. 1, pp. 437–41.

18. In connection with the temple of King Mausulos, al-Muwaylihi once again displays the level of his erudition by treating his readers to an extract from a dialogue between the dead king and the philosopher Diogenes: see *Misbah al-sharq* 133 (14 December 1900); *Al-Mu'allafat al-kamila*, Vol. 1, pp. 453–4.

19. See *Misbah al-sharq* 192 14 February 1902; 193 21 February 1902; and 196 14 March 1902.

20. See *Misbah al-sharq* 192 14 February 1902); *Al-Mu'allafat al-kamila*, Vol. 1, p. 525.

21. See *Al-Mu'allafat al-kamila*, Vol. 1, pp. 457–8

22. See *Misbah al-sharq* 192 (21 February 1902); *Al-Mu'allafat al-kamila*, Vol. 1, p. 532.

23. While I was conducting the research for my doctoral thesis in Cairo in 1966–7, a number of Egyptian intellectuals shared with me an admiration for *Hadith 'Isa ibn Hisham* that might be termed 'guarded', since it had been a 'set text' for the *Thanawiyya 'amma* (Secondary Education) examination, and the amount of vocabulary involved was substantial. I was reminded of my own attitude as a schoolboy towards Chaucer's *Canterbury Tales*, similarly a required text – in those days – for what were then called O Level exams in England.

24. See *Misbah al-Sharq* 193 (21 February 1902).

25. See Roger Allen, *A Period of Time*, pp. 10–11.

26. Al-Muwaylihi's explanation of the encounter was published under the title *Hadithat daraktus* in *Misbah al-sharq* 229 (8tNovember 1902). When 'Ali Yusuf, the editor of the rival newspaper, *Al-Mu'ayyad*, began a campaign against

al-Muwaylihi under the title *'Am al-kaff* (*The Year of the Slap*), al-Muwaylihi published an injudicious response entitled *Jarida 'ammiyya*' (implying something akin to 'gutter press'): *Misbah al-sharq* 230 (15 November 1902).

27. The family home was and still is in the city of Hulwan to the south of Cairo.

28. Entire chapters on the shaykhs of al-Azhar, for example, the princes of the Royal family, and anecdotes about Muhammad 'Ali. They have now been 'restored' to their former positions in the narrative in Muhammad al-Muwaylihi, *Al-Mu'allafat al-kamila*. For further details on these omissions and the text of the fourth edition of *Hadith 'Isa ibn Hisham*, see Roger Allen, *A Period of Time*, pp. 41–4.

29. Muhammad al-Muwaylihi, *Al-Mu'allafat al-kamila*. Vol. 1, pp. 285–305.

8

Ataturk Becomes ʿAntar: Nationalist-vernacular Politics and Epic Heroism in 1920s Egypt

Marilyn Booth

From the 1890s, published colloquial Arabic poetry emerged as populist political commentary in Egypt when several factors converged: nationalist anti-imperialist activism crystallised, a non-official press was in place, and some outstanding poets became fierce public commentators and exploited the widening opportunities for print-led circulation.[1] Disseminated through a popular press that included organs dedicated to vernacular expression – then read aloud, memorised and thus circulated orally – their poetry offered alternative political voices that converged on or diverged ambiguously from the varying public political stances of Egypt's nationalist elite. This elite was internally heterogeneous according to origins and professions, comprising a rising bourgeoisie and landowning class (including a secularly educated cluster of reformer-intellectuals), and scholar-bureaucrats trained in traditional Islamic sciences, some of whom composed colloquial poetry.

Mahmud Bayram al-Tunisi (1893–1961) was not a member of any elite. An autodidact reared in the Maghribi fishermen's neighbourhood of al-Sayyala, Alexandria, he became a leading practitioner of vernacular poetic-political art, gaining renown during the political turmoil following the First World War and the rising nationalist pressures on Britain's 'Protectorate' over Egypt. Banished in 1919 after writing poetry attacking Egypt's royals, Bayram's voice remained vibrant locally. He wrote for popular periodicals from exile in France and Tunisia, sending in dialect poetry, essays, *maqamat* mockeries, short stories, memoirs and satiric pastiches of the high poetic and belletristic traditions demonstrating how well read this unschooled young man was. Bayram's transformative exploitation of forms – both 'folk' and 'learned' – was not simply an adoption of appropriate generic vehicles. His was a motivated critical appropriation of forms wherein the genre templates themselves – representative of cultural categories and expressive histories – constituted targets as well as vehicles of satire.[2] While 'the political' in Bayram's corpus incorporates representation of topical public politics, more profoundly his news commentary critiqued cultural categories that buttressed social hierarchies undergirding political authority of the few over the many. Thus he satirically reworked genres associated with 'high' culture but appropriated forms from oral expressive culture, drawing on their structures, imagery, stock characters and epithetic usages to celebrate community-affirming aspects of heritage whilst interrogating received identities through satire. In his art, sought audience, and dissemination modes, Bayram falls into that hard-to-define category of 'the popular' – neither 'folk' nor 'elite' – which the literary scholar Pierre Cachia has critically delineated over the years.[3] Bayram differed, Cachia argued, from other popular-vernacular poets, as one who 'espous[ed] modernistic, mainly nationalist, causes'.[4] Yet, employing techniques and familiar features of both folk art and popular poetry in a partial reversal, even critique, of the value system they underlay, he retained a popular – or populist – narrative outlook that exhibited distrust of elite political formations and their socio-economic elaborations.

Researching Bayram's 1920s corpus for a dissertation directed by Mustafa Badawi and Albert Hourani, I focused on Bayram's narrative *mawwals* and satirical prose texts as critiques of urban Egyptian society and its class and gender hierarchies. I was also fascinated by his topical political commentaries and his utilisation of oral folk tradition to yoke narrative commentary and political critique. In honour of Mustafa Badawi, I return now to texts I wanted to think about then. This modest chapter launches a study of a series of texts published 1921–2 in *Al-Shabab* newspaper. Some reappeared in a small volume, *Muntakhabat al-Shabab* (*Selections from al-Shabab*), vol. 2, issued by *Al-Shabab*'s editor-publisher in 1923. Unsigned in the newspaper, texts in the volume were attributed explicitly to Bayram al-Tunisi; readers already knew he produced *Al-Shabab*'s contents and layout, front- to back-page, from exile. These texts, never fully reprinted in Bayram's 'canonical' later collections, figured political contestation in the thematic-formal mould of the *sira sha'biyya*, utilising expectations the genre raised to cast contemporary events in a satirically 'epic' mock-heroic light.

A Genre, a World

The *sira sha'biyya* (folk epic, folk romance) has long been predominantly an orally performed tradition celebrating historical-mythological heroes who embody values defining Bedouin life: chivalry, honour, protective solidarity and courage to act when collective security is threatened. The tradition is recognised as early as the eighth to ninth centuries, and narrates the hero's life cycle: difficult acceptance in society, love trials, conflicts. Battle scenes evoke themes of *defence* of the group and *quest* as integral to heroic self-realisation and socially integrative duty.[5] Listeners considered these narrated battles and their heroes as part of a glorious history.[6] *Sira* also signified biography: popular folk epic retained focus on individual life stories as the stuff of history.

The monorhymed verse alternating with prose passages, and language and imagery evoking the Bedouin society in which *sira* emerged, would clue readers immediately as to the genre template. The *qasida* with intervening prose passages is one of three forms the *sira* assumed in Egypt. The colloquial poet and collector of *sira* 'Abd al-Rahman al-Abnudi notes that the *qasida* monorhyme recitation form, found in the Delta and Alexandria region, often narrated by performers of religious narrative ballads, is closest to the written form attested for some *siyar*, notably *Sirat 'Antar*.[7] Thus, Bayram was drawing partly on the chapbook-publication form of *sira* with which his urban readers might have been most readily familiar. The monorhyme also accentuates the *sira*'s linkage to the great *qasida* tradition of Bedouin poetry. The language and form of this text-series are distinct within Bayram's poetic corpus.

In earliest publication, most of Bayram's compositions on this model appeared under the shared rubric "'Ala 'l-rababa' (On the Rabab). The *rabab*, or rebec, is a small stringed instrument with one or two strings stretched over a rectangular wooden box or coconut shell, customary accompaniment to recitation of one epic cycle in particular, the *Sirat Bani Hilal*.[8] The collective title evokes a communicative setting highlighting the relationship between poet/performer and audience, a sense of shared social experience, values and status: a common world. But as Peter Heath has argued for *Sirat ʿAntar*, one of the most famous exemplifications of this narrative tradition, Bayram's *sira* series does not merely entertain: it affirms community by evoking a familiar, shared history from a particular narrative perspective.[9] However, Bayram teaches *contemporary* history via the lineaments of popular heroism.

In Egypt, ʿAntar ibn Shaddad became an eponymous symbol of the redoubtable epic hero: the 'deeds' or 'feats' of ʿAntar (*ʿamayil ʿAntar*) remain alive in Egyptian colloquial Arabic, signifying 'doing the nigh-impossible'. Remke Kruk calls ʿAntar 'the Arab Hercules, whose strength and valour have become proverbial . . . the personification of Arab manly virtue, *muruwwa*, stoically enduring hardship, generous, protector of the helpless and a paragon of knightly skill, *furusiyya*'.[10] Bayram updates the hero. Mustafa Kemal Ataturk – founder of the Turkish Republic and, earlier, leader of the resistance to Greek incursions into Anatolia – and Saʿd Zaghlul – leader of Egypt's nationalists – become the modern ʿAntar, doing the nigh-impossible on behalf of Turks, Egyptians and all others resisting Europe's encroachment.

The ''Ala 'l-rababa' texts also signal a debt to tradition by mimicking the oral recitatory performance of the *sira shaʿbiyya*, through announcing a *rawi* (reciter/narrator). But, in the context of newspaper publication, this *rawi* is the emerging reporter, a correspondent who reports on doings of central government *to* constituents, and reports *from* a popular constituency to the central authorities, conveying petitions and critiques.[11] These texts cast contemporary political conflict as the *sira* while appropriating the spaces of the newspaper and the café as sites of collective and critical newspaper consumption. It is no accident that these poems appeared in column one on page one of the newspaper: an ongoing news commentary that continued through late 1924 with 'editorials' on the British–Egyptian negotiations.

Bayram's first audience was composed largely of urban newspaper readers, but not necessarily well-educated ones, and oral audiences who were collective consumers of newsprint. That such works were heard as well as read, whether in cafés, at home or on the street, is important to the communally oriented satiric potential of imitating folk epic formally. Such an audience would know *sira* recitation and likely be familiar with cheaply printed chapbook versions of epic circulating in Egypt.[12] Bayram utilised the alternation of prose and verse found particularly in printed versions, though some of his

''Ala 'l-rababa' compositions are simply monorhyme poems unbroken by prose.

Sira sha'biyya and/as Contemporary Politics

At least four Bayramic *sira* compositions narrate the Turkish–Greek contestation for possession of Asia Minor in the context of postwar intra-European negotiations for neocolonial primacy. I label this group the 'Sira Kemaliyya': it is a succession of narrative 'cartoon' editorials on Great Power politics as played out in the eastern Mediterranean. As I have suggested, casting these commentaries in the mould of the *sira sha'biyya* shaped a particular narrative perspective for an anticipated Egyptian readership: an alliance of solidarity and shared challenges with the 'local' (Turkish) hero. These were preceded in *Al-Shabab* by at least two ''Ala 'l-rababa' poems on the postwar Egyptian–British negotiations over independence. They turned on the opposition between Sa'd Zaghlul (1859–1927) as *batal* (hero) and the British government and Lord Milner (1854–1925), who headed a 1921 'fact-finding' mission to Egypt, as his adversaries. Thus, through the 'Sira Sa'diyya', readers of the 'Sira Kemaliyya' had been introduced to Bayram's framing of contemporary world political events as folk epic-romance. That he explored both issues through this genre template linked Egyptian nationalist anti-colonial politics to the Greek–Turkish struggle, hence to the imperialist politics of European powers in their support for Greece. 'Banu Zaghlul' and 'Banu 'Uthman' (the tribe of Zaghlul and the tribe of the Ottomans) evoke clan solidarity within and across national and imperial borders.

Thus the context of composition and first reception was the immediate post-First World War European powers' competition and local manoeuvring to carve up the Ottoman carcass. The four texts – including the one I present below – confront the conflict between Greece and Turkey 1919–22. The hostilities of those years were a culmination of struggles for domination in the Ottoman Empire's heartland. Constructing a memory of the ancient Byzantine Empire, some Greeks saw its resurrection, replacing the Ottomans, as destiny. Others envisioned Greece prevailing regionally as a modern nation state and regional economic-political power. Either way, the 'Great Idea' of Greek expansion fueled a series of conflicts: between Turks and Greeks in Crete, between Macedonians and Bulgarians, and between Anatolian Turks backed by nationalists and Anatolian Greeks backed by politicians in Athens. A closer look at the political context is needed to understand Bayram's topical and satiric renditions of the national-heroic.

Having increased its territory massively through the Balkan Wars (1912–13), Greece's government set its sights on controlling the Izmir/ Smyrna region of Asia Minor with its sizeable ethnic Greek population.[13] This was not a new mission. As Richard Clogg notes, 'the incorporation of Smyrna and its hinterland within the bounds of the independent Greek state had long been a cherished element of the Great Idea'.[14] Smyrna was 'the heart of Hellenism in Asia Minor', as Richard Llewellyn Smith describes it.[15] Greek politicians had voiced mounting concern about the treatment of Greeks in Anatolia, though the outbreak of the First World War suspended their campaign temporarily.[16]

The savvy Cretan politician Eleftherios Venizelos (1864–1936), Prime Minister of Greece for periods before, during and after the Great War, had impressed Allied leaders with his political skills and his support. He was able to further Greek irredentist ambitions in the postwar negotiations, in particular with the British leader Lloyd George (1863–1945) who looked favourably on Greece's ambitions to control extensive Ottoman territory, perhaps especially since he and Venizelos had developed a strong personal bond. Following the 1918 armistice, Venizelos got Allied agreement that Greece would deploy troops in Smyrna to protect Greek ethnics – a decision 'taken suddenly, casually, and in great secrecy', without 'thought for the consequences'.[17]

Greek troops landed in mid-May 1919. 'In this somewhat haphazard and casual way began the Greek occupation of western Asia Minor, an occupation that was to culminate three years later in a disaster of truly tragic dimensions.'[18] Fighting soon broke out between Greek soldiers and local Turks. Though the Venizelos-appointed governor of the occupied territory Aristides Stergiadis (1861–1949) worked to suppress discrimination against the Turkish populace, this did not end the violence or suppress growing Turkish nationalism, which the occupation helped to foster.

The rising Turkish nationalist leader Mustafa Kemal's (1881–1938) call for an independent state was gathering momentum. In February 1920, Kemal announced a break with the Ottoman government. A year on, he made agreements with France and Italy; Turkish Nationalist forces began to challenge British troops stationed near Istanbul. The Ottoman Empire was formally dismembered in August 1920 with the Treaty of Sèvres. But Mustafa Kemal was not party to the treaty and did not accept its harsh terms. The Venizelists allowed themselves to believe that, as Lloyd George had supported them earlier, he would support an offensive into Anatolia. But Venizelos's election defeat in November 1920 and the likely return of King Constantine (no friend of the Allies) brought other views to the fore in Athens and London. Purges of Venizelists occurred, including the replacement of General Paraskevopoulas, commander of Greek troops in Anatolia, by General Anastasios Papoulas who was '[c]onceited, gullible, not blessed with a penetrating intelligence' and soon proved to lack strength of character.[19] Though he tried to keep political factionalism muted, about five hundred Venizelist officers retired, left their posts or were made to leave, weakening Greece's military presence in Asia Minor.[20]

At an attempted mediation summit in February 1921 Lloyd George seemed again to give tacit encouragement to Greece's ambitions, whilst France and Italy supported the Turkish nationalists who insisted Greek troops leave Asia Minor. On 23 March 1921 the Greeks launched their offensive. They made serious inroads into Anatolia but were under-armed and overstretched, and did not take Turkish military preparedness seriously enough. As summer turned to autumn, their advance towards Ankara was halted by lack of supplies, exhaustion and a Turkish counter-attack in early September.

'The retreat from the Sakarya [River] marked the end of the Greek hopes for imposing a settlement on Turkey by force of arms ... the government recognized that a face-saving settlement must come through the diplomacy of the Powers'[21] But the Allies' proposal for Greek evacuation raised fears in Greece about the treatment of Asia Minor's Christians under Turkish governance, while the Turks would not sign an armistice that did not stipulate immediate Greek withdrawal. Diplomatic initiatives seemed at a weary end, and army morale was low. Meanwhile, 'Mustafa Kemal was preparing a devastating counterattack along the 200-mile Greek front at a time when the Greek army was impeded by the replacement as commander in chief of General Papoulas by the idiosyncratic General Hadjianestis' (or Hatzianestis), both of whom make cameo appearances in Bayram's poems.[22]

Ataturk's offensive began on 26 August 1922, a 'shattering and bloody assault'.[23] Soon Greek forces were making a quick, disorganised retreat. The Greek governor left Smyrna on 8 September and by 19 September no remnants of the Greek army remained in Asia Minor. Though the Turkish army's takeover of the city was at first quiet, violence erupted, the Armenian, Greek and Frankish quarters were levelled by flames, and 250,000 people fled to the harbour. This 'catastrophe', as it was known in Greece, led to massive immigration of Turkish-speaking ethnic Greeks to Greece and a smaller number of Turks moving in the opposite direction. The Treaty of Lausanne (July 1923) formalised Greece's withdrawal of claims to Smyrna/Izmir and eastern Thrace. Bayram's poetic 'cycle' narrates episodes in this conflict from spring 1921 on.

The Battle Imagined, the Hero Made

What was likely the first salvo of the 'Sira Kemaliyya' appeared in *Al-Shabab* 69 on 21 May 1922 – after the Greek offensive was repelled and Mustafa Kemal had rejected any compromise leaving Greek troops in Asia Minor, but several months before his final offensive and takeover of Smyrna. Narrated partly in the Greek royalist 'vizier' Gounaris's 'voice', it narrates the Greek pullback amidst surprise at the strength and persistence of the Turkish forces and the Powers' unsuccessful attempts to make the Turks accept less than full Greek evacuation. That the presence of the Turkish 'epic hero' Kemal and the strength of his troops are 'voiced' by the adversary heightens the irony contained in this counter-image which challenges the orientalist chimera propagated by Lloyd George, of the Turks as simultaneously weak and menacing. Below I present a partial translation and analysis of this text.

The News-bulletin *Sira*

Bayram evokes the *sira* form through interleaved *saj'* (rhymed and rhythmic prose) and verse, a battlefield setting (followed by the 'battlefield' of negotiations) and the use of poetic 'dialogue' between characters which are actually opposing monologues enacting an utter lack of common ground. Familiar folk epithets of heroism announce the vehicle of satire and the editorial perspective. But paratextually the reader-listener has already been prepared:

Bayram makes use of – plays with – the conventional extended title form that chapbook versions of *Sirat 'Antar*, *Sirat Bani Hilal* and the like often bore:

> *'Ala l-rababa*
> *harb al-Turk wa-l-rum*
> *wa-ma gara fiha bi-l-tamam*
> *wa-l-kamal*
> *wa-l-hamdu lillah*
> *'ala kull*
> *hal*

On the Rebab: / the War of the Turks and the Greeks / and what happened in it fully / and completely [or: through Kemal] / praise be to God / for every / situation [or: in any case].)[24]

This title is multiply ironic. *Rum*, an ancient signifier for Greeks/Byzantines, specifically those of Greek-provenance churches, could imply 'Christians' more generally. Beneath the specific reference this intimated a semantic field that cast the conflict as a larger one between Muslims/Easterners and Christians/Europeans, drawing on long-standing tropes of ethnic-religious belonging as bases for political community. Such usages permeate the *sira* tradition, ascribing identity through religious labelling. Heath and Kruk note the anachronistic appearance in the 'Antar cycle of 'Frankish crusaders' as the Byzantine (Rum) emperor's allies.[25] That a medieval-origin epic ('Antar) featured conflict between Arabs and Byzantines furnished an historical template for Bayram's 'epic' of great-power politics and ethnic-religious (political) rivalries in his era's eastern Mediterranean.

The phrase *wa-ma gara fiha bi-l-tamam wa-l-kamal* was a formulaic expansion associated with the genre. The title on an undated chapbook printing of a Hilaliyya episode shows how Bayram mimics this pervasive phrasing partly by exaggerating its physical layout:

> *Qissat*
> *Khadra al-sharifa*
> *wa-ma gara laha ma'a waladiha al-amir*
> *Abu Zayd bi-l-tamam wa-l-kamal*
> *wa-l-hamdu lillah 'ala kull hal*

(The Story of / Khadra the Honourable / and what happened to her with her son the emir / Abu Zayd fully and completely / and praise be to God for every situation.)[26]

In Bayram's rendering, *kamal* (completion, fullness, perfection) puns on the hero's name, Mustafa Kemal. Set off by a line break, *wa-l-kamal*'s double signification is emphasised. Similarly, *ʿala kull hal* could signify a straightforward thanks offering, '[God be praised] for/in every situation/state', as in chapbook *sira* titles, but also a sardonic, shrug-it-off 'whatever the case'.

The text elaborates the opposition of identities, launching the narrative with a conventional invocation tailored to the events to be narrated. This opening echoes, or mimics, epic featuring pre-Islamic heroes (such as ʿAntar) that insert Islamic references, including the narrator's invocation of the prophet of Islam as he opens the 'performance'.[27]

> I offer prayers on behalf of the great warrior Muhammad
>> who laid down conditions for peacemaking and muster

First-person address establishes the presence of the *rawi*, the reciter-narrator (poet). As in origin the *sira* is a work of storytelling in a communal venue, the choice of genre template gives the *rawi*'s political narrative a declarative and public cast, whilst the opening gestures to the affective contact and cultural bond between audience, *sira* narrator and interactive performance tradition. For conventional *sira* performance, storytellers' 'exclamations . . . praising God, describing the situation of the hero . . . elicited similar responses from the audience'.[28]

The descriptive expansion foreshadows the 'negotiations' to come, hinting that it is the Muslim 'side' who adhere to fair conditions in peace and war. Muhammad is called on as ultimate hero and basis of legitimacy, posed implicitly in contrast to the secular Western Powers. Thus the narrator-figure bestows a religious-cultural legitimacy on (one side in) the conflict and evokes the foundational peacefulness yet fighting readiness of the Muslim *umma* in times of crisis, while signaling the text's narrative perspective, the positionality from which it speaks. *Rawi* and audience speak *with* the prophet and the hero, Mustafa Kemal, the link even stronger in that one epithet of the Prophet is al-Mustafa, 'the chosen'. The invocation implies that the entire community of Islam stands behind its hero. In the traditional *sira*, the hero fights the enemies of Islam, even anachronistically.[29] Often the hero is linked by bloodline to the family of Muhammad and has the aid of religious figures in his quest. Bayram plays seriously with this linkage via the opening reference to Muhammad and epithetic *al-sayyid*, suggesting more than a linkage of faith between Mustafa Kemal and the Prophet. The figure of a hero sanctioned through linkage to Islamic history and fighting on behalf of the faith-as-community sets up the narrative perspective unequivocally, just as the hero's name offers rich possibilities for heroic punning, both Mustafa as the epithetic 'chosen one' and the 'complete and perfect' Kemal. Thus, in taking up the *sira sha'biyya*'s terms, the text immediately signals to genre-savvy consumers that international-regional political conflict is managed here through the interpretative lens of 'local' (regional) community and heritage. It establishes legitimacy as a collective expression of solidarity while hailing these readers/listeners as part of the collectivity the *rawi* addresses. It recognises – or reorganises – the conflict as both saturated by international power relations and born within and prolonged by 'local' ideological–cultural dichotomisation. The poet characterises Turks and Greeks as opposing, fighting tribes and their leaders as legendary, fantastical figures. This adheres to the genre template, wherein opposing factions are identified by ethnicity and religion, sometimes anachronistically, and characterised as swearing by the sign of their identity.[30]

The next lines are narrated by *al-wazir* (the vizier) Gounaris, speaking for Greece's government. On one level simply Arabic for 'government minister', *wazir* evokes Ottoman governance and earlier Muslim empires, reminding listeners of the Anatolian Greeks' former status as Ottoman subjects. Dimitrios Gounaris (1866–1922), ally of King Constantine and opponent of Venizelos, was Prime Minister briefly in 1915, spent time in exile, and returned to Greece in 1920 as a key political force driving the Royalist government after Venizelos's electoral defeat. Already a behind-the-scenes player, from early April 1921 to mid-May 1922 he was Prime Minister. His resignation (days before Bayram's poem appeared) did not mean immediate loss of power. But, when the government was deposed following widespread army rebellion after Mustafa Kemal's victory, Gounaris was one of the Six who were tried for treason, found guilty and executed in November 1922. His plaint in Bayram's poem foreshadows what is to come: the evocative *ya wayl* (O woe) serves as both descriptor and curse: 'woe betides' and 'woe betide'.

The scene utilises stock figures of folk narratives and epithets common to epic. The vizier – aide and counsellor to the ruler – may be treacherous or good. 'The youth' (*al-fata*) is Papoulas; a positive term, *al-fata* connotes vigour, yet here belittles Papoulas, suggesting inexperience and naivety – an heroic term inverted through satire when applied to one of the villains. Gounaris was an implacable opponent of Venizelos, caricatured as an irresponsible 'distant' 'Grey Beard' and doer of vile deeds through Gounaris's oath: *yikhzik wa-yikhzi 'amlatak ya ba'id*, a negative inversion of 'Antar's *'amayil*, as disasters wrought rather than deeds accomplished. That 'the Greeks' speak Egyptian is perhaps the biggest joke of all.

> Said Vizier Gounaris of what plagued and beset him,
>   as tears from his eyes rolled far on and on:
> 'Woe betides he who picks fights with fierce lions,
>   Woe to the one stirring *sayyid* Kemal's rage!
> When the youth Papoulas poked there 'neath the lid
>   he stumbled on foes well armoured in iron,
> He learned that al-Kemal [the Perfect One], if war came in winter
>   would furnish the field with carpets to cover
> The Rum armies entered, and those trailing after,
>   lacking nothing but newborns, they would find out.
> The Turks' swords shone bright – and the sword only gleams
>   when gripped by a people of stamina strong
> Anatolian foxes erect in grape bowers
>   counted their swords felling each cluster
> The Anatole vulture had his fill of our flesh
>   and built his nest of meat-strips the sun bleached drier
> If one Turk departed, there'd rise in his place
>   one hundred before us, and the dead one's a martyr
> If we lost one [of ours] 'neath the hooves of their horses,
>   where to find a new dupe to waste in our muster?
> True, we have (it is said) a 'back' to support us
>   but Kemal! his chest and back both are still stronger

Entering fifty banks in the lands of Londara

    I came out with saddle bags bulging only with forearms

O Grey-Beard! the Rum army descended,

    to meet Kemal's troops – that Valiant knight-saviour

But it's me must await the disaster of disasters

    God wreck you and your doings, you faraway punter!'

The battlefield scene is dramatised through the legend-like imagery of a wild bestiary: the wily 'Anatolian foxes' coming out of their lair (the Greeks did not expect such strength from the waiting Turks), the vulture satiated on Greek flesh that, drying in the sun like the takings of the Bedouin hunter, to form strips of dried meat (*al-qadid*), was so abundant it could be heaped up to make shelters. The Greeks are heroes inverted – Gounaris weeps and moans his loss, as will Constantine – and are presented as passive and feminised. By contrast, through 'Gounaris's' description of his adversary, 'Kemal' is indeed the 'perfect' epic hero: fierce, bold, militarily capable and staunchly defensive of his people against invaders. Here is the image of masculine strength, buttressed further as the army is described as one powerful body. Drawing on the vocabulary of heroism with its epithets and formulaic usages (*usud kawasir, al-sayf, al-fata, al-faris, al-sandid*), the poem also puns on colloquialisms. The Greeks may have *dahr* (back, as backing), but Kemal has both 'back' and 'chest', support behind and ahead, and courage. 'Forearms' – or 'helping hands' – as the sole yield from a visit to London's banks may suggest the 'moral' support unaccompanied by material help the British gave the Greeks. This is the counter-image to the powerful figure of the autonomous Bedouin warrior, with his camel saddlebags, carpets, swords and loyal following whom he furnishes as necessary. 'Grey Beard' and the 'faraway punter' are Venizelos, who spent early 1922 in Europe and America with a wealthy supporter he had just married, though secondarily 'the vizier' might be cursing Lloyd George for supporting the Greeks – in word only – in an untenable adventure for which Gounaris must now assume responsibility.

    The first prose section opens paratextually: *qala l-rawi* (the narrator said). Reprising the 'I' of the opening invocation, the *rawi* as arbiter of the narrative perspective describes the situation that frames the 'conversations' in verse.[31] As Heath notes, 'printed versions of Arabic popular narratives . . .

emphasize[ ] oral provenance with the stock formula *qala r-rawi'*, thus evoking the storytelling or performance context.[32] Bayram follows this double invocation of context, oral and written, using the 'oral' narrative formula but following the print conventions in his title (as seen above) and internal structure. Orally performed *siyar* such as the Hilaliyya relied strongly on verse with its mnemonic advantages, less on prose: 'the oral versions have a much higher percentage of poetry . . . while written versions are primarily composed of rhymed prose with only occasional sections of verse, most often the speech of characters rather than narrative description'.[33] Bayram utilises this prose–verse division of narrative duties. His rhyming prose accentuates the hilarity of this modern urban 'tribal' stand-off as the *rawi* describes the Big Souvlaki versus the *tarbush*-wearing knight-hero as a fantastical 'Azrael' (*shuwaalaaki* may also echo *shuwaal*, big sack, connoting in colloquial Egyptian a man without a will of his own).

> Said the *rawi*: This is what the vizier said – that Big Souvlaki. As for what was, from the horsed warrior of the age [*amma ma kan. Min faris al-zaman*]. The lion of the Ottoman Tribe and death-angel of the dynasty of Tribe Greece [*asad bani 'Uthman wa-Azrael dawlat Bani al-Yunan*]. He removed his *tarbush*, and shouted, O armies, O armies [*ya juyush ya juyush*]. Around him gathered the tribes and every horseman ran with blood. He opened the sealed letter, brought by the messenger of the Kings of the Rum, and read what was in it, may God preserve him.

The next poetic segment is this letter: the offer of 'compromise' from the defeated Greeks (behind whom the European Powers lurk). Inappropriately 'familiar' Turkish interjections in the Arabic mock the notion that the Rum 'speak the same language' as the Turks; worse, the letter addresses the Turkish leader as 'Abu Darwish', an informal appellation for 'Mustafa'. And then, the language of bureaucratic address creates a travesty of formal government-to-government communications: *bash nizami*, senior civil servant, a Turkish term evocative of Egypt's Turkish bureaucratic (and colloquial) heritage.

> To the fierce hero of Turkish lands called
> > Kemal al-Mustafa, lion of great men
> *Afarim* [Bravo]! armies of the *bash nizami*

Afarim, Abu Darwish, *Afarim*
Your guns fell all who tower high
   Your swords put to sleep those alert of limb
For the Greeks, Havas and Reuters announced
   Defeat on defeat, strong lad, and victims
Constantine sat in the cool morn weeping
   Gounaris came to us, a-sea and upstream
Enough, Banu 'Uthman, enough, no more battles!
   Abu Darwish, you've taken booty to the brim!
Our aim is truce, for war destroys:
   Ruins its folk when peace lasts for them.

Reversing the order of Kemal's name emphasises his link to Islam's first family; turning *mustafa* into an epithet again plays on the notion of a sancti-fied 'chosen' to heighten his heroic presence. But the Greek plea, in defeat, goes unheard.

The following prose interlude pairs a better epithet with Kemal, *al-ghazi* (Turkish *gazi*), the Fighter, signalling the *rawi*'s alignment with him and distance from the narrated Greeks with their insulting letter. This title the Turkish parliament officially bestowed on him in September 1921. Characteristic external physical description presents the Gazi's soldiers as fierce and animal-like, associated with flame, maintaining the imagery encap-sulating legendary *sira* heroes.[34] In traditional nomadic poetry the rising dust cloud signals a distant Bedouin raiding party, thus a warning of peril to come. Melding the heroes of new Turkish nationalism with Arab Bedouin expressive forms, the text intimates a populist pan-Islamic or neo-Ottoman solidarity against external threats.

> The *rawi* said: When the Gazi finished reading this letter, the soldiers mut-tered and stamped their feet, mouths opening to murmur. Flames shot from their fangs and from beneath their claws rose the dust in a cloud. The noisy tumult grew abundant and the horn was blown. The Gazi shouted . . .

Here the narrative collapses into Turkish and pseudo-Turkish strings, albeit with identifiable (to Arabic listeners) loanwords and familiar religious-based invocations that serve also as popular evocations of approval or surprise (*ma shaʾ Allah*). Kemal summons 'Yusuf Kemal': Yusuf Kemal Tengirsenk, Turkey's Foreign Minister 1921–2. He is *al-batal al-dirgham*, as Kemal is called by the Rum, a lion or powerful stallion: metaphorically, a valiant, graceful and courageous individual.

> The hero emerged to say *Labayk* (Here I am, how can I serve you?). He said, Take this letter of mine to the Kings of the Rum. Write what I dictate to you. Yusuf grasped the pen, Mustafa raised the flag, and composed: Prayers on behalf of the Father of al-Zahraʾ the Virgin.

Mustafa Kemal's dictate appears in verse, where, once again, 'dialogue' becomes monologue. Introducing his 'letter' with reference to Muhammad, Kemal is at once *rawi* and hero. And the speaker's *risala* (letter, message) bears echoes of an earlier *risala*, the message and mission of Muhammad, whilst perhaps gesturing to cross-sectarian unity (*al-injil*, gospel). As the speaker sets conditions, we are reminded of the text's opening, Muhammad as arbiter of war and peace.

> I offer prayers for the Easterner, the Hijazi, Muhammad
>   The messenger named in the gospel with grace
> Says the angry youth, Perfection/Kemal of the Warriors [*kamal al-fawaris*]
>   Kemal of Bani ʿUthman, Consummate/Kemal of his
>   generation and place [*kamal al-jil*]
> To the Rumish Kings convey a message from me
>   setting out our conditions, every detail and trace
> First, that anyone who's stamped o'er our country
>   is rightly prisoner or a corpse in each case
> Second, we say, as we write our response:
>   our lands the Greeks must leave, first, leaving no trace
> Third, the Treaty of Sèvres we'll see adjusted
>   for the sword has made adjustments here apace
> Fourth, in the period of two months or three,
>   we will have gained two thousand miles' space . . .

The next prose section enacts the European 'negotiations', through diction that evokes much earlier stand-offs ('the country of the *franj*') and is a hilarious mêlée of British 'etiquette', colonial patronising and local identity markers. The text demonstrates Bayram's mastery at mimicking the colonists through their own usages. The Turks are made unappealing promises by each European power in turn; the Italians, caricatured linguistically, support the Turks yet will not insist on a Greek evacuation. (Throughout the torturous discussions over Asia Minor, the Italians and French were more favourable to the Turks while London held to its support for Greece.) As Kemal was 'Azrael', angel of death to the Greeks, here the British are Iblis, or Satan, the fallen angel, attempting to seduce the Turks. The text thus appropriates satirically a vision of history setting human experience within a divine plan: the imperialists are on the side of the always-already-fallen. The European powers emerge as stupidly condescending and unrealistic. The unequivocal response must come in Turkish (*yok efendim*: No, sirs).

> Said the rawi: The messenger arrived, entering the country of the Franj with flutes and drums. Bells were struck and lamps were lit, the dinner cloth was rolled out, set with tea and biscuits, fowl and meat and *halqum*-sweets. When they had eaten and washed their hands, the talk circulated and Iblis came to them:
>
> O messenger of Kamal [or, of perfection]. Good and decent man [*ya bn al-halal*], do lift the sword away until winter vanishes and summer is in sight. Then we'll give you Ankara, and two metres of the shore of Marmara, and the Greeks will leave when the time comes.
>
> *Yok efendim.*
>
> France: We'll give you Izmir, and the big mountain. And the Greeks will leave the line to you, and stop and stay at the shore.
>
> *Yok efendim.*
>
> Italy: La la la la. Izmiro is for the Turko. Anatolo is for the Turko. Istambulo is for the Turko. Kullo [*kull*, all] is for the Turko. But leave-o the Grigo [Greeks] *shwayya* [a little].
>
> *Yok efendim.*

In a final prose section titled 'Yusuf Kemal's speech', Turkish and mock Turkish interspersed with Islamic phrases predominate, culminating in the religious invocation, equally belief and utter rejection of the outcome of this narrative, *la hawla wa-la quwwata ila billahi al-ʿali al-ʿazim, salam ʿalaykum wa-rahmatu Allah*. Thus the text ends in the interlingual chaos of one-sided 'negotiations', the Turks standing linguistically firm and thus politically so, affirming identity and political stance. This text is set after the Turks' first defeat of the Greek forces but before the final rout. The Greek offer of a truce without complete withdrawal is enacted satirically: the true players – European Powers – 'speak for' Greece. The poem's inconclusive ending narrates its own historical moment and highlights the play of language, politics as fiction. This is but a *qissa* – a story, one episode in a larger heroic cycle; and narration of it, as news, will be ongoing. The terse repeated *yok efendim* signals that Turkey's leader and indefatigable hero refuses to speak the Europeans' language of false negotiation.

I have argued that Bayram deployed the genre template of the *sira shaʿbiyya* strategically to invoke a collective identity based on shared heritage, while stretching it to embrace a regional resistant politics posed against Europeans' ambitions and their support for 'local' clients. Given the genre's horizon of expectations, setting up hero versus villain(s) animates a satiric political inversion: Greeks, backed by the truly powerful (but herein ineffective) Europeans, are the snivelling inverse of the Arab/Turkish/Muslim hero. Casting contemporary political conflict in epic yet populist terms, Bayram manages the duality of heroic posturing as a heavy-handed colonialist tactic versus the effective heroism of Mustafa Kemal. In later texts in this series, more ambiguity over the effectivity and sincerity of the modern epic hero would surface.

Bayram's 'epics' of the early 1920s follow the structural genre markers of the *sira shaʿbiyya*, constructing binary oppositions between political heroes (Zaghlul, Ataturk) and forces against which they struggled, embodied as individual villain-adversaries (Milner, Venizelos and Gounaris, Papoulas). This dyadic agonistic structure mirrors the *sira*'s male heroic figure, echoing the great epic cycles. The hero's quest consists in defeating adversaries in the interests of community maintenance. That the epic hero is larger than life – for these heroes are always 'innately indomitable'[35] – allows Bayram to magnify national/ist heroes but also opens the door to a caricature of pomposity, self-deception, greed and incapacity.

Bayram brings together the narrative context of *sira* – the *samar*, or evening session of narration and conviviality – as the space of the *watan* (homeland) and *qawm* (national community) but also in its regional-identitarian context, with the heroic content, nationalist defiance of Europe's imperialist regional blueprint. In form, language and thematic compass, the text constructs an audience as a collective identity of and beyond nation. At times, the identity posited in this series is a strategically hybridised one that layers nationalist, anti-colonial identities upon regional-confessional ones. The quest moves toward immediate political triumph but further toward the self-definition and realisation of independent polities in the context of imperial Great Power politics, seen for what it is through the lens of populist irony. By articulating this quest in a form long associated with popular and orally performed Arabic culture, the author thematises cultural *and* political self-realisation, and announces a history of heroism and an indigenous expressive culture as 'the back and chest' of a collective, proud political body. As Heath notes, the *siyar sha'biyya* 'form a cohesive genre by reason of their shared emphasis on heroes and heroic deeds of battle, their pseudo-historical tone and setting, and their indefatigable drive toward cyclic expansion: one event leads to another, one battle to another, one war to another'[36] and by doing so they accumulate a historical self-consciousness for the community. Did Bayram mean to gesture to these conflicts as never-ending, parts of a cycle that would ever and always be rehearsed, an ongoing commentary on the self-conscious national 'heroism' required of the less powerful in the late imperial age?

Notes

1. Marilyn Booth, 'Colloquial Arabic Poetry, Politics, and the Press in Modern Egypt', *International Journal of Middle East Studies* 24:3 (1992), pp. 419–40; Marilyn Booth, 'Insistent Localism in a Satiric World: Shaykh Naggar's "Reed-Pipe" in the 1890s Cairene Press', in Hans Harder and Barbara Mittler (eds), *Asian Punches: A Transcultural Affair*, New York and Heidelberg: Springer Verlag, 2013, pp. 187–218; Ziad Fahmy, *Ordinary Egyptians: Creating the Modern Nation through Popular Culture*, Stanford, CA: Stanford University Press, 2011; Marilyn Booth, 'Poetry in the Vernacular', in M. M. Badawi (ed.), *The Cambridge History of Arabic Literature: Modern Arabic Literature*, Cambridge: Cambridge University Press, 1992, pp. 463–82.
2. Marilyn Booth, *Bayram al-Tunisi's Egypt: Social Criticism and Narrative Strategies*, Exeter: Ithaca Press, 1990.

3. Pierre Cachia, *Popular Narrative Ballads of Modern Egypt*, Oxford: Clarendon Press, 1989, chs 3, 7, 8; Pierre Cachia, *Exploring Arab Folk Literature*, Edinburgh: Edinburgh University Press, 2011.

4. Cachia, *Popular Narrative Ballads*, p. 86.

5. Peter Heath, 'Other *Sira*s and Popular Narratives', in Roger Allen and D. S. Richards (eds), *Arabic Literature in the Post-classical Period*, Cambridge: Cambridge University Press, 2006, p. 327.

6. G. Canova, '*Sira* Literature', in Julie Scott Meisami and Paul Starkey (eds), *Encyclopedia of Arabic Literature*, London and New York: Routledge, 1998, Vol. 2: p. 726.

7. 'Abd al-Rahman al-Abnudi, *La Geste hilalienne*, trans. Tahar Guiga, Cairo: Al-Hay'a al-Misriyya al-'Amma li'l-Kitab, 1978. See also Dwight F. Reynolds, '*Sirat* Bani Hilal', in Roger Allen and D. S. Richards (eds), *Arabic Literature in the Post-classical Period*, pp. 307–18.

8. See Reynolds, '*Sirat* Bani Hilal'.

9. Peter Heath, *The Thirsty Sword: Sirat 'Antar and the Arabic Popular Epic*, Salt Lake City: University of Utah Press, 1996.

10. Remke Kruk, 'Sirat 'Antar ibn Shaddad', in Roger Allen and D. S. Richards (eds), *Arabic Literature in the Post-classical Period*, p. 292.

11. Marilyn Booth, 'Disruptions of the Local, Eruptions of the Feminine: Local Reportage and National Anxieties in Egypt's 1890s', in Anthony Gorman and Didier Monciaud (eds), *Between Politics, Society and Culture: The Press in the Middle East before Independence*, Edinburgh: Edinburgh University Press, forthcoming.

12. I have found many of these (generally undated) in Cairo's antiquarian book markets. Versions or portions of 'Antar appeared in Cairo and Beirut from the 1860s (Heath, *Thirsty Sword*, p. 29; also Reynolds, '*Sirat* Bani Hilal', p. 308).

13. This account follows Richard Clogg, *A Short History of Modern Greece,* Cambridge: Cambridge University Press, 1979, pp. 99–132; and Michael Llewellyn Smith, *Ionian Vision: Greece in Asia Minor 1919–1922*, London: Allen Lane, 1973.

14. Clogg, *Short History*, p. 112.

15. Ibid., p. 29.

16. Ibid., pp. 30–2.

17. Ibid., p. 81.

18. Clogg, *Short History*, p. 113.

19. Llewellyn Smith, *Ionian Vision*, pp. 175, 228–30.

20. Ibid., pp. 173–9.

21. Ibid., p. 234.
22. Clogg, *Short History*, p. 117.
23. Llewellyn Smith, *Ionian Vision*, p. 288.
24. [Bayram al-Tunisi], "Ala al-rababa . . .', *Al-Shabab* 69 (21 May 1922). This text does not appear in *Muntakhabat al-Shabab*. All translations are mine and drawn from this text. I transliterate according to the printed text not colloquial pronunciation.
25. Kruk, 'Sirat 'Antar ibn Shaddad', p. 296; Heath, *Thirsty Sword*, pp. 30–1.
26. *Qissat Khadra al-sharifa* . . ., Cairo: Maktabat al-jumhuriyya al-'arabiyya, n.d.
27. Kruk, 'Sirat 'Antar ibn Shaddad', p. 297.
28. Heath, *Thirsty Sword*, pp. 32–8; quotation, p. 38.
29. H. T. Norris, 'The Rediscovery of the Ancient Sagas of the Banu Hilal', *Bulletin of the School of Oriental and African Studies* 51:3 (1988), pp. 462–81.
30. Heath, *Thirsty Sword*, pp. 16–17.
31. Canova, *'Sira* Literature', p. 726. Heath sees this functional interrelationship differently for *Sirat 'Antar*: prose used descriptively for 'object of the moment', poetry fulfilling a generalising, expansive function (*Thirsty Sword*, pp. 109–15).
32. Heath, *Thirsty Sword*, p. 151.
33. Reynolds, *'Sirat* Bani Hilal', p. 318.
34. Heath, *Thirsty Sword*, pp. 120–2.
35. Ibid., p. 71.
36. Ibid., p. xvi.

9

Jewish Arabs in the Israeli Asylum:
A Literary Reflection[1]

Miriam Cooke

In the 1950s two of Mustafa Badawi's Jewish students left Iraq for Israel. Life in Baghdad had become untenable for Sasson Somekh and David Semah, and they made the perilous trip to the young Zionist state. There they learned Hebrew and became integrated into the predominantly Ashkenazi culture. However, unlike many of their Mizrahi Jewish contemporaries, they held on to their mother tongue and nurtured their interest in Arabic literature and culture. During the late 1960s and early 1970s, both pursued their doctorates on Egyptian men of letters under the supervision of Mustafa Badawi. Sasson Somekh analysed the early novels of Najib Mahfuz, and David Semah focused on the Egyptian critics ʿAbbas Mahmud al-ʿAqqad, Muhammad Husayn Haykal, Taha Husayn and Muhammad Mandur. In 1973, Brill published Somekh's dissertation with the title *The Changing Rhythm* and a year later they brought out Semah's *Four Egyptian Literary Critics*. Both went on to pursue distinguished careers in the Israeli academy. This chapter examines the lives and writings of a few Mizrahi intellectuals who, like Badawi's students, succeeded despite the challenges they faced as Jewish Arabs.

In 2002, an Iraqi Muslim named Samir (b. 1955)[2] directed *Forget Baghdad*, a documentary about Iraqi writers in Israel. Having heard so much about the Jews and the role they had played in his country, he wanted to know what happened to them after they left in the 1950s. How had they been welcomed and how were they living in the Jewish state?

'They bought us,' responds Samir Naqqash (1938–2006). 'We became their slaves . . . They sent us back 100,000 years.' Author of five collections of stories, three plays and four novels, Naqqash was one of the last Iraqis in Israel to write in Arabic.

Reliving his traumatic encounter with Hebrew, Shimon Ballas (b. 1930), Professor of Arabic literature at Haifa University, recalls: 'I tried to forget Arabic, not to read a single letter.' Then one night in the 1960s Arabic exacted her revenge by bombarding him with words and phrases that kept him sleepless until morning. Since then he has written in Hebrew, but 'carried' Arabic with him wherever he goes. Author of ten works of fiction – including *The Transit Camp* (1964)[3] – he has also produced several Hebrew translations and studies of modern Arabic literature.

The prize-winning author Sami Michael (b. 1926) comments wryly on life in Israel decades after immigration, 'We were completely integrated into life in Baghdad, but in Israel I felt like a visitor, a stranger'.

'In the Arab world we're Jews,' says the critic Ella Shohat (b. 1955) who was born to Iraqi parents in Israel and immigrated to the United States in the early 1980s, 'and in Israel we're Arabs. We always have the wrong identity.'

Samir's interviews reveal these intellectuals' continuing alienation in and from Israel and their determination to remember Baghdad. Since the 1990s, several Jewish Arabs have found national recognition, and they have begun to highlight their stigmatised difference.

In a landmark anthology of non-European Jewish writings in Israel, entitled *Keys to the Garden: New Israeli Writing* (1996), the critic Ammiel Alcalay traces the development of a Mizrahi consciousness:

> Originally a component of the pejorative label used to institutionally categorize non-European Jews (*benei ʿedot ha-mizrah* / 'offspring of oriental ethnic communities'), the word *mizrah* (East) and *mizrahi* (Easterner) gradually took on qualities of pride and defiance as the *mizrahim* (plural) came to describe themselves.

Celebrating this literary recognition, Alcalay asserts that some of the most important and vital literary oeuvres in Israel

> have emerged precisely out of the *mizrahi* problematic, with all its attendant concerns about identity, memory, language, and minority/majority

relations . . . By remaining connected to the sources of their own particular pain and experience, these writers refuse to accept the universality of what has, ideologically, come to be construed as Jewish 'fate,' applicable to all Jews, in all places, at all times, sooner or later. Most paradoxically, this refusal is expressed through insisting on the fact of exile, both personal and collective, within the promised land, within the space of return itself.[4]

Mizrahi writers have found literary inspiration in their experience of alienation as oriental Jews. Unlike European Jews, they do not consider the Holocaust to be their nation's greatest tragedy and shaping experience. For them to be eternal exiles within the utopian space of return is the source of their suffering.

Looking at the first wave of immigration and its aftermath through novels, poetry, autobiographies and films, I argue that Israel is an asylum. In the first instance, it was an asylum for European Jews (Ashkenazis) until they turned the asylum into their state. From that point on, they created asylums for various constituencies, including Jewish Arabs.

Foreigners in the Asylum of the Promised Land

Established only sixty-five years ago, Israel's mission was to construct a nation state that would gather in all Jews who had been millennially scattered. Although all Jews by virtue of their religion should have had the 'right of return' to Zion, not all Jews enjoyed this right equally, especially when they came from Arab countries. These Jewish Arabs presented a conundrum because, although they were co-religionists, they shared the ethnicity of the enemy. Where Arabs and Jews are considered mutually exclusive identities, Jewish Arabs don't quite fit. Their story contests the myth that Israel is a melting pot for all Jews. Rather, Israel was and continues to be what sociologist Bryan Turner calls an enclave society.[5]

There are many enclaves in multicultural, multiethnic Israel for those who do not quite fit the ideal notion of what an Israeli should be. The enclave of interest in this chapter is the one that houses Jewish Arabs, especially those who came from Iraq. Unlike the mostly illiterate North Africans[6] who chose to go to Israel, Iraqi immigrants were generally from the urban middle class. The transition from an Arab Muslim society, where they lived comfortably as a minority, to the Jewish nation state was unexpectedly painful.

The twenty-four women and men in Alcalay's anthology, who include Arabs, Iranians, Indians and Turks, articulate that pain. Although many wrote during the 1960s, they were so marginalised that it was as though they had not written. While Naqqash remained above the fray by refusing to use Hebrew and writing for Arabs outside Israel, others were hurt by this critical neglect. For Tikva Levi, erasure of Mizrahi culture was tantamount to a 'covert Holocaust . . . This is sometimes much more difficult to deal with than a wall with a closed border . . . we're inside Racism parallel to Holocaust / awfully close to the graveyard.'[7] The analogy is shocking, but it compels attention to what she considers to be a form of cultural genocide. How is it possible that this national home for all Jews should quickly prove to be cruel to some Jews?

For Jewish Arabs life in Israel was a long-term experience of asylum. The asylum is a refuge, but it is also a place of isolation, discipline and exile; it mirrors society by locating the norm in the negative: this, thank God, I am not. A 'total institution', to use Erving Goffman's term, the asylum is a closed world where the expectations and values of society are learned and internalised. The asylum molds individuals into compliant social actors. It is in such places, writes the Algerian Jew Jacques Derrida, that the new arrival becomes a foreigner, a

> guest who is wrong, illegitimate, clandestine, liable to expulsion or arrest . . . From the point of view of the law, the guest, even when he is well received, is first of all a foreigner, he must remain a foreigner (who) is not the other, the completely other who is relegated to an absolute out-side, savage, barbaric, precultural and prejuridical, outside and prior to the family, the community, the city, the nation, or the State.[8]

The one who comes from elsewhere is first of all a foreigner, or an illegiti-mate guest. The foreigner's acceptance into the new community is contingent upon conformity with the host's expectations. One might say that the for-eigner dwells for a time in a *barzakh*. This Qur'anic term refers to the meta-physical space between this life and the hereafter that is both and neither.[9] For the Jewish Arabs in Israel, the physical *barzakh* was the transit camp that bridged the Arab past and the Israeli present; both were at once present and absent.

Acculturation in the Asylum

Foreigners must learn the rules of the desired home and prove to their hosts that they are assets to be embraced and not parasites to be shunned. In Asia's pre-Israeli transit camps where they awaited transfer to the Promised Land, Mizrahi Jews learned the protocols of Zionist citizenship. In 1943, an emissary to Asian Jews in a camp in Abadan wrote patronisingly about his charges: 'With the help of science it is possible to succeed in removing people from dark corners to brighter corners . . . The main thing is to extricate these people from the Levantine morass in which they are mired.'[10] This is the language of European colonialism: the European Jews must extricate non-European Jews from this primal, polluting Levantine morass.

After transfer to Israel, these 'foreigners' were held in transit camps until permanent housing could be identified. While Europeans were also penned in camps, their experience was generally shorter and less bitter. In his 2007 autobiography *Baghdad Yesterday*, the literary critic Sasson Somekh (b. 1933) recalls Operation Ezra and Nehemiah.[11] Over 100,000 Jews left Iraq in 1951 unready 'for the drastic transition from an Arab country to the new Jewish state'.[12] They were taken to a camp near Haifa run by Yiddish-speaking Ashkenazis, the term used for European Jews. Although Somekh refuses to write of the 'difficulties of absorption and the challenges posed by our having to start a new life in a new language', he does note that 'life in Israel could be cruel as well, and many of my generation, who were scalded in the melting pot of the fifties and sixties, were distanced from their native culture because of the continuous conflict with the Arab world' (p. 10, p. 174). Awarded some of Israel's most coveted prizes, Somekh prefers not to critique the state that has honoured him. Yet he does hint at the ordeal of the first years when he and other Jewish Arabs were scalded in Israel's 'melting pot'.

Jewish Arab intellectuals' descriptions of the transit camps and their persistence in the mind recall the philosopher Giorgio Agamben's states of exception where what is being excluded in the camp is *captured outside*, that is, it is included by virtue of its very exclusion . . . the birth of the camp . . . takes place when the political system of the modern nation-state . . . decides to undertake the management of the biological life of the nation directly as its own task . . . The state of exception, which used to be essentially a temporary suspension of the order, becomes now a new and stable spatial arrangement inhabited by that naked life that increasingly cannot be inscribed into the order.[13]

Jewish Arabs wrote about their 'naked life' in an Israel, one that excluded Arabs, both Palestinian Israelis and Jews migrating from Arab countries. Sharing the race of the Arab enemy, Jewish Arabs had to remake themselves into Ashkenazis to be accepted, to be fully clothed.

The process of acculturation in the asylum of the camps has figured importantly in Mizrahi literature. Writing about literary representations of the immigration of Iraqi Jews to Israel, the historian Moshe Gat cites several fictional accounts of the horrors of the camps where Arab culture was to be stripped away and replaced by the veneer of Europe.[14] The Iraqi Israeli journalist Nissim Rejwan (b. 1924) is scathing: 'Having shattered his personality, the Ashkenazis proceed to ask that he be an Ashkenazi like unto themselves . . . integration of the new immigrant into Israeli society and culture [meant] "remoulding" the newcomer from Asian and African countries into something very much like the self-image of the veteran, non-Oriental, Jewish settler'.[15] Shattering the personality, demanding mimicry and remoulding in the image of the Ashkenazi were the crucial elements of the Mizrahi acculturation. They were stripped of what Goffman calls 'identity equipment'.[16] Without past or culture or dignity, they could no longer present their usual image of themselves to others. Simultaneously included and excluded from the society into which they sought admission, they were forced to change and to reject the identity equipment they had brought from afar, to become worthy of inclusion in the modern family of the nation state.

Transit Camp

When a character in Ballas's *The Transit Camp* asks what transit camps mean, he is told they were a 'passage' to complete integration into the life of the state. I looked for the word in the Bible and found it in the Book of Samuel: a passage about Jonathan 'going between the passes, and they had "a sharp rock on the one side, and a sharp rock on the other side." There's a "transit" camp for you! A rock on one side and a rock on the other side. Go ahead and try to break those rocks! Isn't this just another way of saying exile?'[17] The narrator is not the illiterate ignoramus the authorities think he is, for he immediately goes to the Bible to find the real meaning of *ma'bara*, or passage. He finds Scylla and Charybdis on either side of the passage and beyond. This 'passage' signals the return of the millennial condition of exile. Now, however, exile is in the *barzakh* between the forbidden Arab past and the unattainable Israeli present; Jewish Arabs are simultaneously in both and neither. They are condemned to exist in the limbo of the asylum.[18]

Somekh and his compatriots were outraged when they realised that they had been reduced to inconvenient commodities:

> The clerks called this process *siddur* which means literally, 'arrangement' . . . Because of the linguistic similarity between Hebrew and Arabic, the word *siddur* and its related forms sounded very much like the Arabic *tasdir* which means 'the exporting of goods.' We angrily protested the fact that overnight we had been transformed from people into goods, imported and exported by Yiddish-speaking clerks.[19]

Somekh's knowledge of Arabic reveals the truth lurking in the Hebrew: Jewish Arabs were reduced to the naked life of commodities at best, of parasites at worst. It would take a long time for them to cease to be foreigners.

For the Moroccan Albert Swissa, the first days in Israel felt like living in 'a penitentiary, or area of containment'. His parents soon realised that 'they and their kind were pariahs, ostracized from the economic, social, cultural and – worst of all – spiritual life of the nascent state of Israel . . . it fell to the Oriental Jews to fight on all fronts of Israeli society, to fight against the society itself, and to fight against the image Israeli society ascribed to them'.[20] They were Derrida's foreigners who might never earn the right to membership in the new nation.[21]

Religion and the Secular State

How could these 'foreigners' achieve nationalisation? The process was contradictory: through religion and not-religion. Israel embodies a paradox:

it is both a modern, thus secular, nation state and a premodern, religious belonging. How could it be both modern and premodern, both secular and religious? The answer is that it was modern for some (Ashkenazis) and provisionally premodern for others (Mizrahim). Let me explain.

During the first half of the twentieth century, European Zionists – with the help of British colonial powers – paved the way for the establishment of a nation state that would provide a national identity, national rights and citizenship to all Jews regardless of their place of origin. Palestine was chosen to be this new national home for the Jews. From the end of the nineteenth century, Zionists transformed secular Palestinian territory into a religious European place. Once stripped of its secular, national markings, Palestine was overwritten with a religious national identity that, ironically, was newly secularised.

The sociologist Yehouda Shenhav chronicles the earliest instances of the paradoxical process. European emissaries to Asian transit camps, he explains, attempted 'to nationalize the Arab Jews through religion'.[22] The very first step involved erasing the dangerous Arab ethnicity and replacing it with a religious identity. Once Jewish Arabs had become just Jews they could begin the journey toward alignment with the European Jews. In other words, religion would erase, or at the very least overwrite, the offending ethnicity. The catch, however, was that modern European Jews in Palestine and then in Israel were deemed to be secular because modernity is by definition secular. It was not enough, therefore, to emphasise their religious identity to become modern Israelis, Jewish Arabs had to secularise their newly acquired religio-national identity.

How did this confusing situation come about? The paradoxical outcome of the Enlightenment secularisation of human rights in the late eighteenth century, Israel is a modern nation state with a premodern religious core identity. Enlightenment human rights guaranteed freedom and equality for citizens of internationally recognised nation states, and not for members of religious communities. Premised on ethnic homogeneity, modern nation states excluded those who did not fit the new national profile, thus creating internal and interregional minorities living 'outside normal legal protection', and without guaranteed rights.[23] That was what happened to Jews in twentieth-century Europe. They became minorities in need of a state that would give secular national rights to Jews, namely people sharing a religion.

The birth of the Israeli state transformed European Jews from stateless refugees into citizens of an internationally recognised nation state. Their unmarked identity was to become the norm for all who aspired to be Israeli citizens, and assimilation became the sine qua non. Although all asylum seekers had the moral claim to first admittance into the new Jewish state, in that they had what was called 'the right of return', the state had the reciprocal right to impose conditions. Acquiescence to these conditions then determined whether to grant citizenship or asylum. If, for example, a Jewish Arab seemed more Arab than Jew, citizenship might be postponed until such time that the Jew predominated. But then this new Jew without ethnicity had to transform the religious identification into a cultural identity. Israel was a state for Jews who did not identify as religious but rather as cultural citizens. In this politically ambivalent system, Palestinian non-Jews and Jewish Arabs became minorities outside normal legal protection.

Newly nationalised through premodern religion, Jewish Arabs were confronted with a conundrum: how to retain and balance religious, ethnic and cultural affiliations and identities? Held in asylums on the margins of society, Jewish Arabs had to learn how to become both modern and culturally Jewish. But how could Jewish Arabs secularise their newly emphasised religious identification without falling back into the dangerous Arab ethnicity? If they were to be successful, they might jeopardise the very process that qualified them to be Israeli. How were they to deal with the racialised imbalance between Ashkenazis and Jewish Arabs that was articulated in terms of modernity?

For Ella Shohat, it is racial prejudice that divides Israeli society into asylums containing Jewish Arabs and Palestinians, and the racialisation of Jewish Arabs goes back to nineteenth-century European colonial practices. In *Taboo Memories*, she writes about the violence done to Egyptian Jews by the European appropriation of the Geniza documents. In 1864 Solomon Schechter of Cambridge University travelled to Cairo where he 'discovered' some documents in the Ben Ezra synagogue. For 850 years, Egyptian rabbis had stored documents carrying 'scriptural traces of God's name'. Assuming the local community did not value this treasure, despite the fact that they had safeguarded it for centuries, British Jews transferred it to the safekeeping of the Taylor–Schechter collection in Cambridge. Thus 'inadvertently began a process of symbolic displacement of Jews from the East from their geo-cultural space . . . While the Geniza documents testify to the rootedness of the Jews in a vast region stretching from the Mediterranean to the Indian Ocean, the textual "witnesses" themselves ironically were uprooted and displaced.'[24] What we learn from this account is that when the Geniza documents became part of an unmarked, universal Jewish patrimony their Mediterranean/ Arab origins were erased.[25] In turn and with time, this 'universal' cultural legacy was racialised to become Ashkenazi. This, Shohat explains, is what happened to Jewish Arabs who 'suddenly became simply "Jews"' (205) when they arrived in Israel. It was not enough to be Jewish to become Israeli; as good colonial subjects, they had to mimic their European co-religionists.

In her controversial study of the filmic representation of Mizrahis, Shohat tore the veil off anti-Arab racism. Between 1967 and 1977, a new genre of farce called 'bourekas' emerged. Folkloric outsiders, Jewish Arabs were stereotyped as lazy and primitive but also cunning: 'Since the target audience is the Oriental public, the films are necessarily permeated by social and ethnic tensions. In the world of the oppressed, the oppressor is a constant (historical) presence in relation to whom the repressed must either assimilate or rebel.'[26] One of the best-known boureka films is Ephraim Kishon's 1964 *Sallah Shabbati*. It opens with refugees disembarking from a plane: the first to leave are the wealthy Ashkenazis, elegant, urbane and encumbered with numerous suitcases; next, out tumble some dirty, raggedy Mizrahis, and a little girl appears on the conveyor belt having stowed away with the luggage. The eponymous hero is taken with wife and seven children to a filthy transit camp, out of which they are promised immediate transfer to permanent housing. The only immediate, however, is the realisation that this promise is bogus. Vignette after hilarious vignette follows Shabbati's wily struggles to obtain the permanent housing that all Jews were promised upon arrival in Israel. After failing to sell his beautiful daughter to a fat chauffeur or to the neighboring kibbutz, he lights on a plan. In this new world you get what you do not want, so he organises a demonstration against permanent housing. He gets the coveted transfer. The film ends with the motley crowd disappearing into the concrete jungle of a soulless housing development. Questions linger: Will permanent housing be different from the asylum of the camp? Can

Shabbati ever become fully Israeli? Or will he continue to carry the camp with him wherever he goes?

The Moroccan Sami Shalom Chetrit provides an answer in his elliptical 'Getting to Know a Friendly American Jew: Conversation'. An American interrogates a Jewish Arab:

> – And you are, I mean, you're Israeli, right?
> – Yes, of course.
> – Your family is observant?
> – Pretty much . . .
> – Excuse me for prying, but I just have to ask you, are you Jewish or Arab?
> – I'm an Arab Jew . . .
> – Arab Jew? I've never heard of that . . . Look, I've got nothing against Arabs. I even have friends who are Arabs, but how can you say 'Arab Jew' when all the Arabs want is to destroy the Jews?
> – And how can you say 'European Jews' when the Europeans have already destroyed the Jews?[27]

Neither Shabbati nor Chetrit's Jewish Arab will escape the asylum. Like Tikva Levi, who compared the situation of Jewish Arabs in Israel with the Holocaust, writing 'we're inside Racism parallel to Holocaust', Chetrit juxtaposes the Holocaust – here unnamed but clearly indicated – and Ashkenazi anti-Arab racism. But the poem is making another vital point: the Holocaust is past; more, it must be forgotten in the newly muscular Israel. The weak diasporic past of European Jews has been transcended, and the present reality is a nation state surrounded by Arab enemies.

The Iraqi Jews' Exodus

Why did over 200,000 Jews in Arab countries leave their homes and prosperous businesses in the early 1950s and start from scratch in a brand new state? While some challenge the Zionist narrative of Arab pogroms, others lament betrayal by Muslim friends and neighbours.

Nissim Rejwan is among those who deny the story of local persecutions: 'it was the fashion to speak of mass *aliya* from Muslim lands as '"rescue immigration", implying that these ancient Jewish communities were virtually ejected from the lands of their birth'.[28] Half a century after leaving Iraq,

Rejwan exonerates the Iraqi state, claiming that there were other reasons for Jews to leave, notably encouragement from European Zionists and provocation by German Nazis. In other words, Zionists were trying to attract Jewish Arabs to swell the Israeli ranks, or German Nazis had incited anti-Semitism in Iraq.

Like Rejwan, Naqqash and Ballas hesitate to criticise their Iraqi neighbours. In his 2004 novel *Shlomo the Kurd*, Naqqash implicates the Germans in the *farhud* – the Arabic term for pogrom. In June 1941, the British put down a nationalist coup against Nuri Said, their puppet Prime Minister. Nationalists were pro-Nazi and so they turned their anger against the Jews who were wrongly suspected of being pro-British and therefore pro-Zionist. One hundred and fifty Jews were massacred. Shlomo, head of the Kurdish Jewish community, jumps back and forth across the twentieth century to tell a surreal story about the new wandering Jew. We read the *farhud* through a First World War predecessor in Azeri Sablakh. In 1917, Shlomo fled famine[29] and also Russian, Ottoman and Persian forces fighting for control of his native town. Naqqash indicts the outside forces and praises the Jews' unwavering loyalty to their Muslim and Christian neighbours: 'Azrail [the angel of death] came to stay in Sablakh when the foreigners arrived' (p. 324). Czarist Russians occupied the city and killed Muslims, assuming them to be allied with their Ottoman enemies. Mourning the fate of the Muslims, Shlomo exclaimed that they 'are still our brothers and family as they have been from the beginning of time. Neither war nor ordeal can change us . . . God blesses all who give shelter to their neighbour' (pp. 180–4, pp. 208–9, p. 257). He gave shelter to the displaced people of the town until almost all had gone. The Ottomans' promise 'not to leave a single Jew or Christian alive' (p. 348) prefigures the *farhud* and also rumours of Hitler's call for 'No more Jews on the face of the earth!' In this version, Iraqi Jews were caught between the British, European Zionists and Hitler. Not knowing whom to trust, Shlomo asked, 'Is this a return of Sablakh in Baghdad? The English leave and invite the Nazis.'[30] The perpetrators are not identified beyond accusations of British and Nazi complicity. The townsfolk in First World War Sablakh like their successors in 1941 Baghdad remain loyal to each other despite their different religions and terrible fates.

In *The Other One* (1990), Ballas joins Rejwan and Naqqash in exculpating Muslim friends and neighbours. He blames the Zionists for using unscrupulous methods to bring Jewish Arabs to Israel:

> Israeli agents got what they wanted when they planted bombs in the synagogues, for they managed to sow panic among Jews who hadn't exactly rushed to sign on for immigration at first. They worked hand in hand with the authorities to realize the Zionist program, and Jewish money worked on the decision makers who had made a covenant with the enemy.[31]

The European Zionists are violent and unscrupulous in this account of Iraqi Jews' decisions to leave. More, they are in cahoots with the Nazis.

While recalling his grief at leaving his Baghdad home, Sasson Somekh is less absolute than Naqqash and Ballas in defending Muslim friends and neighbours and their role in the *farhud* and also afterwards: 'for weeks and months the community remained in mourning and shock. How could yesterday's neighbours have become wild animals in an instant? Was the *Farhood* a one-time event, or might it signal the opening of a new, problematic era in Muslim–Jewish relations?' .[32] Somekh answers his own question by describing what happened after 1948 and the founding of the Israeli state: the Iraqi government cracked down on Jewish-run businesses and Jewish civil servants said to be working on sensitive documents. Universities stopped admitting Jews; people started to curse and spit on 'dirty Jews' who feared leaving their homes.[33] The 1950 Citizenship Waiver Law deprived any who left for Israel of Iraqi citizenship and allowed seizure of any assets they might possess. In 1950 and 1951, Jewish sites were bombed.[34] For Somekh, the Iraqi government was active in the purge of Jews.

Language and the Asylum

Israel was founded on the right of all Jews to return to Zion. But before they could fully return to the land from which they had been millennially excluded, they had to pass through the asylum of the transit camp. A condition of release was mastery of Modern Hebrew. Language was crucial in their self-fashioning. Some Iraqi writers assert that, whereas Ashkenazi Jews passed quickly into Israeli society, Jewish Arabs did not. Rejwan notes that there were even conditions for learning the language. Jewish Arabs, he writes, had to be 'intelligent,' exceptional, and 'clean,' or whatever, to be taught the elements of the Hebrew language! . . . Newcomers from 'certain European' countries simply cease to be 'new immigrants' as soon as they have acquired a smattering of Hebrew – so that in a sense the appellation 'new' applies exclusively to immigrants from Oriental lands, though they may have been as long as fifteen years in the country . . . the integration of Oriental Jews into Israeli society can be attained 'only through Ashkenazisation' . . . [the Iraqi Jew] was not a simple Jew among other Jews, but some nameless 'Oriental' among 'Westerners,' a man who was to be 'raised' to the standards of his new society, to be 'cleansed and purified . . . from the dross of Orientalism'.[35]

Rejwan denounces the contempt with which he and fellow Iraqi Jews were treated. Highly educated and full of hopes, they had been relegated to the pre-cultural of Derrida's foreigners. Only the intelligent, exceptional and clean could be taught Hebrew, the civilising tool essential in the transformation of Arabs into Europeans.

One character in Ballas's *Transit Camp* confirms this linguistic condition. Mastery of Modern Hebrew did not apply to Europeans. Not only were they quickly released from the camps with little or no Hebrew, but some Yiddish-speaking Ashkenazis from Central and Eastern Europe also held positions of authority. In exasperation he exclaims: 'the God of [the State of] Israel is also Yiddish!' (p. 89). In an interview with the anthropologist Smadar Lavie, Ballas mused about the difficulty of transitioning from Arabic to Hebrew. The two languages could not co-exist; one had to replace the other and so he had 'felt forced to un-learn my Arabic and re-fracture my identity'.[36] Language in this context is not merely a skill, it is an essential part of identity that must be broken to change.

Linguistic deviations warned of a reversion to a pre-Israel Arabness. Since this Arab identity no longer attached to a nation state, reversion was to a state of statelessness. Statelessness meant the return of a desire for the birth nation, and for another identity, i.e. Arab, i.e. enemy. The challenge was how to perform loyalty, or mimicry, without losing all sense of self-respect, how to learn citizenship while still in the asylum.

Asylum of the Mind

In poems, fiction and memoirs, Arab Jews record their ongoing sense of living in an asylum; they are outside Israeli society but also captured in it. In 'December '86 by the Rivers of Babylon', Tikva Levi laments the fate of the eternal strangers

> On a park bench
> They sit and also cry
> In their transmigratory company
> My elders
> Thirty-six years in the Land
> Still foreigners . . .
> From Babylon to Israel
> And from Palestine in the refugee camps
> This is no ambrosia
> But a bitter cup
> Drunk daily
> Years upon years
> Of hope compounded
> To return to their borders
> To their country to their homeland.[37]

In a few short lines, the reader lives the couple's thirty-six years of bitterness. The finality of their situation is sealed in their constant sense of exile in the place of return and in the hopeless longing to return to Babylon, their birthplace.

The Jewish Arab asylum in Israel, like Agamben's camp, is neither temporary nor restricted to a particular place. Once established, the camp becomes systemic and a state of mind. Permanent consciousness of the asylum is illustrated in Rejwan's depiction of the transit camp or *ma'bara*. The physical camp persists in 'the "other" *ma'bara* of prejudice, of indignity and of enforced inferiority. This *ma'bara* is far from liquidated as yet' (Rejwan 2006, pp. 89–90).[38] It is the '*ma'bara* of the mind' or a 'mental transit camp'. The logic of the transit camps pursued Jewish Arabs even after they left its physical confines.

Only their children might escape. The birth of his daughter made Sami Michael realise that while he would remain 'a *stranger*, for her, this is her home, her country. So I settled here because of her'.[39] His use of the word 'stranger' when talking with Samir recalls Derrida's foreigners or asylum seekers and Foucault's strangers who are 'judged not only by appearances but by all that they may betray and reveal in spite of themselves'.[40] Nothing of the Arab stranger/foreigner should betray and reveal itself. But the stranger/foreigner is so hard to erase.

Political Awakening

Over the past twenty years, some Jewish Arab intellectuals have embraced their stigmatised difference and written confidently from the place of their alienation, from the metaphorical asylum.[41] Several have achieved recognition, including three Israel Prize laureates, the literary critic Sasson Somekh, the sociologist Sami Smooha and the novelist Sami Michael. Recognition and perhaps also a sense of immunity from the racism directed against their compatriots have empowered them to demand attention to their writings and to the ongoing marginalisation of many Jewish Arabs.

Writing about non-European Jews who are fighting against the status quo, Sami Chetrit hails

> an emerging Mizrahi alternative to Ashkenazi Zionism in all aspects – religious, social, economic, and cultural. At the same time, Mizrahi electoral power is a contested field for which most Israeli political parties vie . . . The 'New Mizrahim' is a term for an unorganised but growing wave of young people . . . who have created a new discourse with their critique of Israel's Ashkenazi-dominated social, economic, cultural and political structures . . . [they] want none of the Ashkenazi Zionist collective memory and seek to form a Mizrahi collective memory from which a Mizrahi consciousness and alternative vision for the State of Israel will emerge . . . Unlike their predecessors, they are not asking for 'acceptance' or 'integration' but are questioning the fundamental premises of the state.[42]

The majority in Israel, Mizrahi and especially the youth with their electoral power, are challenging the Ashkenazi status quo. Unlike their grandparents who had accepted the humiliating terms of Israeli citizenship, they are reclaiming a non-Ashkenazi identity with its different memories of the past and visions for the future. Implicit in their challenge is the mandate to rethink communal history, recall taboo memories and rewrite their lives.

But the asylum persists. For Shenhav 'the gaps between Israeli-born Ashkenazis and Mizrahim have not decreased in the past thirty years and in some cases have increased'.[43] During the 1990s, Somekh and a group of his established Iraqi friends realised that they were the 'last generation of Jewish Arabs. We therefore attempted to establish a solidarity association with the Iraqi people . . . and to document the cooperation and good neighborliness between the Jews and other Iraqis, so that the coming generations would know about this wonderful connection that had characterized Jewish life in the Arab world for 1,500 years'.[44] They were seeking reconciliation between their memories and identities. For the literary critic Hanan Hever, they were trying to displace the binary opposition between Jews and Arabs onto Baghdad, a site in which Zionist nationality will not fulfill a meaningful function'.[45] Nostalgically celebrating their Iraqi identity and their Arabness, they could finally connect Baghdad with Israel without anxiety. They could demand respect for Jewish Arabs and recognition of their literary contributions to Israeli society.

The asylum is the symptom of Israeli society; it is where terrible histories are captured outside. A repository of memory, the asylum is a *lieu de mémoire* that everyone knows exists, refuses to engage and can remember to forget to remember. That is how it lives on in the mind.

Notes

1. I want to thank Ranjana Khanna, Charlie Piot, Shai Ginsburg, Banu Gokariksel, Erdag Goknar, Ellen McLarney, Sasson Somekh and, of course, Bruce Lawrence for their helpful suggestions for revisions and further readings.
2. He does not use a surname.
3. It is the first of many Hebrew novels about the experiences of Jewish Arabs in 1950s Israel that came to be known as '*sifrut hama'abarah*', or literature of the transit camps.
4. Ammiel Alcalay, *Keys to the Garden: New Israeli Writing*, San Francisco: City Lights Books, 1996, pp. viii–xi.

5. Bryan Turner, 'Managing Religions: State Responses to Religious Diversity', *Contemporary Islam* 1: 2 (2007), pp. 130–1.
6. Some middle-class North African Jews migrated to France after the Second World War. In 1988 Gisele Halimi, a Tunisian lawyer for Algerian freedom fighters, wrote about her childhood as a Jew in Tunisia. Halimi looks back on her life from its humble beginnings in the Goulette fishing port of Tunis, through years of anti-colonial and feminist activism, to her migration to France (Gisele Halimi, *Le lait de l'oranger*, Paris: Gallimard, 1988).
7. Alcalay, *Keys to the Garden*, p. 341, p. 346.
8. Jacques Derrida, *Of Hospitality: Anne Dufourmantelle Invites Jacques Derrida to respond*, trans. Rachel Bowlby, Stanford: Stanford University Press, 1997, pp. 59–61 and pp. 71–3.
9. The *barzakh*, literally isthmus, 'is never an extreme separation; it is like the line that separates between the sun and its shadow, and like God's saying: He let forth the two seas that meet together, between them a *barzakh* they do not overpass' (Qur'an 55: 19–20).
10. Yehouda Shenhav, *The Arab Jews: A Postcolonial Reading of Nationalism, Religion and Ethnicity*, Stanford: Stanford University Press, 2006, p. 73.
11. Rejwan explains the Biblical reference: 'the exodus of Jews to Babylon in the early sixth century BCE' (Nissim Rejwan, *Outsider in the Promised Land: An Iraqi Jew in Israel*, Austin: University of Texas Press, 2004, p. 33).
12. Sasson Somekh, *Baghdad Yesterday: The Making of an Arab Jew*, Jerusalem: Ibis, 2007, p. 181. Originally published 2004 in Hebrew.
13. Original emphasis. Gioirgio Agamben, *Means without End: Notes on Politics*, trans. Vincenzo Binetti and Cesare Casarino, Minneapolis: University of Minnesota Press, 2000, pp. 38–43.
14. Moshe Gat, 'The Immigration of Iraqi Jewry to Israel as Reflected in Literature', *Revue Européenne de Migrations Internationales* 14:3 (1998), pp. 52–6.
15. Rejwan, *Outsider in the Promised Land*, p. 113, p. 175.
16. Erving Goffman, *Asylums: Essays on the Social Situation of Mental Patients and other Inmates*, New York: Anchor Books, 1961, p. 44, p. 21.
17. Ammiel Alcalay, *Keys to the Garden: New Israeli Writing*, p. 238.
18. Nancy Berg, *Exile from Exile: Israeli Writers from Iraq*, Albany: State University of New York Press, 1996.
19. Somekh, *Baghdad Yesterday*, p. 186.
20. Alcalay, *Keys to the Garden*, p. 186, p. 188, p. 190.
21. In her study of Mizrahi writers, Smadar Lavie has called Israel 'an exilic Arab

home for the majority of Israeli Jews, the *Mizrahim*, who immigrated to Israel from third World countries . . . Israel is not home but their diaspora's diaspora' (Smadar Lavie, 'Blow-ups in the Borderzones: Third World Israeli Authors' Gropings for Home', *New Formations* 18 (Winter 1992), p. 85).

22. Shenhav, *The Arab Jews*, p. 81.

23. Hannah Arendt, *The Origins of Totalitarianism*, New York: Harcourt Brace, 1973, p. 290, p. 297, p. 275.

24. Ella Shohat, *Taboo Memories Diasporic Voices*, Durham, NC: Duke University Press, 2006, p. 204.

25. When Shlomo Dov Goitein later tried to make sense of this cultural treasure in his five-volume *Mediterranean Society* (Berkeley: University of California Press, 1967–83), he celebrated the centuries of commerce and interchange among Mediterranean Jews, Muslims and Christians that the Geniza documents revealed.

26. Ella Shohat, *Israeli Cinema: East/West and the Politics of Representation*, Austin: University of Texas Press, 1986, pp. 124–38.

27. Alcalay, *Keys to the Garden*, pp. 362–3.

28. The term *aliya* means immigrating to Zion. Rejwan, *Outsider in the Promised Land*, p. 191.

29. The famine takes up much of the book with a wife eating her husband's corpse (p. 317).

30. Samir Naqqash, *Shlumu al-kurdi wa ana wa al-zaman* (*Shlomo and I and Time*), Cologne: Al-Kamel Verlag, 2004, p. 46. Further references are given in the text. Translations from Arabic are mine.

31. Ammiel Alcalay, *After Jews and Arabs: Remaking Levantine Culture*, Minneapolis: University of Minnesota Press, 1993, p. 242.

32. Somekh, *Baghdad Today*, p. 131; see Rejwan, *Outsider in the Promised Land*, p. 132.

33. Conversation with Somekh in Durham, NC on 29 September 2007.

34. Somekh, *Baghdad Yesterday*, pp. 148–53; Rejwan, *Outsider in the Promised Land*, p. 25.

35. Rejwan, *Outsider in the Promised Land*, p. 2, p. 93.

36. Lavie, 'Blow-ups in the Borderzones', p. 94.

37. Alcalay, *Keys to the Garden*, p. 346.

38. Rejwan, *Outsider in the Promised Land*, pp, 89–90.

39. Samir, *Forget Baghdad*, Dschoint Ventschr Filmproduktkion, 2002.

40. Michel Foucault, *Madness and Civilization: A History of Insanity in the Age of Reason*, New York: Random House, 1965, pp. 249–50.

41. Lavie was prescient when she wondered in 1992 whether Mizrahi writers could 'use the categorization of race/class attributed to them as a means to mobilize against the Euro-centre' (Lavie, 'Blow-ups in the Borderzones', p. 99).

42. Sami Shalom Chetrit, 'Mizrahi Politics in Israel: Between Integration and Alternative', in *Journal of Palestine Studies* 29:4 (2000), p. 51, pp. 59–61.

43. Sami Smooha confirms that the gap between Mizrahi and Ashkenazi communities in Israel is growing. See http://jewishrefugees.blogspot.com/2008/05/iraqi-jews-in-israel-took-long-hard.html (accessed 9 May 2008).

44. Somekh, *Baghdad Yesterday*, pp. 174–5.

45. Hanan Hever, 'Mapping Literary Space: Territory and Violence in Israeli Literature', in Laurence J. Silberstein (ed.), *Mapping Jewish Identities*, New York: New York University Press, 2000, p. 212.

10

Strange Incidents from History: Youssef Rakha and his *Sultan's Seal*

Paul Starkey

Youssef Rakha's *Kitab al-tughra* (*Book of the Sultan's Seal*),[1] his first novel, set in the spring of 2007 and completed at the start of 2010, was published less than a fortnight after mass protests centred on Cairo's Tahrir Square had forced the resignation of the then Egyptian President Hosni Mubarak on 11 February 2011 – a move that prompted the transfer of power to the Supreme Council of the Armed Forces (SCAF), and everything that has followed since. As Mona Anis observed a few weeks later in *Al-Ahram Weekly*,[2] this may have been an unfortunate rather than a fortunate coincidence, since 'a historical event of such wide import as the Egyptian uprising will naturally overshadow the appearance of any new novel, no matter how accomplished'. Fortunate or not, however, the timing of the novel's publication makes an attempt to relate its appearance to current developments in Egypt and the wider Middle East almost inevitable – not only because of the obvious relevance of its central themes (to which we shall return later) to contemporary developments and debates but also because the setting of much of the work overlaps with that of the uprising itself – an area of central Cairo renamed by Rakha, in his 'alternative map' of the city, 'World's Gate' (*Bab al-dunya*).[3]

The appearance of Rakha's work prompted enthusiastic – not to say hyberbolic – reactions in some literary circles. Mona Anis herself was complementary but restrained, describing the work simply as 'an outstanding first novel by an author who has a special ability to deal with modern and classical material, both Arab and western, with equal ease', and adding that '[one] looks forward to further novels with eager anticipation'. Others had higher hopes for the work. Writing in her 'Arabic Literature in English' blog, M. Lynx Qualey noted that:

> Another novel that was published just at the time of the uprising in Egypt – that I'm expecting will be nominated for the IPAF [International Prize for Arabic Fiction] – is Youssef Rakha's *Book of the Sultan's Seal*, published by Dar el Shorouk. Of course, to be nominated, Rakha must be willing to agree to do a little song and dance ... The winner and the short-listed authors must agree, by having submitted their works, to be available for promotional activities such as tours and media appearances related to the Prize, both in the Arab world and abroad. Which is one reason why one should not expect to see Sonallah Ibrahim's latest novel on the IPAF lists.[4]

In the event, for whatever reason, nothing came of M. Lynx Qualey's prediction. In the meantime, however, others had been less restrained in their enthusiasm. The Palestinian-Israeli writer-turned-academic Antun Shammas, for example (author of the Hebrew *Arabeskot* (*Arabeques*),[5] is quoted by Rakha himself as e-mailing him in the following terms:

> I finished your magnum opus [Kitab at Tugra] two days ago, with tears in my eyes, and I've been intoxicated since, in the most *Faridian* sense of the word. Among other things, no one (REPEAT: NO ONE) has ever written so wondrously about love and sex in Arabic the way you did in the last two chapters of the novel, i.e. making the Arabic language make love as it has never done before. Ibn al-Farid should feel so comfortable, and so privileged, and so sexy in your company. But that's not your major achievement, No Sir. You managed to write a perfect (REPEAT: PERFECT) Arabic novel, on so many levels. Very few writers have done that, and to enter the Hall of Fame with a first novel is nothing short of miraculous. Your meticulous attention to what turns a text into a stunning novel is absolutely amazing ... But above all, I think, your major achievement is in being what Foucault would call 'a discourse initiator' – someone who single handedly

changes a discipline, and in this case the discipline of the Arabic novel. You are my al-Jabarti of the Arabic novel.[6]

Elsewhere in the press or on the Web, three of the eleven authors canvassed for their favourite books of 2011 in the *Egyptian Independent* mentioned Rakha's work, with Mansoura Ezz Eldin echoing Shammas and characterising it as 'represent[ing] a significant shift in writing in Egypt', while Ola El-Saket (echoing Mona Anis) suggested that, as with some other novels, the current publishing difficulties in Egypt meant that it had been published at an inopportune moment.[7] Meanwhile, writing in the FluentCityBlog, Matthew Lundin included Rakha's work in his list of 'Five Arabic novels worth learning Arabic for', and helpfully summarised the essence of the plot, in graphic if perhaps slightly unsophisticated terms, as follows: 'The narrator Mustafa Chorabji wanders around Cairo with a weird cast of non-friends and realizes that his wanderings and dreams are pointing to the discovery of a theosophical plot to return the Islamic Umma to its former glory with the help of the ghost of an Ottoman Sultan', before opining that *Kitab al-tughra* is 'insane. It is part morose stream of consciousness, part social commentary on contemporary Egyptian society, part Islamic civilization-referencing surrealist fantasy. Yeah, it's insane. And awesome.'[8]

In this short chapter, I shall attempt to take a slightly more measured view of the author and his work than either Shammas or Lundin – a view inevitably coloured, however, by my experience of translating the novel into English.[9] For although one may certainly have doubts about Shammas's assertion that Youssef Rakha has 'single handedly changed the discipline of the Arabic novel' (as indeed, about his allusion to al-Jabarti), few readers would deny that this is an interesting and original work, which is worth discussing not only in its own right but also in the context of the development of contemporary Egyptian (and Arab) literature more generally.

The author himself, Youssef Rakha, was born in Cairo in 1976 and studied English and philosophy at Hull University in England, from where he received a first-class degree in 1998, as well as being awarded the Larkin Prize for English and the Chris Ayers Prize for Philosophy. Since then, he has worked in Cairo, and lived in Beirut, as well as spending some time in Abu Dhabi, where he helped to found and worked as a features writer for the

English daily *The National*. Before the publication of *Kitab al-tughra*, he was probably best known for his extensive writing for the Cairo-based English-language newspaper *Al-Ahram Weekly*, where he has worked as reporter, copy editor, and cultural-editor-cum-literary-critic, and for which he has interviewed a wide variety of prominent personalities from the Arab literary world as well as from other walks of life. As a result, until 2011 his name was almost as likely to be familiar to the English-speaking Middle Eastern expatriate as to the small elite of Arab readers able or likely to embark on his writings in Arabic. His work in English has also featured in US and UK publications including *The Daily Telegraph*, *The New York Times*, *McSweeney's* and *The Kenyon Review*, among others.

Newspaper and journal writing aside, Youssef Rakha's published works to date include, in addition to *Kitab al-tughra*, a collection of short stories (Cairo: Dar Sharqiyyat, 1999); two travel books, including *Bayrut, shi mahall* (*Beirut, Some Place*) (Alexandria[?]: Amkena Books, 2006), and a new short novel entitled *Al-Tamasih* (*The Crocodiles*) (Beirut: al-Saqi, 2012). In addition to my own forthcoming translation of *Kitab al-tughra*, an English translation of *Al-Tamasih* was due to be published in autumn 2014;[10] this work is described on the Seven Stories Press website as 'an echo of clamor of the Egyptian revolution [that] describes with feeling how and why youth turn to revolution . . . [and how] years of unbounded excesses in sex, drugs, and alcohol dovetail with an honest search for authenticity and total freedom, and a hatred of the mercantile values of society'.

In October 2009, Youssef Rakha was selected as one of the thirty-nine authors of the Beirut39 project, devised as a collaboration between the Hay Festival and Beirut World Capital of the Book 2009, to identify and promote the thirty-nine most promising writers from the Arab world under thirty-nine years of age.[11]

Kitab al-tughra itself is a work of formidable proportions, extending to over five hundred pages, of which the last thirty or so are probably to be classified as 'paratext' (to use Gérard Genette's term):[12] these consist of 'Appendices' (*malahiq*), and include (1) some notes on 'A History of the Ottomans'; (2) details of well-known historical figures (*A'lam*) mentioned in the text, drawn, in contemporary style, 'from Wikipedia and other sources', and (3), most interestingly, perhaps, a glossary of potentially unfamiliar terms and expressions (*Fihrist fi lughat al-kitab*). The latter include a wide variety of types of lexis, ranging from standard Egyptian colloquial usages potentially unfamiliar to non-Egyptian Arab readers, such as *eeh* ('what?'), *badri* ('early') or *bta'* ('belonging to'); to commercial references to, for example, the '128: a type of Fiat car that until recently was the most popular in Egypt'; and a list of foreign (mostly English) words and expressions written in the novel in Arabic script, which include, to take a few examples more or less at random: airbus, CIA, cliché, Ecstasy, erotica, espresso, Hip Hop, Oprah Winfrey, pixels, platitude, porno, tomboy, Twin Towers, weekend, Wikipedia, YouTube and zombie.

If this list promises a sort of voguish, Western-orientated modernism, however, the extended title of Youssef Rakha's work, with its characteristi-cally medieval parallelism and rhyming format (*Kitab al-tughra aw ghara'ib al-tarikh fi madinat al-Mirrikh* 'The Book of the Sultan's Seal, or Strange Incidents from History in the City of Mars') suggests that the author, far from espousing a rigorously iconoclastic stance, is at least as much concerned to place his work squarely in an older Arab literary tradition. In this respect, Rakha's title seems (to me, at least) to faintly echo the title of the greatest masterpiece of Arab-Israeli literature, Emil Habibi's *Al-Waqa'i' al-ghariba fi ikhtifa' Sa'id Abi al-Nahs al-Mutasha'il* (*The Pessoptimist*), though whether such an allusion is intentional I have no idea. Be that as it may, this ground-ing in the medieval tradition is continued in the text of the book itself, which opens with a prologue, or proclamation (*khutba*), in which the author describes the founding of the city of Cairo in AD 969, and explains the rationale for the name *al-Qahira*, an allusion to the planet Mars (in Arabic *al-Mirrikh*, but known to some Arab astronomers as *al-Qahir*), which was in the ascendant at the time.[13] Brief as it is, it is worth devoting some atten-tion to this prologue, as it not only helpfully outlines the main theme and rationale of the book but also provides, both directly and indirectly, useful further information on the rationale for the work's complex structure. The work, so the author informs us, revolves around a series of journeys in Cairo undertaken by the journalist Mustafa Nayif al-Shurbaji [Çorbacı][14] between 30 March and 19 April 2007, his account being cast in the form of 'Epistles' or 'Treatises' (*rasa'il*) 'in the style of the old Arabic books' (*'ala tariqat al-kutub al-'arabiyya al-qadima*); these are addressed to a friend, a psychiatrist named Rashid Jalal al-Suyuti, who has lived in London since 2001. The prologue goes on to list the route of each of these nine journeys, undertaken mainly by car, together with the relevant dates and the main event or events associated with it, and the 'theme' or scientific discipline underlying that particular journey. This table is worth reproducing in full, as it provides a key to the progression of the narrative through the book:

From Maadi to Dokki (on marriage)	Separation	30 March
From Dokki to Isaaf (sociology)	First dream and its fulfilment	31 March–7 April
Desert Road journey (psychology)	Finding the ring	7–8 April
From Isaaf to the other world (paranormal)	Meeting the sultan	9 April
Tour of libraries and the internet (on history)	Discovering the Ottoman State	10–12 April
North Giza journey (on friendship)	Divorce and completing the picture	13–14 April
Tour of Islamic Cairo (on love)	Meeting the beloved	15 April
The Muqattam–Cairo Airport journey (erotica)	Finding a clue / Departure	16–19 April
(Later) Cairo Airport	Journey to Beirut	After 19 April[15]

(Note, incidentally, that Rakha here uses the transliterated English terms for 'sociology', 'psychology', 'paranormal' and 'erotica' rather than their Arabic equivalents.)

As if this complex structure were not all enough, the author goes on to explain that, for the sake of variety, only five of the chapters are narrated directly by Mustafa himself. Parts 3, 6 and 8, by contrast, are related 'by an unknown storyteller whose situation is specified by a plural . . . and who sometimes refers to "our planet" as if it were a viewpoint as all-seeing as destiny'; while the ninth part is 'a miscellany made up of the storyteller's words and texts from Mustafa's notebooks'.[16]

Two further features of the novel require a brief mention at this point, before we turn to a discussion of its themes. The first is that the narrator-cum-'hero', Mustafa, is not only a writer, journalist and intellectual (like

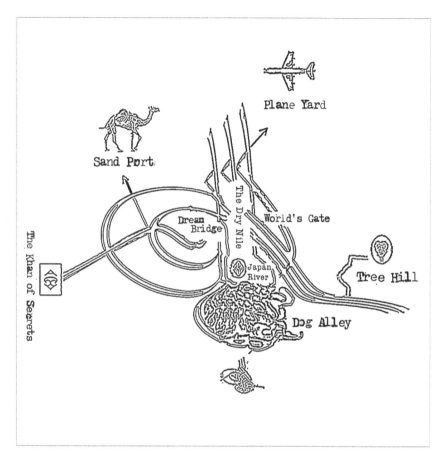

Figure 10.1 From *The Book of the Sultan's Seal*. Image courtesy of Youssef Rakha

Rakha himself, of course) but also a photographer, artist and aspiring calligrapher, who illustrates his journeys at intervals through the book with sketches which, when superimposed on each other at the end of the work, come together to form the shape of an Ottoman *tuğra*, as in Figure 10.1. In this respect, the novel may perhaps be regarded as an attempt by the author/narrator to create a *khitat*[17] of modern-day Cairo. Although initially closely based on the actual geography of contemporary Cairo, however, Rakha's *khitat* (like that of the older writer Jamal [Gamal] al-Ghitani's *Khitat al-Ghitani*)[18] quickly also acquires a more personal dimension in the course of the work, as the narrator decides that:

I just had to give the places new names.

Without any effort, I had already named the whole of the downtown area Bab al-Dunya ('World's Gate'). Now I sat thinking: if Isaaf was the point of departure, then Dokki, with the Dokki Bridge and the Dry Nile Dock – yes, I found myself calling the 6 October Bridge the 'Dry Nile', its ramps becoming harbours – must be the bed that gave me dreams. Let's make Dokki (and with it Mohandiseen, Agouza, and the University) a bridge, yes, 'Dream Bridge'.

Thus we find that Maadi has become *Darb al-kalb* (Dog Alley); Dokki and the areas adjacent to it, *Jisr al-manam* (Dream Bridge); downtown Cairo, as already mentioned, *Bab al-dunya* (World's Gate); and the beginning of the Cairo–Alexandria Desert Road, where the Carrefour supermarket is located, the *Khan al-sirr* (Khan of Secrets). Individual chapter titles then appear in a curiously mixed form, in which Rakha's modern, personal nicknames blend with medieval-type formulae, with results such as the following:

> *al-Qism al-Awwal*
> *al-Risala al-Zawjiyya*
> *Min Darb al-Kalb ila Jisr al-Manam*
> *Ma qalahu Mustafa fi infisalihi ʿan zawjatihi wa-ma adda ilayhi*
> *al-Jumʿa 30 Mars*

> Part One
> The Epistle on Matrimony
> From Dog Alley to Dream Bridge
> Mustafa's Account of his Separation from his Wife and its Consequences
> Friday, March 30th

As if this curious mixture, with its intertextual allusions to the stylistic characteristics of an earlier age, were not enough, Rakha also intersperses his narrative with direct quotations from earlier authors – medieval, premodern and near-contemporary. These include, by way of example, in the *khutba*, al-Jahiz, and Shams al-Din al-Dhahabi quoting Ibn Iyas; and, in subsequent chapters, ʿUmar Ibn al-Farid, Ibn Hazm, al-Maqrizi, al-Hallaj, Ibn Khaldun, al-Jabarti, the *Lisan al-ʿArab*, Sargon Boulos, and several others. Transitions from section to section are again erratically indicated, sometimes simply by means of a heading such as *Fasl* ('chapter', or 'section'). Such liberal, and deliberate, use of the medieval tradition is in stark contrast to some of Rakha's language, which is a curious mixture of registers, from the most formal of *fusha* to the most informal of Egyptian colloquialisms, and including a fair sprinkling of imported foreign words (mostly from English) for which he makes no apology, defending them on the basis that he wishes to echo the voices of the people he is writing about. In this regard, Rakha's early quotation from the medieval writer al-Jahiz is especially significant, for he here invokes arguably the greatest master of medieval Arabic prose in support of his approach:

> If, in this book, you come across any solecism, or speech lacking correct grammatical inflection, or expression used in an unusual way, you should know that I have left it as it is because grammatical inflection in this sort of discourse makes it sound unattractive and out of place.[19]

Writing elsewhere on the Web, Rakha explains that 'the book attempts to produce a contemporary equivalent of the "middle Arabic" in which the great Cairo historians al-Jabarti and Ibn Iyas wrote: a language that juxtaposes fixed formal grammar with an idiomatically distinct contemporary vernacular, rich in non-Arabic vocabulary'.[20] Space forbids a detailed discussion of how this approach is played out in practice, but we may note in this context, by way of example, Rakha's use of verbs such as *fidil* and *baqa* in their Egyptian vernacular rather than their *fusha* sense (i.e. respectively 'to remain continue' and 'to be/become' rather than 'to be left' and 'to remain');[21] the expressions *il-waqt* and *dil-waqti* used interchangeably with the standard Arabic *al-an*; *sa'at* often used in the sense of 'sometimes', rather than 'the hours'; and the consistent use of *narfaza* in the sense of 'anger' rather than 'nerves'. Current expressions and idioms taken from the media are also not infrequently used, as in, for example, *asta'in bi-sadiq*, one of the options sometimes available to participants in multiple-choice question competition shows of the 'Who wants to be a millionaire?' variety.[22]

A further indicator of Rakha's sensitivity to the details of language usage and register is provided by his attempts to mimic, or describe, the pronunciation of individual speakers (including non-native Arabic speakers) in the course of his narrative. These include the effeminate African Aldo

Mantenzika, who 'would soften the "s" in Safsaf, as he did with all the Arabic consonants'.[23] Mustafa's colleague Wahid al-Din, pressed to explain why he has not yet married, exclaims: 'Heh! . . . Mr Mantenzika, marriage is all a matter of fate' – the point being given additional emphasis by the author's gloss that 'he pronounced the "g" in marriage the classical way, and sounded the "q" in "*qisma*"'.[24] Transmuted into the Ottoman caliph Vahdettin, Wahid al-Din's pronunciation acquires a distinctively, and carefully described, Turkish resonance:

> There was a clearly articulated 'd' before every soft 'g', for example. Those letters that are difficult for foreigners – *Ha'*, *'ayn* and *qaf* (he pronounced his *qaf*s, unlike ordinary Egyptians) – were articulated softly, and the 'w' turned, fully or partially, into a 'v' (like a Persian 'w'). There was a French-like influence on the letters of prolongation and the vowels. When he said Wahid al-Din, especially when he was absorbed in what he was saying, it sounded like Vahdettin.[25]

In the same vein, we may note the author's description of Claudine's (the narrator's eventual lover) speaking English:

> Far from showing off the languages she knew and pronounced well like Yildiz – witness the ostentatious way she switches from English to French to German and vice versa – Claudine hadn't developed a faux American accent like most of the graduates of the American University. When she spoke English she retained all the mistakes of French pronunciation, like substituting a 'z' or an 's' for 'th', would you believe it?[26]

So much, for the moment at least, of Rakha's attitude to, and use of, language. What, then, of the narrator's journeys themselves, and of the overall themes that emerge from the complex narrative that conveys them? Space forbids an extended discussion of the highly complex set of events, and in the outline that follows I merely reproduce Rakha's own website summary of his work, which 'fills out' the information presented in table form in the introduction to the work itself and provides as convenient a summary of events as any other:

• The first journey takes place on 30 March 2007, when, after separating from his nameless wife (who plays only an insignificant part in the story),

Mustafa makes the journey from his marital home in Maadi to the house of his parents in Dokky. This section, according to Rakha, is a treatise on marriage.

- Between 30 March and 7 April, Mustafa recounts his daily journey from Dokky to downtown Cairo, where he works as a journalist, and has the first in a series of dreams, providing an occasion to describe the social disintegration around him. The collapse of public life mirrors the collapse of his private life. This section is associated with sociology.

- On 7 and 9 April Mustafa makes a journey to the shopping mall at the start of the Desert Road, and there – as well as having a strange encounter that seems to be related to the dream – he finds a ring with a calligraphic seal. This section is associated with psychology.

- On 9 April, Mustafa meets and is given an assignment relating to a lost manuscript by the ghost of the last Ottoman Sultan, whose seal the ring bears. This section is associated with the paranormal.

- On 10–12 April, following the encounter with the Sultan, Mustafa makes an intellectual journey in books and on the internet, finding out about the Ottomans. This section is clearly associated with history.

- On 13–14 April, Mustafa visits several quarters of Cairo, divorcing his wife and discovering what it is all about: the dream, the ring, his encounter with the Sultan. The central journey is to the camel market. This is a treatise on friendship.

- On 15 April, further confirming what he has discovered, Mustafa journeys through Islamic Cairo and encounters a new lover. This is Rakha's treatise on love.

- On 16–19 April, Mustafa makes the journey from the house of his lover in Muqattam to Cairo Airport, having found the object he needs to start undertaking his assignment. This is a treatise on eroticism.

- After 19 April, we find Mustafa in Beirut undertaking his assignment. This is not so much a journey as an event, and replaces the treatise with a series of parables mimicking the eight previous sections.[27]

At this stage, it may be worth reminding ourselves that, as well as the additional complexity introduced by the alternation of the narrative voice between Mustafa himself and the 'unknown storyteller' already mentioned, the degree of interaction between the supposed 'subject' of each section (marriage, sociology, psychology etc.) and the text itself varies considerably from chapter to chapter, as does the use made of quotations from earlier authors – the latter being particularly extensively employed in Section 8, where a series of quotations from the Egyptian mystical poet Ibn al-Farid's *Nazm al-suluk* and other works is employed as a sort of counterpoint to the progress of Mustafa's short-lived love affair with Claudine. (The longest of these quotations extends to some six lines.)[28] In light of this, some other of the author's interpretations of his own work to be found on his website may seem slightly forced; indeed, faced with Rakha's statement that 'some chapters are not so much parodies as miniature, post-millennial versions of specific canonical classics: Ibn Khaldun's *Prolegomenon* (5), al-Jahiz's *Book of Misers* (6), Ibn Hazm's *The Ring of the Dove* (7), Ibn al-Farid's *Diwan* (8)',[29] some readers may well feel that he is pushing his analysis, or his analogies, a little too far. It is, however. difficult to disagree with Mona Anis's judgement that 'the intertextual references in this thoroughly hybrid work are astonishing', extending as they do not only to the medieval Arabic tradition but also to popular (Western) horror and zombie literature, most notably George Romero's 1968 film *Night of the Living Dead*.

Between Heritage and Modernity

What, then, of the actual themes that emerge from this complex web of journeys and events, underpinned as they are by intertextual references and quotations from this vast range of sources? As is his wont, Youssef Rakha has given the critic a convenient starting point in the form of his own commentary, which highlights (and indeed, further develops) what he identifies as the main theme of the book: the contemporary Arab/Muslim's (and in particular, of course, the Egyptian/Muslim's) search for a sense of identity. This theme, which Rakha chooses to explore largely through a discussion of the history of the Ottoman state, is succinctly if elliptically summed up in the final sentence of the novel, in which the second, 'unknown' narrator provides a sort of *apologia* for writing down the story at all:

> Even if it was all fantasy, even if he'd made it up, there were things in it
> that needed to be documented, not because they'd lead to great events, nor

because I particularly agreed with their contents. But because the story of Mustafa Çorbaci and his sudden transformation during twenty one days from a Europeanized intellectual to a semi-madman who believed he could perform magic deeds to resurrect the Islamic caliphate – and this is what I'd really become convinced of – the story of Mustafa Çorbaci was not just a set of fairy tales.[30]

In an article entitled 'Hail, Prince of Believers: On Fiction and the Caliphate', Rakha throws further light on his motivation for focusing his novel on this theme. 'I was searching', he explains,

> for both a nationhood and a positive perspective on religious identity as a form of civilisation compatible with the post-Enlightenment world. The closest development I could come up with, aside from Muhammad Ali Pasha's abortive attempt at Ottoman-style Arab empire . . . was the original model, starting from the reign of Sultan-Caliph Mahmoud II in 1808. I was searching for Islam as a post-, not a pre-nationalist political identity, and the caliphate as an alternative to the postcolonial republic, with Mahmoud and his sons' heterodox approach to the Sublime State and their pan-Ottoman modernising efforts forming the basis of that conception . . . The aggressively secular orientation of Kemalism had . . . broken with even the highest peaks of Muslim heritage; and it was such severance and complete identification with Europe that eventually gave rise to Islamism. In Egypt, the Muslim Brotherhood emerged in response to Kemal abolishing the caliphate altogether in 1924.[31]

This is not the place to discuss the plausibility of Rakha's views on the relevance of the caliphate to the course of recent Islamic history or to the predicament of contemporary Egypt. Suffice it to note that his preoccupation with the caliphate is played out in the novel on a number of levels, most notably in Parts Four and Five – the first of which sees Mustafa's work colleague Wahid al-Din transformed into the last of the Ottoman sultans, Vahdettin (Mehmed VI);[32] while the second sees Mustafa himself conducting an intense period of research in the libraries of Cairo, as well as on the internet. As already noted, and as if to reinforce for the reader the centrality of Ottoman history to his work, Rakha also includes in his Appendices a

section entitled 'Ta'rikh Al 'Uthman (sitt hikayat)', which provides information on snippets of Ottoman history spanning the period from AD 1277, at
the very beginning of the Ottoman dynasty, to 1924 at its very end. Most
fundamentally, of course, it is the *tughra* (or 'tuğra' as it is spelled in modern
Turkish), the seal of the Ottoman sultans, that not only gives Rakha's book
its title but also, as it were, 'underwrites' Mustafa's progress through Cairo;
for, as previously noted, the hero/narrator is not only a writer, journalist and
intellectual but also a photographer, artist and aspiring calligrapher, who, in
his attempt to create his own personal *khitat* of Cairo, illustrates his journeys
with sketches in his notebooks that eventually come together to form the
shape of the Sultan's seal. In this way, the historical aspects of the debate
about the caliphate are seamlessly integrated into Rakha's vignettes of contemporary Cairo – vignettes that at times convey an impression of a city
teetering on the point of collapse under the weight of its own contradictions.

In this respect, the external world of the city mirrors and echoes the inner
turmoil of the hero himself, whose private life has been turned upside-down
with the collapse of his marriage to a wife who remains unnamed, but who
is significantly characterised as being 'between two cultures'.[33] Mustafa's subsequent search for emotional and intellectual fulfilment leads him eventually
to the rediscovery of Claudine, the sister of another work colleague, who like
his ex-wife, is herself a 'product of two civilisations'; but, following a short
period of intense and graphically described love-making, he leaves Claudine
and travels to Beirut, a city whose attractions are spelled out in unambiguous
terms by the 'unknown' narrator, whose experiences to some extent mirror
those of Mustafa:

> I suffered the same confusion [as Mustafa] between heritage and (God help
> us all!) modernity. This is the reason for my coming to take up residence
> here, to be honest – plus the fact that living in Beirut is a little easier for
> someone who likes to drink every day, likes to live on his own, likes to see
> women in the street, and hates the sights and practices of Islamization that
> are spreading in Cairo like the plague. The Lebanese have taught me to love
> life. I savor my food, enjoy sex and wine, and I dance . . .[34]

If the contrast between the hedonistic atmosphere of Beirut and the
creeping Islamisation of Cairo is here expressed in apparently unambigu-

ous terms, the inherent tension between the traditional values of Muslim society and the West is a little more difficult to pin down. As already noted, Mustafa's ex-wife is characterised as a 'cool woman between two cultures', 'between two cultures, like me',[35] and it is at least implied – not least, by his derogatory references to England as a 'rotten island' that he is 'no longer dazzled by' ('England, indeed – forget that shit, man!')[36] – that this somehow contributed to the breakdown of the marriage. The cultural orientation of Claudine's family, however, with whom he finds such intense, if short-lived, sexual fulfilment in the Eighth Part of the novel, is even more complex, for Claudine's father, a certain Dr Murad, had

> despite his humble Upper Egyptian origins . . . married a rich woman from an upper-class family who claimed Turkish roots. Kariman Hanim, Yildiz's[37] mother, had resolved on this name [Yildiz, Mustafa's work colleague] for her second daughter, after Dr Murad had insisted for their first daughter on a European name whose Old French and Latin origins he particularly appreciated, Claudine.[38]

The tension between heritage and modernity that forms a central concern of the book thus finds yet another expression in the etymology of the two sisters' names, though like the other tensions discussed it remains a statement of a problematic, lacking any resolution even through Mustafa's erotic encounter with Claudine.

At this point, we should perhaps return to Antun Shammas's somewhat hyperbolic description of Rakha and his work as having 'singlehandedly changed the discipline of the Arabic novel' and his mention in this context of al-Jabarti. To my mind, both parts of this statement are somewhat off-target. To take first the question of language register, although Youssef Rakha's statement of purpose and his invocation of al-Jahiz are more carefully formulated than those of most authors, examples of the 'corruption' of *fusha* with various kinds of non-*fusha* expressions (whether they be colloquial Arabic or foreign importations) can be found during most, if not all, periods of Arabic literary development, and are almost certainly becoming more rather than less common.[39] The debate about the use of dialect in written fiction moreover remains an ongoing one, which can still evoke strong passions on both sides of the argument. In terms of narrative technique, some aspects of

Rakha's work also appear to be direct developments of techniques employed by earlier writers in Egypt and elsewhere – not least the intertextual devices so beloved of many of the so-called 'Generation of the Sixties'.[40] In this respect, we may think in particular of Jamal al-Ghitani's *Al-Zayni Barakat*, which makes extensive use of quotations from, and parodies of, the medieval historian Ibn Iyas, and which, like Rakha's work, also employs figures drawn from history to illustrate and explore contemporary issues.[41] None of this, of course, is intended to belittle Rakha's achievement in this fascinating work, but whether it has changed, or will change, the direction of the Arabic novel seems to me highly doubtful.

Shammas's comparison of Rakha with al-Jabarti also seems to me a rather debatable one, since, in literary terms, al-Jabarti was arguably not an innovator at all: his importance derives rather from his good fortune in having been able to chronicle a period when the history of his country was being irrevocably changed by the shift in the relationship between the Middle East and the West encapsulated in Napoleon's invasion. Only time will tell whether Rakha's work will prove to have appeared at a similarly pivotal point in contemporary Egyptian history. A more plausible literary analogy to my mind is hinted at in the article already referred to by Mona Anis,[42] who, after suggesting that the book shares features with works by Emile Habibi (previously mentioned in connection with the book's title) and Yahya al-Tahir, goes on to characterise Rakha's novel as 'Rabelaisian' – an adjective not infrequently used of that pioneering mid-nineteenth-century masterpiece of imaginative prose writing, Faris al-Shidyaq's *Al-Saq ʿala al-saq fi ma huwa al-Fariyaq*.[43] And indeed, to my mind there is more than a touch of al-Shidyaq in Rakha's work – both authors sharing an apparently boundless energy and curiosity about the world (and especially the delights of the Arabic language), an uninhibited attitude to love and sex and a zeal for literary experimentation – as well as a tendency to bite off more than they chew, with results manifest in extravagant, sprawling works of fiction.

Quite what Mustafa Badawi would have made of Youssef Rakha's work, I do not know. The two men, however, had at least one thing in common: an ability to use Arabic and English with almost equal fluency, and to navigate the literary traditions of the two languages with almost equal ease. I am not sure that Mustafa Badawi would have been totally convinced by some aspects of Youssef Rakha's 'modern middle Arabic'; but I am confident that he would have admired Rakha's erudition and free-spirited approach, and I like to think that he would have enjoyed reading the account of his fictional namesake's progress through Cairo, and through life, as much as I have enjoyed translating it.

Notes

1. *Kitab al-tughra: Ghara'ib al-tarikh fi madinat al-Mirrikh*, Cairo: Dar al-Shuruq, 2010 (*sic*).

2. Mona Anis, 'Between Worlds', *Al-Ahram Weekly Online*, 26 May–1 June 2011, available at http://weekly.ahram.org.eg/2011/1049/cu3.htm (last accessed 14 January 2014).

3. Curiously, however, Tahrir Square itself, which acquired (and retains) almost iconic status during the anti-Mubarak protests, plays almost no part in Rakha's novel at all.

4. http://arablit.wordpress.com/2011/06/17/and-the-nominations-for-the-international-prize-for-arabic-fiction-begin/ (last accessed 15 February 2014).

5. Originally published in Hebrew as *Arabeskot*, Tel Aviv: Am Oved Publishers, 1986; English translation by Vivian Eden, as *Arabesques*, New York: Harper & Row, 1988.

6. http://yrakha.com/2013/05/24/book-of-the-sultans-seal/ʿmore-2798 (last accessed 20 January 2014).

7. http://www.egyptindependent.com//news/year-review-11-authors-choose-their-favorite-books-2011 (last accessed 20 January 2014).

8. http://fluentcityblog.com/five-arabic-novels-worth-learning-arabic-for/ (last accessed 20 January 2014).

9. *The Book of the Sultan's Seal: Strange Incidents from History in the City of Mars*, translated by Paul Starkey, Northampton, MA: Interlink Books, forthcoming.

10. *Crocodiles*, translated by Robin Moger, New York: Seven Stories Press, forthcoming. See also http://www.sevenstories.com/news/youssef-rakha-in-the-new-york-times/ (last accessed 20 January 2014).

11. For further details, including lists of nominees and selected authors, see https://www.hayfestival.com/beirut39. The exercise led to a publication itself entitled *Beirut 39: New Writing from the Arab World*, edited by Samuel Shimon, London etc.: Bloomsbury, 2010.

12. See Gérard, Genette, *Seuils*, Paris: Editions du Seuil, 1987 (translated by Jane

E. Lewin as *Paratexts: Thresholds of Interpretation*, Cambridge: Cambridge University Press, 1997).

13. *Kitab al-tughra*, p. 14.

14. The Turkish origin of this name (itself discussed in the text) creates an obvious spelling problem for anyone writing about the work in – or translating it into – a language using a non-Arabic script. Writing in English on the Web about his own work, Rakha himself uses the form 'Çorbaci', though, strictly speaking, the correct modern Turkish spelling should have an undotted 'ı': 'Çorbacı'.

15. *Kitab al-tughra*, pp. 12–13.

16. Ibid., p. 13.

17. For the *khitat* form, see Nezar AlSayyad, Irene A. Bierman and Nasser Rabbat (eds) *Making Cairo Medieval* (Idaho Falls, ID: Lexington Books, 2005), especially pp. 30ff. For an introduction to the *khitat* in a modern context, see also the article 'Mapping Cairo' by Samia Mehrez available at http://english.ahram. org.eg/NewsContent/18/0/212/Books/Mapping-Cairo.aspx (last accessed 16 February 2014).

18. Jamal [Gamal] al-Ghitani, *Khitat al-Ghitani*, Cairo: Maktabat Madbuli, 1991.

19. This translation is based on that by R. B. Serjeant, *The Book of Misers* (Reading: Garnet, 1997), p. 32. Unfortunately, Serjeant's translation as it stands is somewhat problematic, as he has interpreted *taraknaha* to mean 'I have left it out' rather than 'I have left it in' or 'I have left it alone', which makes a nonsense of Rakha's use of the quotation. In this context, Charles Pellat's French translation ('nous les avons conservés', *Le livre des avares de Gahiz*, Paris: Maisonneuve, 1951, p. 57) is perhaps more helpful.

20. See yrakha.com/2013/05/24/book-of-the-sultans-seal (last accessed 7 February 2014).

21. Definitions taken from Martin Hinds and El-Said Badawi, *A Dictionary of Egyptian Arabic*, Beirut: Librairie du Liban, 1986, and Hans Wehr, *A Dictionary of Modern Written Arabic*, fourth ed., Wiesbaden: Harrassowitz, 1979, respectively.

22. This account draws heavily on the author's own observations in a private e-mail sent in the context of discussion on my English draft translation.

23. *Kitab al-tughra*, p. 59 – 'Safsaf' being Aldo's nickname for the narrator, Mustafa.

24. Ibid., p. 63.

25. Ibid., p. 177.

26. Ibid., p. 334.

27. yrakha.com/2013/05/24/book-of-the-sultans-seal (last accessed 7 February 2014).
28. *Kitab al-tughra*, p. 422.
29. yrakha.com/2013/05/24/book-of-the-sultans-seal (last accessed 7 February 2014).
30. *Kitab al-tughra*, p. 465.
31. http://weekly.ahram.org.eg/News/1048/23/Hail,-Prince-of-Believers.aspx (last accessed 18 February 2014).
32. For Vahdettin, see Geoffrey Lewis, *Turkey*, London: Benn, 1965, pp. 52–74; Bernard Lewis, *The Emergence of Modern Turkey*, London: Oxford University Press, 1968, pp. 239–59.
33. *Kitab al-tughra*, p. 24.
34. Ibid., pp. 461–2.
35. Ibid., p. 24.
36. Ibid., p. 17.
37. = 'star' in Turkish.
38. *Kitab al-tughra*, p. 48.
39. For a discussion of 'Middle Arabic', see C. H. M. Versteegh, *The Arabic Language*, Edinburgh: Edinburgh University Press, 1997, chapter 8. See also J. S. Meisami and Paul Starkey (eds), *Encyclopedia of Arabic Literature*, London a New York: Routledge, 1998, pp. 189–91, 'Dialect in Literature (Medieval)' and 'Dialect in Literature (Modern)'.
40. On this, see Luc Deheuvels, Barbara Michalak-Pikulska and Paul Starkey (eds), *Intertextuality in Modern Arabic Literature since 1967*, Durham, NC: School of Modern Languages and Cultures, 2006.
41. *Al-Zayni Barakat*, Cairo: Dar al-Mustaqbal al-ʿArabi, 1971; English translation by Farouk Adbel Wahab, London: Penguin, 1988.
42. 'Between Worlds', *Al-Ahram Weekly Online*, 26 May–1 June 2011, available at http://weekly.ahram.org.eg/2011/1049/cu3.htm (last accessed 14 January 2014).
43. On which see, for example, Kamran Rastegar, *Literary Modernity between the Middle East and Europe: Textual Transactions*, Abingdon: Routledge, 2007, pp. 101–25. A bilingual edition of *al-Saq ʿala al-saq* in four volumes, with Arabic and English translation on facing pages, has been published: *Leg over Leg, or the Turtle in the Tree, Concerning the Fariyaq, What Manner of Creature Might He Be*, edited and translated by Humphrey Davies, New York and London: New York University Press, 2013/14.

11

Towards a Comparative Approach
to Arabic Literature

Abdul-Nabi Isstaif

I ntroducing his contribution to the Blackwell *Companion to Comparative Literature*, entitled 'Comparison, World Literature, and the Common Denominator', Professor Haun Saussey, the former President of the American Comparative Literature Association (2009–11), and the author of the Association's *Report on the State of the Discipline*, 2004, which appeared later in book form, edited and introduced by him under the title: *Comparative Literature in an Age of Globalization* (2006), writes:

> I think the job of the comparatist is to invent new relations among liter-
> ary works (and relations with things that have not been previously classed
> among literary works).[1]

Bearing in mind this suggestion from a distinguished authority on comparative literature, students of Arabic literature, if they ever thought of studying this literature comparatively, might wonder if they need to look for relations between Arabic literature and other world literatures, and whether, if they do not find them, they need to invent such relations. Fortunately, the student of Arabic literature has no need to look too hard for such links, let alone to invent them, for they are as old as Arabic literature itself.

In the first place, Arabic literature's relations with other literatures of the world go back to pre-Islamic times, if not earlier, when the Arabs of the Peninsula were in close contact with the various surrounding nations and empires. Their relationships with their neighbours were not only commercial but also political, military, social and cultural. One aspect of the outcome of these ties is reflected in the many foreign words which permeated the Arabic language from Aramaic, Syriac, Greek, Latin, Persian, Amharic, Ethiopic and other languages of the Ancient Near East.[2] It is enough to refer in this context to the foreign vocabularies in the Qur'an, the claimed linguistic miracle of the Prophet Muhammad which the eloquent Arabs were challenged and failed to imitate. 'Language', as René Wellek rightly states, 'is the material of literature as stone or bronze is of sculpture, paint of pictures, or sounds of music. But one should realize that language is no mere inert matter like stone but is itself a creation of man and is thus charged with the cultural heritage of a linguistic group.'[3] Therefore, if the Arabic language, the medium of Arabic literature, was so exposed to other ancient languages, the literary masterpieces produced in this medium must also have been touched by the cultures of these languages whose loanwords became an integral part of Arabic.

As for the literatures of these languages, they have been in continuous interaction with Arabic literature ever since the authors from the various neighbouring nations established any form of contact with the Arabs. The advent of Islam then produced the greatest interaction between the Arabs and the other peoples of the Ancient World. Describing this interaction in his *Cultures in Motion: Mapping Key Contacts and Their Imprints in World History*, Peter N. Stearns writes:

> One of the great cultural contact experiences in world history involved the spread of Islam, from its initial base in the Arabian Peninsula and the Middle East to a host of areas in Africa, Asia, and Europe. Islam appealed to people in a variety of societies and cultures, bringing important changes as a result of contact while often in some respects merging with the established local belief systems.[4]

In fact the spread of Islam, accompanied by the acquisition of Arabic as the language of worship and daily life, and later as a medium of literature, consolidated even further this interaction, which had become so deep that it involved the very process of creative writing in Arabic which was widely used by the newly converted Muslims. Keen as they were to prove their allegiance and commitment to the new faith, it was quite natural for them to articulate their new experience under the banner of the newly formed Islamic state in the language of the Qur'an, which they used to recite in their prayers five times a day. Thus, Sir Hamilton Gibb was right when he wrote in his *Arabic Literature: An Introduction*:[5]

> Classical Arabic literature is the enduring monument of a civilization, not of a people. Its contributors, nevertheless, under the influence of their Arab conquerors, lost their national languages, traditions, and customs and were moulded into units of thought and belief, absorbed into a new and wider Arab nation.

As for the Europeans, they had been the closest neighbours to the Arabs for many centuries, and to Muslims since the advent of Islam in the seventh century, 'neighbours in constant contact and communication, often as rivals, sometimes as enemies, and with attitudes towards each other formed and confirmed by centuries of experience, and for the Europeans, of fear'.[6] Spain, for nine centuries, and Sicily, for almost four centuries, where the interaction between Arabic and European literatures, first in Latin and later in the various Latin vernaculars, reached its zenith, were, in fact, the springboards for the process of the dissemination of Arabic and Islamic influence throughout Europe. Summing up the outcome of this enduring interaction, Peter N. Stearns adds:

> The Muslim period in Spain and Portugal had vital consequences. Muslim rulers developed an elaborate political and cultural framework while largely tolerating Christian subjects . . .
>
> Muslim artistic styles long influenced Spanish architecture and decoration, even after Islam itself had been pushed out. Music, including the guitar, an Arab instrument, merged traditions as well – and from Spain the new styles would later spread to the Americas. Centers of learning, like Toledo, drew scholars from all over Europe, eager to take advantage of Muslim and Jewish science and philosophy; the result helped spur change and development in European intellectual life.[7]

The experience of the Crusaders in the Levant, which lasted nearly two centuries and which had left a profound influence on those who survived it and who returned safely to their home countries, consolidated this process yet further, and transformed much in Europe in the following centuries.

As for sub-Saharan Africa,

> important interactions occurred during the postclassical period . . . and by the late twentieth century about 40 percent of all sub-Saharan Africans were Muslim. Trade with Muslim North Africa developed quickly, transported across the Sahara Desert by camel and horseback. The trade was vital to Ghana for tax revenues and supply of horses. The king of Ghana also hired Arab Muslims to keep records, because they had writing and bureaucratic experience. But contacts also facilitated raids by Muslims from the north, often encouraged by local Islamic groups. The kingdom of Mali, which flourished after Ghana collapsed in about 1200, regularized interactions with Muslims. Rulers like Sundiata more systematically utilized Muslim bureaucrats and converted to Islam as a gesture of goodwill toward the North African trading partners.[8]

Down the East African coast, Arab traders and missionaries in the Indian Ocean worked directly from Egypt southwards, and widespread conversions occurred:

> Farther south, Swahili merchants – the word in Arabic means 'coasters' or 'people who work along the coasts' – established a lively commerce between Indian Ocean ports and interior villages. In the process they also brought the Arabic language and Muslim religion and political ideas. Many traders intermarried with the African elite, as Islam began to provide cultural unity for upper classes all along the coast. Conversions were voluntary, but Islam represented high social status and the kind of generalized religion useful to far flung trade – a religion that local African cultures did not provide.[9]

The spread of Islam to the east covered central Asia, India and at a later stage the south-eastern areas of the continent. As a matter of fact, Islam was the first external religion to penetrate the region of central Asia, which had, as a whole, remained untouched by the surrounding civilisations until the beginning of the eighth century. The systematic spread of Islam in central Asia, involving the two dominant patterns of Muslim contact, force and persuasion, was most effective, resulting in the majority of its population being Muslim today.[10]

Owing to the major differences between Islam and Hinduism, the initial trading contacts and even successful Arab raids on Indian territories had little cultural impact. A few pockets of Muslims developed, but as small minorities. Hindus largely tolerated these groups. Changes in Hinduism, including more emotional rituals and use of popular languages rather than the scholarly Sanskrit, bolstered this religion's position. As is common when two major cultures encounter each other, influences moved in both directions. Muslims learned about Indian science and mathematics, including the numbering system that passed to the Middle East, where it was later adopted by Europeans.[11]

Unlike other areas in the three continents, where both force and persuasion were used to spread the message of Islam, the final divine message was introduced into south-east Asia during the late fourteenth century entirely by persuasion. The upright conduct of Muslim merchants, who came from Arabia and the Indian subcontinent, attracted the people of the Malay Peninsula to the message of Islam. While the merchants worked on establishing social and commercial contacts with the elites of the coastal towns and centers of the peninsula, the Sufis operated among the inland people, and soon the entire area was dominated by the followers of the new faith. Peter N. Stearns, again, relates the last chapter of the story of the spread of Islam in the premodern era:

> Muslim trading ships from Arabia and particularly from India brought both Muslim merchants and Sufis to the Malay peninsula and the islands that now form Indonesia. Merchants established crucial contacts in the coastal towns, where they influenced the ruling classes. By the fifteenth century, most elites in these cities had been converted. From the coastal towns, Sufis traveled inland, setting up schools and preaching in each village. Islam appealed to inland peoples as a way of integrating with the coastal populations, in a period of expanding trade. By the sixteenth century Islam had become a dominant religion in the Indonesian islands, save for pockets of Hinduism and for isolated, polytheistic peoples in remote parts of the interior. It had won powerful influence on the Malay Peninsula and in the southern part of the Philippines. Its spread was stopped only by the arrival of European naval and commercial superiority during the sixteenth

century. Even so, it was not pushed back; Indonesia is the largest Muslim nation in the world today.[12]

Turning to the modern era of contact between the Arab world and the rest of the globe, it is clear that the era of colonisation by Western powers of most of the Muslim and Arab worlds brought the process of interaction between Arabic and other literatures to a new phase. The presence of European missionaries, traders, travellers, diplomats, writers, administrators and soldiers throughout the Arab world started late in the eighteenth century, providing ample space for encounters that engulfed almost all aspects of life in the Arab world and later in Europe and the Americas. Furthermore, the movement of Arab immigration from the mid-nineteenth century to North and South America as well as to western Africa and Australia, and to all parts of Europe in the second half of the twentieth century created more diverse opportunities for interactions, producing a distinct brand of Arabic literature, namely the early Mahjar (Diaspora) literature, written mostly in Arabic, and the new Mahjar literatures written in languages such as French, English, Spanish, German, Portuguese, and Italian. In fact, there is hardly any aspect of modern Arabic writing which has not been touched by these encounters, and it is impossible to study these writings without taking this into consideration.

In short, every point of contact between Arabic literature and other world literatures is a space of interaction between the two literatures involved in the process, and each space needs thorough investigation. For example, classical Arabic literature is the outcome of the most fruitful partnership among various nations, peoples and traditions in the ancient and medieval worlds, while modern Arabic literature is the outcome of an all-embracing interaction between this centuries-long tradition and the various cultural and literary traditions of the rest of the modern world. In other words, viewed as one of the most important aspects of the Arab–Muslim contribution to world civilisation, Arabic literature has a unique experience of encounter with the literatures of the world in both ancient, medieval and modern times, from East to West, and South to North. Yet this long, extensive, diverse and rich experience of cross-cultural encounter is regrettably either neglected or ignored by comparatists from both East and West.[13] Although comparative literature is meant to be 'a discipline of tolerance',[14] scholars on both sides of the divide tend to deny stubbornly the importance of this interaction in bringing about the changes we witnessed in the histories of Arabic and other world literatures. Ethnocentricity and Eurocentricity seems to have affected the attitudes of both Arab scholars and their European counterparts, who tend to play down the role played by national literary traditions in inspiring any changes that took place on both sides of the divide between Europe and the Islamic and Arab worlds.

To cite one example of this intolerance, one may refer to the role played by the Andalusian literary heritage, particularly the *Muwashshah* (Hispano-Arabic strophic poetry composed in classical Arabic) and the *Zajal* (Hispano-Arabic strophic poetry composed in vernacular Arabic) in the emergence of the 'courtly love' phenomenon in Europe in the late Middle Ages. Writing on 'courtly love', in his monumental masterpiece *The Allegory of Love*, C. S. Lewis describes this phenomenon as 'a revolution', to which the Renaissance itself, when compared with it, 'is a mere ripple on the surface of literature'.[15]

> Every one has heard of courtly love and every one knows that it appears *quite suddenly at the end of the eleventh century*[16] in Languedoc. The characteristics of the Troubadour poetry have been repeatedly described. With the form, which is lyrical, and the style, which is sophisticated and often 'aureate' or deliberately enigmatic, we need not concern ourselves. The sentiment, of course, is love, but love of a highly specialized sort, whose characteristics may be enumerated as Humility, Courtesy, Adultery, and the Religion of Love. The lover is always abject. Obedience to his lady's lightest wish, however whimsical, and silent acquiescence in her rebukes, however unjust, are the only virtues he dares to claim. There is a service of love closely modelled on the service which a feudal vassal owes to his lord. The lover is the lady's 'man'. He addresses her as *midons*, which etymologically represents not 'my lady' but 'my lord'. The whole attitude has been rightly described as 'a feudalisation of love'. This solemn amatory ritual is felt to be part and parcel of the courtly life.[17]

Yet this sudden emergence of courtly love, with its distinctive characteristics, and 'the abrupt appearance of complex Occitanian lyric in the early years of the twelfth century'[18] which points to a possible connection with an earlier literary phenomenon in neighbouring Andalusia, namely the two newly invented poetic genres of the *Muwashshah* and *Zajal*, is viewed as a sort of transmutation that could be easily attributed to the genius of the Troubadours, but never to any external, non-Western element. Although 'the court culture of the eleventh-century Arabic Spain was by all accounts brilliant, sophisticated, and particularly interested in artistic creation', and despite the fact that 'secular as well as mystical love was a frequent topic of both lyric and didactic works; theories of profane love had been well worked out before 1100', and that 'motifs (such as the need for secrecy), styles (such as difficult composition), and concepts (such as *raqib* or "guard") similar or identical to those of the troubadour poetry appear in the amorous verse of Muslim Spain',[19] all these parallels were not seen as enough proof of any connection between the Troubadour lyrics and the *Muwashshahs* and *Zajals* of Andalusía. Furthermore, what is really missing in all the arguments against the so-called Arabic theory is the fact that in both the *Muwashshahs* and *Zajals* on the one hand, and the Troubadours' songs on the other, the music reigns supreme, and this dominance of music points strongly to the original Arabic 'roots' of a significant part of the three lyrical genres, 'given the pre-dominance of Anadalusian musical instruments, many of whose names are still distinguishably Arabic'.[20] Nevertheless, Meg Bogin, in her 'Historical Background' to *The Women Troubadours*, quotes René Nelli's assertion that the poems of the troubadour Guilhem IX

> contain the basic canon of ideas – homage to the lady, true love as endless suffering, chastity as the highest expression of true love – that Arab poets had already codified in works such as *The Dove's Neck Ring*, a mid-eleventh-century treatise by the Cordoban Ali ibn-Hazm, which contained a chapter on 'The Submissiveness the Lover Owes His Lady.[21]

Then she adds:

> Guilhem by all accounts did not begin to write until 1102 just after his return from the Crusades. He had spent a year semi-imprisoned at the court of Tancred, where, presumably, he would have been exposed to Arab poetry. Not only the Crusades but the *Reconquista* – the continuing effort to re-conquer Spain from Islam – had created an important network of

connections between Occitania and the resplendent courts of Christian Spain, where Moorish poets and performers were in residence. Spain was Occitania's closest neighbor, and there was a constant flow of people back and forth across the Pyrenees . . .

The influence of Arab culture was so pervasive that it was hardly necessary to leave Occitania to hear the melodies of Andalusia and Arabia. Much of southern France had been conquered by Moslem invaders in the mid-eighth century. Although the Saracens, as they were called, did not maintain their hold for long, they left their mark in place names and, undoubtedly, in the folk imagination.[22]

Yet we still hear voices in the West which continue to deny any role played by the *Muwashshahs* and *Zajals* in the emergence of the twelfth-century Troubadour songs. In fact, the role of the Arabs in the medieval literary history of Europe is often overlooked and the Arabs themselves are always excluded entirely from the historical scene – an omission which led the late Professor Maria Rosa Menocal to write in her book:

This academic conceptual banishment of the Arab from medieval Europe was to have extraordinary power. While versions of the Arabist theory were to be brought up again and again, it would not be reinstituted as part of the mainstream of philological thought. The sporadic suggestions of Arabic influence on this or that aspect of medieval European literature or on salient features of its lexicon, such as trobar, were largely ignored, were dismissed as unworthy of serious consideration, or at best were subjected to unusually heated and vitriolic criticism. The proponents of such ideas, predominantly Arabists, were dismissed as individuals who simply had an axe to grind rather than a conceivably legitimate contribution to make and who, in any case, were not knowledgeable in the field of European literature.[23]

There are some exceptions to this unfair dismissal of the Arabs from the realm of the verbal arts of medieval Europe. These include in particular three major masterpieces produced by oriental authors which were appropriated and freely used by Western writers, namely Ibn al-Muqaffaʻ's translation of *Kalila wa dimna*, Ibn Tufayl's *Hayy bin Yaqzan* and *Alf layla wa layla*, all of which have been, in Sandra Naddaff's words, emblematic works of world literature, that have 'circulated far beyond their linguistic and cultural points of origin' adapting, as they travel, 'to various media, genres, and contexts'. *Alf layla*, for example, has been an intertext in so many literary and artistic works to the extent that:

> One might productively develop a literary history of nineteenth and twentieth century European and American literature using *Alf Layla wa Layla* as the generative source text. Innumerable Western writers – Beckford, Coleridge, Dickens, Mallarmé, Stevenson, Proust, Yeats, von Hofmannsthal, Twain, Borges, among many others – testify to the influence and importance of this work in the development of their own literary imagination. The short story form, and the *conte fantastique* in particular, were responsive to the intertextual possibilities of the *1001 Nights*. Two examples suffice: Théophile Gauthier's 'La Mille et deuxième nuit' (1842) and Edgar Allan Poe's 'The Thousand-and-Second Tale of Scheherazade' (1845) represent a general fascination with Scheherazade's fate once she moved beyond the narrative time of 1001 nights into real time as the wife of Sultan Shahriyar.[24]

It seems that, when acknowledging the impact of the *Arabian Nights* and other works for that matter, Western scholars do so only as way of emphasising their contribution to the disseminations of these works throughout the globe, ignoring, on the whole, the other most interesting, even exciting, spaces of interaction between Arabic, Western and other literatures of the world such as those of the Iberian space and its extension in Latin America. Conversely, we still witness several Arab scholars strongly objecting to the idea that modern literary genres such as the novel, short story and drama were all inspired by the Arabs' encounter with Europe from the late eighteenth century onwards, claiming that they were merely developments of Arabic literary traditions in narrative, such as the *maqama* and dramatic performances.[25]

In short, the interaction between Arabic literature and other literatures of the world has continued, expanded and deepened, so that by the onset of the new millennium, it involved almost all the literatures of the world – ancient, medieval or modern – and covered both East and West, North and South. In fact, of the great literatures of the world, Arabic literature is unique in a way that cannot be claimed by other literatures, namely through its long, continuous living presence as a verbal art.

In calling for a comparative approach to the study of Arabic literature, the following points are of particular relevance:

- The study of the relationships between Arabic and other World literatures cannot be accomplished by one scholar, or even by a team of scholars from one nation. Such comparative study entails partnerships, both Arab and non-Arab, which would offer opportunities for co-operation between insiders and outsiders, each of whom would bring their vision and insights to the study of the spaces of literary interaction. Such complementarity will lead to more rounded, less subjective approaches.
- The study of Arabic literature comparatively on such a large scale by specialists in the various literatures involved will enrich the theoretical foundations of the comparative approach to literature in general. There is a widespread feeling among comparatists all over the world that their work suffers from Western-centricism,[26] due simply to the circumstances surrounding the birth of the comparative approach and development over the last two centuries. Tapping the contributions of scholars from the rest of the world and drawing on a much expanded circle of materials of interaction between world literatures would help to rectify the unhappy present state of the art.

To give just a brief example of the potential of this expansion, one can refer to Michael Crichton's interaction with *Ibn Fadlan's Journey to Russia*,[27] as embodied in his novel *Eaters of the Dead*. In his 'A Factual Note on *Eaters of the Dead*', the Afterword which he added to the 1993 edition, Crichton acknowledges his debt to *Ibn Fadlan's Journey to Russia*, stating that:

> In the tenth century, an Arab named Ibn Fadlan had travelled north from Baghdad into what is now Russia, where he came in contact with the Vikings. His manuscript, well-known to scholars, provides one of the earliest eyewitness accounts of Viking life and culture. As a college undergraduate, I had read portions of the manuscripts. Ibn Fadlan had a distinct voice and style. He was imitable. He was believable. He was unexpected. And after a thousand years, I felt that Ibn Fadlan would not mind being revived in a new role, as a witness to the events that led to the epic poem of Beowulf.

> Although the full manuscript of Ibn Fadlan has been translated into Russian, German, French, and many other languages, only portions have been translated into English. I obtained the existing manuscript fragments and combined them, with only slight modifications, into the first three chapters of *Eaters of the Dead*. I then wrote the rest of the novel in the style of the manuscript to carry Ibn Fadlan on the rest of his now-fictional journey. I also added commentary and some extremely pedantic footnotes.[28]

He also stresses that all references in his Afterword are genuine, while the novel, including its introduction, text, footnotes and bibliography, should properly be viewed as fiction.[29]

The student of this space of comparative interaction would certainly feel comfortable with applying all the three conditions of the so called 'French School': that the comparative study should be confined to the question of influence between different literatures; that the difference between literature should be based on difference in languages; and that the relationship between the two works is real. He would also be happy to consider the various relations between Ibn Fadlan's text and other forms of knowledge required to reach a better understanding of the text, including geography, medieval Muslim and European history, anthropology, ethnology, sociology, psychology and so forth, as suggested by the 'the American School', particularly in Henry Remak's version.[30] This approach also provides an opportunity to conduct a case study in translation, as well as in comparative stylistics, such as that proposed by René Etiemble in his *Crisis of Comparative Literature*.[31] Furthermore, the two texts involved in this comparative study can be considered from the receptionist perspective, exploring all forms of passive and positive reception, including what I have called elsewhere[32] the critical and inspirational forms of reception, a practice which would meet the requirements of the so-called 'school of reception' in comparative literary study. As for those comparatists interested in imagological studies, they will find in the image of the Arab/Muslim Ibn Fadlan, as reflected in Crichton's novel, an appropriate example. Finally, as the novel was made into a successful film entitled *The 13th Warrior*, directed by John McTiernan[33] (Touchstone Pictures, 1999), with Antonio Banderas (98 mins), comparatists can explore the transformations undergone by the narratives of Ibn Fadlan and Crichton in the movie. We should not forget that a postcolonial contrapuntal reading is also tenable, particularly in view of the fact that some scholars may see Crichton's novel and the subsequent making of the novel into a film as an appropriation of the Arabic text on a large scale in both Western literature and cinema. In short, expanding our perspectives on the comparative study of literature will lead to an inevitable expansion of the Western or world literary canon, and will enrich the theory of comparative study in general.

The study of Arabic literature from a comparative perspective will help to undermine self-centricism, be it national, racial, continental or even cultural, thus allowing a more humanist perspective to dominate the field. This will shake the hierarchical tendency that permeates most comparative studies of influence published nowadays.

The domination of the humanist perspective in comparative literature will help to ease the existing tension between Islam and the West, and will replace the spirit of confrontation adopted by both sides with a spirit of collaboration and co-operation. This should produce a better class of comparative study free of any form of power – a virus that has contaminated Western scholarship for centuries.

Finally, to expand the study of Arabic literature comparatively is compatible with the many recent academic calls for the comparative study of regional, continental and even global literatures. Here one can refer in particular to *The Comparative History of Literatures in European Languages*, published by the International Comparative Literature Association (ICLA), in co-operation with the Hungarian Academy of Science; also to *Latin American Literature: Comparative History of Cultural Formations*, published by Oxford University Press,[34] and to the current research programme 'Travelling Traditions: Comparative Perspectives on Near Eastern Literatures' directed by Friederike Pannewick (Centrum für Nah- und Mitteloststudien/Arabistik, Philipps-Universität Marburg) and Samah Selim (Rutgers University, New Jersey), and sponsored by the project Europe in the Middle East – the Middle East in Europe (EUME).

The call for a comparative approach to Arabic literature is a methodological necessity dictated by the very nature of this literature: its medium, the Arabic language, which has interacted openly with all living languages since pre-Islamic times; its complex network of relations with other literatures and cultures throughout its long and continuous history; the ethnic diversity of its producers, and, finally, the multi-cultural nature of the new Mahjar literatures produced by Arab writers all over the world in Arabic and other living languages. There is a growing feeling among Arab comparatists that the experience of encounter between Arabic and other literatures of the world deserves a comprehensive reassessment. This is fully justified. The study of Arabic literature comparatively is urgently needed both for its vital importance to our understanding of a fascinating and complex chapter in the history of interaction among world literatures and for the promising contributions it will make to theories of comparative literature which have been dominated for too long by Western perspectives.

Notes

1. Haun Saussy, 'Comparison, World Literature, and the Common Denominator', in Ali Behdad and Dominic Thomas (eds), *A Companion to Comparative Literature*, Oxford: Blackwell, 2011, p. 60.
2. Arthur Geoffrey, *The Foreign Vocabulary of the Qur'an*, Baroda, Oriental Institute, 1938, and Kees Versteegh, 'Linguistic Contacts between Arabic and Other Languages', *Arabica*, 'Linguistique arabe. sociolinguistique et histoire de la langue', 48:4 (2001), pp. 470–508.
3. René Wellek and Austin Warren, *Theory of Literature*, third edition, London: Penguin Books, 1980, p. 22.
4. Peter N. Stearns, 'The Spread of Islam', in his *Cultures in Motion: Mapping Key Contacts and Their Imprints in World History*, New Haven and London: Yale University Press, 2001, p. 46.
5. Oxford University Press, 1974, p. 1.
6. Bernard Lewis, *Islam and the West*, New York and Oxford: Oxford University Press, 1993, p. 17.
7. Stearns, 'The Spread of Islam', p. 49.
8. Ibid., pp. 50–1.
9. Ibid., p. 51.
10. Ibid., p. 52.
11. Ibid., p. 54.
12. Ibid., pp. 54–5.
13. Abdul-Nabi Isstaif, 'al-hudur al-mughayyab li'l-tajriba al-'arabiyya fi'l-dars al-muqaran', *Thaqafat* (University of Bahrain) 17 (2006), pp. 41–50.

14. Rey Chow, 'A Discipline of Tolerance', in Behdad and Thomas (eds), *A Companion to Comparative Literature*, p. 15.
15. C. S. Lewis, *The Allegory of Love*, New York: Oxford University Press, 1958, p. 4.
16. My emphasis.
17. Lewis, *The Allegory of Love*, p. 2.
18. Gerald A. Bond, 'Origins', in F. R. P. Akehurst and Judith M. Davis (eds), *A Handbook of the Troubadour*, Berkeley and London: University of California Press, 1995, p. 237.
19. Ibid., p. 243.
20. Maria Rosa Menocal, *Shards of Love: Exile and the Origins of the Lyric*, Durham, NC, and London: Duke University Press, 1994, p. 166.
21. Meg Bogin, *The Women Troubadours: An Introduction to the Women Poets of 12th-century Provence and a Collection of Their Poems*, New York and London: W. W. Norton and Company, 1980, pp. 45–6.
22. Ibid., pp. 46–7.
23. Maria Rosa Menocal, *The Arabic Role in Medieval Literary History: A Forgotten Heritage*, Philadelphia: University of Pennsylvania Press, 1987, p. 83.
24. Sandra Naddaff, 'The Thousand and One Nights as World Literature', in Theo D'haen, David Damrosch and Djelal Kadir, *The Routledge Companion to World Literature*, New York and London: Routledge, 2014, p. 491.
25. See for example: ʿAli ʿUqla ʿArsan, *Al-Zawahir al-masrahiyyah ʿInda ʾl-ʿArab*, third ed., expanded and revised, Damascus: Arab Writers Union, 1985.
26. Sukehiro Hirakawa, 'Japanese Culture: Accommodation to Modern Time', *Yearbook of Comparative and General Literature* 28 (1979), pp. 46–50; Werner P. Friedrich, 'On the Integrity of Our Planning', in Haskell M. Block (ed.), *The Teaching of World Literature*, Proceedings of the Conference at the University of Wisconsin, April 24–25, 1959, Chapel Hill: The University of North Carolina Press, 1960, pp. 14–15; and Rey Chow, 'In the Name of Comparative Literature', in Charles Bernheimer (ed.), *Comparative Literature in the Age of Multiculturalism*, Baltimore and London: The Johns Hopkins University Press, 1995, p. 109.
27. See Ahmad Ibn Fadlan Ibn al-ʿAbbas Ibn Rashid Ibn Hammad, *Risalat Ibn Fadlan fi wasf al-rihala Ila Bilad al-Turk wa al-Khazar wa al-Rus wa al-Saqaliba*, edited, with commentary and introduction by Sami al-Dahhan, second ed., Beirut: Maktabat al-Thaqafa al-ʿAlamiyya, 1987; and Ahmad Ibn Fadlan, *Ibn Fadlan's Journey to Russia: A Tenth-century Traveler from Baghdad to the Volga River*, translated with commentary by Richard Frye, Princeton: Markus Wiener Publishers, 2005.

28. Michael Crichton, 'A Factual Note on *Eaters of the Dead*', in his *Eaters of the Dead: The Manuscript of Ibn Fadlan, Relating His Experiences with the Northmen in A.D. 922*, London: Arrow Books, 1993, pp. 184–5.

29. Ibid., p. 186.

30. Henry H. Remak, 'Comparative Literature: Its Definition and Function', in Newton P. Stallknecht and Horst Frenz (eds), *Comparative Literature: Methods and Perspectives*, revised ed., Carbondale: Southern Illinois University Press, 1971, p. 1.

31. René Etiemble, *The Crisis in Comparative Literature*, translated, and with a foreword, by Georges Joyaux and Herbert Weisinger, East Lansing: Michigan State University Press, 1966, pp. 8–9.

32. Abdul-Nabi Isstaif, 'The West's Reception of Ibn Fadlan's Epistle' (in Arabic), *Al-Turath al-Arabi* (Damascus: The Arab Writers Union) 31:129 (Spring 2013), pp. 67–76.

33. Touchstone Pictures, 1999, with Antonio Banderas (98 mins).

34. Mario J Valdés and Djelal Kadir (eds), *Latin American Literature: Comparative History of Cultural Formations*, Oxford: Oxford University Press, 2004; see also Mario J. Valdés and Linda Hutcheon, 'Rethinking Literary History – Comparatively', *American Council of Learned Societies Occasional Paper* No. 27 (1994); and Linda Hutcheon, Djelal Kadir and Mario J. Valdés, 'Collaborative Historiography: A Comparative Literary History of Latin America', *American Council of Learned Societies Occasional Paper* No. 35, 1996.

12

Does Literature Matter?
The Relationship between Literature and
Politics in Revolutionary Egypt

Elisabeth Kendall

This chapter investigates the complex links between literature and politics in contemporary Egypt. Literature here is used to mean works of the creative imagination (poems, short stories, novels and so on). That literature is political is beyond dispute inasmuch as its production and consumption cannot occur in a societal vacuum. In Egypt, the very fundamentals of how, what and where one publishes are themselves political decisions in a culture industry that has been the site of successive battles between artists and the establishment. What is less clear is how closely literature is (or should be) tied to the service of a particular political agenda or connected to the masses, and to what extent literature can and does succeed in influencing political reality. Many pundits have attributed widespread failure to predict Egypt's revolution to the dearth of warning signs, but the seeds of revolution were apparent in cultural production in the years leading up to the events of 2011. Novels, poems, films and soap operas drove home the reality and consequences of pervasive corruption in a dysfunctional state.[1] Creative works of the imagination have some advantages over factual forms of discourse. As art and as make-believe, they enjoy a greater capacity to circumvent the various kinds of censorship to which other forms of discourse are subject under authoritarian regimes; they have artistic licence to distill, stress or exaggerate particular features of the world they choose to represent using myriad devices for extra effect, in addition to the simple power of selective presentation; and, finally, their aesthetical qualities have the power to speak to hearts as well as minds. The Afghan writer Atiq Rahimi has described the relationship between literature and politics as 'the power of words against the words of power'.[2]

This chapter attempts to describe, theorise and, to a limited extent, quantify the nature of the relationship between politics and literature in Egypt from both angles of this dialectic. The flurry of literary activity that accompanied the 2011 revolution (and its ongoing aftermath)[3] is generally subject to two assumptions: that it gave expression to the pulse of the Egyptian nation, as new works were created and old works resurfaced; and that, more than just recording the uprising, it formed an integral part of it, and possibly even played a role in inspiring and fuelling it. Both these assumptions are interrogated below. The first half of the chapter looks at the influence of politics on literature, most obviously revealed by the ideologies at play in the content, although form and style can also be significant. Not all can be neatly categorised politically, and this was particularly apparent during the 2011 revolution in which leftist ideologies, which had peppered 'committed' literature from the time of the 1952 revolution until the 1970s and even beyond, yielded to broader and vaguer notions of people power and nationhood. The ability of this literature to link to 'the people', however, even in the context of the recent revolution, is questioned. The second half of this chapter then looks, conversely, at the more complex question of the influence of literature on politics, assessing briefly the relevance of some of the main cultural theories surrounding this question. It then tries to unpack the influence of literature on politics by investigating specific questions regarding the effects of the consumption of literature (in particular poetry) in contemporary Egypt on political participation and democratic views. The discussion is informed by cultural-political analyses drawn from a comprehensive national survey carried out by this author with colleagues following Egypt's first parliamentary elections after the 2011 revolution.[4]

Setting the Scene

It has long been assumed that literature wields at least some degree of influence on its audience or readership. Plato banned poets from his ideal republic owing to the seditious ideas they could spread; the British Empire used novels as a tool for instructing the natives in the greatness of England and its civilising mission. With regard to the specific context of Egypt during the 2011 revolution, El Hamamsy and Soliman describe the literature surrounding it as 'an example of political agency reflected culturally',[5] whilst Elliott Colla recognises it as 'fuel for others to go to the street'[6] and describes the poetry that resounded in Tahrir Square as no mere 'ornament' but rather 'a significant part of the action itself'.[7] Reem Saad echoes this view when she writes of the role of poetry in the recent revolution: 'It was not only a source of inspiration but it also carried more explanatory power than social science'.[8] The second half of this chapter attempts to measure some aspects of this alleged agency. Leaving agency to one side, however, it is important to stress that literature in Egypt can in fact be considered inherently political, even where its political stance is not obvious, for any one of three reasons: practical, experiential or stylistic. First, practically, the division of the cultural field into overlapping spheres of establishment and independent control makes the very decision of where to publish into a political statement. Second, experientially, the political frustration of writers and artists at their inability to change the status quo caused them to shift from overt dissidence to more subtle cultural expressions, a move that need not be seen as political demobilisation but rather as 'decentred activism'.[9] And finally, stylistically, even highly experimental works (often labelled postmodern and with no obvious message) carry a latent political message, for they question the established order through eschewing dominant norms of taste and style.[10]

Theory about literary work can generally be split into two spheres, albeit clearly overlapping: the first considers it as a work of art (literary theory and aesthetics) and the second as a social phenomenon (social theory and cultural studies). The latter is our primary focus here. However, it is worth pointing out that even scholars of the first, who consciously limit their analyses to textual close-reading approaches, do so against an implicit assumption that their chosen field, and the work(s) under consideration, carry a certain significance in society. Even if consumers (readers, listeners) are moved solely by a work's aesthetics, this necessarily plays a role, however small, in informing their worldview, which is constantly under (re)construction. In other words, even a purely aesthetic appreciation does not preclude the potential of literary works to shape society and attitudes; in many ways, it simply assumes it.

Where the direct relationship between the literary work and society is freely acknowledged, this can happen in two ways. A work can reflect or at least reveal something about society, real or imagined; in other words, politics influences literature. Conversely, the author's (re)presentation of society in his or her work can eventually be reflected back into society; in other words, literature influences politics. Some works might achieve both, by exposing society in such a way as to impact and change that society. Assessing the impact that literature exerts on the course of politics is hard to pin down. Harlow recently asked, 'What can literature do, after all?' If it were a verb, 'what would happen if we could all "literature"?'.[11] Identifying the reverse – the ways in which politics can influence literature – is by contrast reasonably straightforward.

The Influence of Politics on Literature

For literary production to influence political thinking, it is naturally helpful (although not a prerequisite) for it to include reasonably transparent messaging about the state of society and politics. In Egypt, this is perhaps best exemplified by the concept of 'commitment' (*iltizam*). From around the time of Egypt's previous revolution in 1952, the literary establishment developed an attachment to works that displayed openly their commitment to a leftist agenda through a socialist realist style of writing. By the 1960s, however, more experimental writers were starting to move away from direct socialist realism as they sought to express their trauma at the state of society – particularly after Egypt's 1967 defeat by Israel – through new forms and styles that eschewed both the left and the right and focused instead on individual experience. M. M. Badawi was in fact the first major critic to write in English about this shift in literary sensibility. While he acknowledged that writers and poets had suffered political disillusionment under the socialist regime, he implied that the real driver behind the focus on existential and metaphysical issues was the growing literary awareness of Arab writers as they caught up with the march of aesthetic developments in the West.[12] Badawi would no doubt be surprised to note how, conversely, recent revolutionary events in Egypt are now proving an inspiration to Western literary production of a more avant-garde nature. Early examples of this new phenomenon are the performance poetry of the Americans Will McInerney and Kane Smego, who convert their first-hand experiences of Egyptian public feeling and social media postings into multimedia performances entitled *Poetic Portraits of a Revolution*;[13] and the Chicago-based writer and artist Amira Hanafi's *Dictionary of the Revolution* which creatively records flash interpretations of revolutionary themes.[14] There is still little evidence, however, of Egyptian literature (as opposed to events) influencing Western literature. Returning to the shifting literary sensibility among some writers in 1960s Egypt, this sprang from a self-conscious home-grown political alienation and hence it was still a political statement. It was therefore less about writers imitating the West by rejecting the notion of political commitment, and more about reinterpreting their commitment away from an ostensibly mimetic (but by now stylised and stale) socialist realism.[15]

Debates about the role of the *littérateur* in society and the 'crisis' in Arabic literature flourished as writers turned their backs on transparent commitment. These debates continued into the 1990s as a new wave (frequently termed 'generation')[16] of writers was in turn castigated by established critics for neglecting to tackle significant issues of social and political life; their apparent complete indifference to politics was deemed to make them irrelevant.[17] Yet, like those writers before them, there is an argument to be made that their work was being judged by outmoded critical tools.[18] It may be that a commitment of sorts, albeit at times coded in nihilism and rejectionism, was there all along. The engagement of Egyptian writers and artists became more publicly visible in the mid-2000s. In 2005, the Writers and Artists for Change movement was founded as an offshoot of the political opposition movement *Kifaya* around the time of the rigged 2005 elections. The writers movement co-ordinated with human rights and political movements to organise protests and meetings calling for democracy and freedom of expression.[19] There was also a discernible shift in the style of literary output around this time. The Egyptian novelist Sahar El Mougy testifies to the metamorphosis of her own and others' work away from making a statement of estrangement and towards a more active 're-engagement' with society.[20]

It was therefore unsurprising to find that the mass protests in early 2011 that swept President Mubarak from power were accompanied by an 'avalanche of popular cultural production that emerged hand in hand with revolutions in the region'.[21] Writers and artists, young and old, wasted no time in recording and interpreting political developments through their creative work. While contemporary Egyptian poets such as Ahmad Yamani, Tamim al-Barghouti and Nasir Farghali declaimed their work in Tahrir Square, older work too was recited, sung and chanted by protestors, appropriated both from Egyptians such as Ahmad Fu'ad Nigm and Amal Dunqul and from non-Egyptians such as the Palestinian Mahmud Darwish and, most famously, the Tunisian Abu 'l-Qasim al-Shabbi. Some of the old committed voices of the 1960s surfaced themselves in Tahrir Square. The poet 'Abd al-Rahman al-Abnudi, whose politically committed poetry had captured the mood after Egypt's defeat by Israel in 1967, appeared as relevant as ever and he performed new work movingly in the Square.

The common denominator in the commitment of past and present is the focus on restoring and serving the nation. The outpouring of desire to define a new national self is plain to see among the literary products collected as part of the Tahrir Documents project, a Web archive of the physical materials passed around during protests in Tahrir Square.[22] Ken Seigneurie, in his fascinating study of the discourses of the 2011 revolution, identifies the emergence of a new contemporary 'progressive commitment'.[23] The resurgence of a more direct political engagement in literary production fits with the predilections of the reading public according to research conducted on popular book downloads by Richard Jacquemond. Readers apparently still favour the transparently socially committed novels of Yusuf al-Siba'i and Ihsan 'Abd al-Quddus from the 1960s and 1970s, although, tellingly, the most popular read is in fact Islamic literature.[24] Amid these new literary activists, however, there is little cultural articulation of commitment to any specific ideology. Some might argue that the closest one finds to ideology is a kind of neo-Nasserism based on broad principles of nationalism and social justice.[25] However, today's commitment is best described as a focus on generalities: the love for one's nation, the idealisation of a single Egyptian spirit, the struggle against corruption and the desire for freedom. That the great ideologies of socialism or Marxism are deemed to have run their course is understandable. However, equally, we find little sign among the literature of engaged artists of the political Islam that undeniably held strong currency for a large proportion of the electorate who proceeded in 2011–12 to vote a Muslim Brotherhood member into the presidency.

Literature and the People

This last point raises obvious questions about the idealised notion of the writer or poet as mouthpiece of 'the people' (a much-claimed constituency in the recent revolution). How in touch are the various currents in the new body of revolution literature really with the pulse of the nation at large? El Hamamsy and Soliman write of it as distinct from previous cultural production owing to its immediacy and 'close connection with the street'.[26] But which street are we talking about? The evidence suggests that the secular liberal urban educated elite, who figured prominently among the protestors and played roles as audience, propagators and indeed creators of revolutionary literature and art, were not representative of Egypt at large. Yet many Egypt observers fell victim to the foregrounding of skewed impressions of the revolution, produced by the reconstruction of realities on the ground into Western media reports and scholarship through a process (often inadvertent) of 'telescoping'. First, there was the heavy focus on Tahrir Square; then the lens zoomed in on those who could be interviewed in European languages; then it zoomed in yet further on those whose views conformed to what we wanted to believe, hear or indeed research (about women's empowerment, secular values, religious freedom and so on). The anthropologist Lila Abu-Lughod spotted this early on, asking poignantly, 'I knew that most Egyptians were not in those streets. Why were reporters not going out to interview people who were not gathering in Tahrir Square?'[27]

Closer examination may reveal that the literature of the revolution circulating in the usual, albeit extended, urban liberal circles was not in touch with 'the street' after all. It may have been in touch with large pockets of Tahrir Square, but the Egyptian people at large apparently wanted something other than a secular brand of nationalism, and their votes succeeded in ushering in a Muslim Brotherhood-led government in 2012, the limited choice in the final run-off election notwithstanding. Hirschkind describes the revolution unfolding 'without the question "secular or religious" ever imposing itself'. Significantly, however, his article carries the subtitle 'An Intellectual Genealogy of Tahrir Square' and, as things turned out, that is exactly what it was.[28] After all, even a Square with a million people is a small proportion of a population of about eighty million.

The very people power and democracy that liberal-minded writers and artists had fought for, both before and during the protests, in practice yielded results that proved an uncomfortable fit with their own values and aspirations for Egypt. However, it is important to note that other kinds of literature, notably Islamic literature, also exist, even if they receive scant attention from either the Egyptian intelligentsia or Western observers.[29] Mehrez's fascinating volume *Translating Egypt's Revolution*, which pulls together analysis of a vast array of cultural production surrounding the revolution, recognises in the final sentence of its introduction that it is a 'selective effort' and that 'many more "versions" of the revolutionary text' exist.[30] Evidence of this could be seen when, in early 2012, Khalid Fahmi, an Arabic literature professor, and Mahmud Khalil, deputy director of Qur'an Karim radio, set up Huwiyya, a group of pro-Islamist writers and academics. This was to be the Muslim Brotherhood's vehicle for promoting Islamic values in literature and helping Islamist writers to penetrate cultural institutions from which they felt blocked. Huwiyya was a response both to the sidelining of Islamist writers and to the perceived failure of those dominating the culture scene to connect to the people: 'the cultural trend is going against the people's choice'.[31] Whilst this might be accurate, it raises the ever-present question in Egypt about the role of the writer and of literature.

The fact that secular liberal writers apparently do not reflect the views of large swathes of the Egyptian public, as expressed through the ballot box although obviously not monolithic, is not necessarily inconsistent with the notion of writers and cultured intellectuals (*muthaqqafun*) as the conscience of the nation or guardian of its values – however they happen to see them. In fact, many of the literary works that sprang up around the revolution appear grossly naive in their portrayal of a new cosy united national self, in which Copts and Muslims, men and women, young and old, work hand in hand for the same higher purpose (often with implausibly virtuous women supporting their fearless revolutionary men from the sidelines). Much of the prose literature bears a transparent thematic programming and stylistic simplicity that rivals the most derivate literature of socialist realist commitment in the 1960s and 1970s. At the extreme of stereotypical sugar-coated portrayals is 'Aliya Badawi's *Thawrat al-mahrusa* (2012). Other examples are Nabil Faruq's *Al-Thawra* (2011) and, to a slightly lesser extent, Ahmad Sabri

Abu al-Futuh's *Ajandat sayyid al-ahl* (2012). One of the many examples from poetry, a genre that has been more prolific than novels, is Hasan Talab's collection *Injil al-thawra wa-Qur'an-ha* (2011) with its celebration of happy religious tolerance and blunt political messaging. Naturally, more sophisticated works also feature among the revolution's output, particularly in the form of literary memoir,[32] which abounds, but the underlying point remains: there was and is a certain disconnect, rightly or wrongly, between secular liberal writers and the masses who, whether they subsequently regretted it or not, had voted in the Muslim Brotherhood.

Writers, artists and intellectuals were quick to take up the political mantle as guardians of the nation. By late 2012, protests featured the following groups that clearly demonstrate the broad intersection between literature or art and politics: Writers and Artists for Change, The Egyptian Creativity Front, The Coalition of Revolution Artists, The National Union for Protecting Rights and Freedoms of Thought and Creativity, The Coalition for Independent Culture, The National Union for Protecting Freedom of Expression and several more. The confrontation between literary and political spheres reached boiling point following the appointment of 'Ala' 'Abd al-'Aziz, an obscure cinema professor, as Minister for Culture in May 2013 – the sixth since the 2011 revolution. Perceiving an attempt to Islamicise Egyptian culture following several prominent culture-industry firings, writers and artists staged a sit-in at the Culture Ministry. Their statement was astonishingly explicit about the perceived role of culture and hence by implication about the relationship between literature and politics. They announced that the current situation 'does not fulfil the aspirations of intellectuals to cultivate a culture that lives up to the hopes of the great revolution' (as defined by them).[33] The Egyptian Centre of the International Theatre Institute simultaneously issued a call for action in which it referred to 'the Islamists' jihad against the arts', couched in terms such as 'we cannot allow' and 'an urgent mission to protect'.[34]

For many writers and intellectuals, the pursuit of greater freedom is apparently not inconsistent with the reversal through force of a democratic election outcome and support now for an authoritarian military-led regime. More than 150 authors and publishers, including prominent novelists like Baha' Tahir and Sun 'Allah Ibrahim who had been thought to stand against authoritarianism, signed a statement backing the military intervention that removed the Muslim Brotherhood and asked that the latter be designated a 'terrorist organisation'.[35] The strength of feeling against the Brotherhood's abuse of its 'freedom to deny freedoms', to borrow a phrase from the novelist and poet Youssef Rakha, is clear from a statement made on Rakha's blog *after* the army had massacred the sit-in in support of the Brotherhood: whilst regretting the 'insane' number of casualties, he writes 'I am all for the state monopolizing the right to use violence, even where that right is subject to abuse'.[36] Ironically, the novelist Alaa al-Aswany, who had for years ended his newspaper column with the slogan 'democracy is the solution', was particularly vocal among those defending the military overthrow of the democratically elected Mursi regime. As far as he and many members of the intelligentsia were concerned, this was democracy in action. 'The people' had changed their minds owing to the disgraceful acts of the Brotherhood-led regime, such that the army had been forced to intervene to put the revolution on a corrective course. Democracy is still the solution, al-Aswany assures us; it was simply that 'the people' had made a mistake first time round. [37] In many respects, the continuing collaboration between Egypt's new regime and the literati appears to hark back to the familiar fault-lines that existed prior to the revolution, when writers and artists of varying ideologies and ambitions often found common ground against religious interference, forcing them into what Mehrez calls 'dubious alliances with the state'.[38] Ominously, however, it was the new 'corrective' regime that soon afterwards upheld a five-year prison sentence against the writer Karam Sabir for allegedly insulting religion in his short story collection *Ayna Allah?* (2010) in a move reminiscent of the occasional token scapegoating designed to appease the Islamist lobby prior to the revolution.

Significantly, these developments accord well with results gleaned from our survey (explained more fully in the final section). We found that those who read or listen to poetry (this accounted for only 6 per cent of the population so could be viewed as a literary elite) proved a positive predictor of support for 'a strong leader to solve the country's problems even if he or she overthrows democracy'. This was not the case among consumers of mass cultural products, in other words the broader public. This result was produced *after* controlling for other possible factors that might influence such a view, including social class, economic position and political activism. In other words, poetry consumers, whilst sharing with the general population their strong support for democracy (defined in the survey as 'multiple parties competing for power through free elections'), were nevertheless more likely to support a strong leader taking non-democratic measures if necessary. This gives an unusual insight into how those *littérateurs* who fought for democratic freedom could then fight against its result.

The Influence of Literature on Politics

The first part of this chapter has demonstrated a number of ways in which politics can influence literature. But it has also shown that a great many writers and artists hold ambitions to influence politics. Assessing whether and how this might happen through their literary works is tricky and riddled with unknowns. Our survey attempted to unravel this question by looking at the political opinions and behaviours of Egyptian literary consumers (a term that encompasses readers, listeners and observers) after accounting for other socio-economic factors that might influence such behaviours. Before discussing the survey conclusions, however, it is worth exploring briefly the theoretical approaches that touch on the socio-political impact of literature. These might be split roughly into three groups with regard to their construction of the role of consumers: functionalist and structuralist; political economy; and poststructuralist and postmodern.

First, functionalist and structuralist approaches favour clearly defined relationships between culture and society. Culture is a derivative of social structure. It provides the values and norms that maintain society, including the political system.[39] Such approaches imply the existence of an absolute truth that can be captured by literary producers, represented in their literary products and communicated to consumers. This suggests the existence of a direct link between literary content, its consumers and the formation of their political attitudes. It was this belief that lay behind the rise of socialist realist political commitment from the 1950s and it holds continuing appeal for literary producers in Egypt's contemporary atmosphere of revolution. It might also be viewed as the attitude that lies behind much Western adoption of Arabic literary works, which are often considered a direct and entertaining route to understanding the social and political workings of an 'alien' society.

At its most extreme, this attitude celebrates the kind of Egyptian writer that one more nuanced contemporary novelist typifies as the 'straight-talking, know-it-all platitude-monger with vaguely left-wing ideals'.[40] There is clear overlap between these types of approaches and our second category of political economy approaches.

Political economy approaches, also sometimes called structuralist and often influenced by Marxist theory, emphasise culture as the product of the prevailing power structure. Literature designed for mass cultural consumption is viewed as an effective medium for influencing values and behaviours, not by revealing the truth but by partially representing the world in a way that perpetuates the social and political ideas of the dominant class, thus encouraging passivity and conformity among mass audiences.[41] It was this kind of thinking that prompted the Egyptian state's successive and in many ways successful attempts to exert control over the cultural apparatus from the 1950s onwards. Political intervention occurred both visibly through laws but also invisibly, through the effective 'institutionalisation' of censorship by control of publication and dissemination outlets[42] and through state complicity with aggressive religious intervention from the street to safeguard public morality from illicit content. This in turn influenced literary production by engendering an underground publishing industry and cultural resistance movements, but also – in both formal and informal outlets – an unquantifiable level of self-censorship. The Nigerian writer Chinua Achebe articulates succinctly the artist's dilemma under dictatorial regimes: 'poetry can be as activist as it wants, if it has the willingness and the energy. . . . But you see, the point is this: A poet who sees poetry in the light I am suggesting is likely to fall out very seriously with the emperor.'[43] This was certainly the case in Egypt under Nasser and to some extent under Sadat, but in fact the final decade of the Mubarak era saw greater freedom for writers with the proliferation of independent publishing houses and opportunities to produce work independently, cheaply and even anonymously in new digital media 'spaces'.

Some political economy theorists argue that even mass cultural products inevitably contain some elements critical of the social order which consumers can latch onto,[44] and in a move away from simple socio-economic class-based understandings, the relationship of culture to political economy has also been viewed through the more nuanced lens of ideology and its mediation through language.[45] These concepts have been developed within cultural studies by Stuart Hall into a sophisticated political economy approach that differentiates more sharply between the consumers themselves. Like earlier Marxist theory, literature for the mass market is still considered to function largely in favour of society's dominant groups. However, the ability of consumers to react to works ('decode their messages') in different ways is acknowledged. While the majority of consumers still accept the dominant (hegemonic) position presented, some negotiate with it and still others directly oppose it.[46] Nevertheless, it is reasonable to suppose that literature produced outside the dominant cultural apparatus holds greater capacity to foster resistance by revealing alternative realities.[47] By these theories then, one could generally expect to see lower political engagement among consumers of mass culture than among consumers of more 'independent' literature (albeit these consumer groups doubtless overlap).

It is certainly possible that recent new independent outlets for literary production, much of it highlighting state corruption, have helped shape the worldview of the urban educated middle class, many of whom were active in the 2011 revolution. Chinua Achebe admits, 'There's a limit to what storytelling can achieve. We're not saying that a poet can stop a battalion with a couple of lines of his poetry. But there are other forms of power.' Yet Achebe makes a distinction between the role of the storyteller and that of the person who agitates, drums up support and ultimately fights for the cause. Unlike them, the storyteller 'recounts the event – and this is the one who survives, who outlives all the others. It is the storyteller . . . who creates history . . . [and] creates the memory that the survivors must have.'[48] However, in Egypt at least, we find writers who in fact blend these roles, not only by recounting events in which they themselves participated but also by telling their stories and performing their art live as the revolution was unfolding. Pahwa and Winegar trace a perhaps even stronger morphing of the roles of activist and creator with regard to graphic artists and performers engaged in the recent revolution.[49] Nevertheless, Achebe's reality check is useful. It is echoed by the Australian novelist Amanda Lohrey, who points out that for a literary work 'to have political influence it must first be read, and read sympathetically, by a large audience', although she does add that literature 'may help to fortify the morale of activists on the ground'.[50]

Third, poststructuralist and postmodern approaches move yet further away from the notion of consumers passively absorbing a literary work's representation of the world to the idea that literature acts as a catalyst for the construction of many different worlds (and truths). For culture is neither derivative of nor dependent on social structure. Both are part of a reciprocal relationship in which each may influence the other. Such approaches are facilitated by the concept of discourses (frameworks of knowledge). Power lies in the ability to create discourses and it can come from anywhere. The discourses that literary works contain relate in complex ways to the discourses of both their producers *and* their consumers.[51] Hence literature can be viewed as a site of political contestation.[52] Seigneurie writes of 'citizen readers', in the context of the 2011 revolution, consuming protest discourse and argues that 'events don't move masses; discourses about them do'. He speculates that the discourse of 'progressive commitment . . . steeled the will to resist and sacrifice for a better future' and the discourse of 'elegiac humanism', part of poetic and religious tradition, 'grounded action in the respect for human dignity'.[53] These conclusions regarding the power of certain discourses undoubtedly hold true some of the time, but the reality is that their reach is small and they require the consumers themselves to process the discourse in a predictable way.

This third category of approaches acknowledges the relationship of culture to politics but demonstrates a more contingent understanding of the role of consumers in producing meaning. Consumers' understanding of cultural products is not informed by the products themselves, but by how they interpret them, a process that involves dispute and is subject to change. This understanding of how a literary work is read undermines the validity of literary commitment as a conscious political project, since both writer and reader are engaging with one another at a subconscious as well as a conscious level, such that the result on the reader cannot be predicted. It is on this basis that Italo Calvino judged the notion of the committed writer 'wrongheaded'.[54] There is no one-directional transfer of knowledge and understanding from product to consumer (from text to reader, from performance to listener). This process is perhaps best understood by thinking about the apparently mechanical act of translation. Far from being a transparent transfer of meaning, translation inevitably involves a process of interpretative reconstruction.[55] This process was in evidence during the 2011 protests in Egypt and is expertly articulated by Mehrez in her account of the challenges involved in rendering the 'Tahrir Documents' into English.[56]

Understanding that meaning derives from the consumer as much as from the cultural product suggests that we would not necessarily expect to find homogeneous patterns of thinking among consumers, just because they have consumed the same or similar products. An example of this in Egypt would be the reaction to *Al-Khubz al-hafi* (1971) by the Moroccan novelist Muhammad Shukri. This was interpreted by some Egyptians as an eloquent encouragement to overcome huge obstacles in order to lead a free and successful life, but by others as an affront to Islam and an incitement to sexual debauchery, to the extent that the American University in Cairo moved to ban it from its syllabus in the late 1990s.

The Survey

We have now looked at a broad spectrum of cultural studies theories with regard to their implications for the relationship between politics and literature, but what of evidence on the ground in today's Egypt? We will look at this question in four stages, using results from the survey. First, what did the survey ask and what are its limitations? Second, what reach does literature have in Egypt? Third, how important do consumers consider the political influence of literature? And fourth, is there evidence that literary consumption impacts democratic support or political participation?

The survey was conducted in face-to-face interviews of roughly 35 minutes each with a nationally representative sample of two thousand individuals drawn from the Egyptian electorate during December 2011 and January 2012.[57] It revealed a clear divide between consumers of poetry and short stories on the one hand, and mass cultural products on the other. Although the survey asked about the consumption of a range of literary genres,[58] it is likely that novels (*riwayat*) and plays (*masrahiyyat*) were understood to encompass soaps and dramas, since respondents overwhelmingly claimed to consume these via television. They should therefore be understood as mass (television) culture in the context of this survey, rather than literary genres, particularly since over 60 per cent of respondents claimed to consume them. By contrast, a staggeringly low 6 per cent of respondents claimed to consume poetry (orally, aurally or visually) and only 14 per cent short stories. Poetry and short stories were accessed mainly via books, and the former also online. The low consumption of poetry may indicate that respondents did not recognise songs and chants as poetry. For example, the lyrics to the hit *Ihna al-sha'b* (2012) by rock sensation Cairokee are adapted from al-Abnudi's poem *Ahzan-i al-'adiya*; and of course the poetry of Ahmad Fu'ad Nigm was prolifically sung and chanted during protests. Given these survey constraints, comments on the role and influence of literature are necessarily confined here to the genres of poetry and the short story, as opposed to mass culture. Naturally the audiences for both overlap and should not be viewed as discrete constituencies. Jacquemond makes this point powerfully, in the context of 'high' versus 'low' literature, using data from popular downloads of books from the website 4shared.com as evidence of diverse reading practices that blur this much-vaunted divide.[59]

To understand the kind of audience that literature reaches today we analysed the profile of literary consumers in comparison with the overall population. What distinguishes the former from the latter is that they are slightly younger, better educated, more urban in the case of poetry, more supportive of a market economy and women's social rights. They were also significantly more pro-revolution than the overall population (64 per cent of poetry consumers and 56 per cent of short story consumers 'strongly agreed' that the revolution was a good thing, as opposed to only 37 per cent of the overall population). Literary consumers certainly share many overlapping features with the overall population and, interestingly, they did not differ significantly in either their voting behaviour or general religious views. Nevertheless, political economy theories in particular tend to rest on literature's ability to reach a broad audience, and that is clearly not the case here.

How much political importance do literary consumers themselves attribute to literary works? Consumers were asked (on a five-point scale) how important they felt each genre was in shaping their political views. Poetry and short stories, with 37 per cent and 38 per cent respectively, were deemed markedly more politically important than mass cultural products with only 23 per cent. Given that people generally dislike the notion of being influenced or manipulated, it is certainly significant that well over a third of consumers consciously consider literature important in shaping their political views.

Literary consumers, like the general population, strongly support democracy. However, we found no evidence to suggest that this can be attributed to their consumption of poetry, although consumption of mass culture did reveal a positive effect. With regard to mass culture then, our results cast some doubt on the validity of political economy theories arguing that these products entrench the socio-political status quo, even if they reflect it. Our results accord better with later variations on political economy approaches, such as the notion that consumers can still focus on the negative aspects of a work, regardless of the producer's intention. However, our results accord best with postmodern and poststructuralist theories, by which consumers interact with a product depending on the specific temporal and spatial context and their own prior experience, and not based on some fixed notion of content.

There are several possible explanations for the lack of evidence to show that poetry generates support for democracy. The test we posed was tough, since the models used controlled for other factors known to generate democratic support, including social class, economic position and political activism. It would have been striking to see the effects of poetry consumption jumping over such a high bar. The point is that consumers may well hold pro-democracy views but that these can be accounted for by social, economic and political factors rather than being specifically attributable to poetry. This is not to deny that democratic beliefs might be sustained and encouraged through poetry. It is this, perhaps, that we saw in action in Tahrir Square.

Finally, we looked at whether literary consumption impacts political participation. Again, we posed a hard test by taking account of other factors that political science literature knows to be significant (the control variables captured income, education, age, urban/rural distributions, trust in parties, evaluation of democratic experience and religion). Surprisingly, given this hard test, we found that poetry has a strongly positive effect on participation in protests and strikes and, together with short stories, also on boycotting. The consumption of mass cultural products has either no effect or a negative effect. The fact that poetry in particular proved so significant, even after controlling for the other predictors, means that it does independently stimulate political activity.

Conclusions

The upheavals in Egypt in 2011 have been described not just as a political revolution but also as a social and cultural revolution. With regard to literature, which intersects with all three spheres, this looks on the surface to be true, particularly given the heavy and often telescopic focus of both the media and scholars on Tahrir Square, but closer inspection reveals a more complex reality. This chapter shows that, in many respects, the relationship between literature and politics is beginning to fall along the same fault-lines that existed in Egypt prior to the revolution as secular liberal writers resort to uneasy alliances with an apparently authoritarian state against religion. Moreover, while the revolution did succeed in sprouting an 'avalanche' of literature, this avalanche looks to be localised largely (and understandably) around the main sites of protest and, arguably, neither reaches nor reflects the masses. Celebratory and committed styles of writing have made a comeback, albeit ideologically vague, and literary consumers continue to account for only a tiny minority of the Egyptian public.

Yet despite all of this, there *is* evidence that Egyptian literature matters politically. Although our survey revealed mixed evidence to support the idea that literary consumption generates support for democracy (pro-democracy ideas might pre-exist among literary consumers owing to other socio-economic factors), it did show that poetry and short stories can independently generate increased political participation. The link between poetry and protest activities was particularly strong. This therefore supports the widely held assumption that poets and writers played a role in encouraging political activity during the 2011 revolution, albeit among a limited public. At the same time, consumers of poetry were actually found to harbour undemocratic views (even while declaring support for democracy) inasmuch as they were prepared to support the idea of a strong leader who could overthrow democracy if required to solve Egypt's main problems. This provides a glimpse into how many of 2011's revolutionaries became 2013's supporters of a military 'coup'.

It is perhaps fitting to let two Egyptian poets have the last word. Tamim al-Barghouti, speaking in 2013, called poetry 'a ruler's greatest threat' on the basis that poetry influences the imagination more than any other form of expression. He states starkly, 'The only power a ruler actually has can be covered by a shirt and trousers; everything else comes from the obedience of others. They will only obey him if they imagine that it is their duty to obey.'[60] And it is literature that gives people the power to imagine otherwise. The poet (and novelist) Youssef Rakha, whilst making equally grand claims for the value of poems, has a more modest view of their reach: 'like words dictated to prophets by archangels, they change the world. What it is important to remember is that they change your private, inner world. They are not revolutions.'[61]

Both poets might be right. Our survey evidence suggests that the reach of poetry is extremely limited, and naturally its power to change the imagination (or inner world) can extend only to those who actually compose, hear or read it. However, it is possible that poetry and some types of fiction are of greater political significance than their limited popularity implies. Certainly, they generate increased political participation among the small minority of Egyptians who consume them. The important question then is: is this minority active enough to wield influence? If so, literature might indeed be a catalyst for political change, revolution even, all without the masses ever having been directly involved.

Notes

1. Some poems that allegedly stirred emotions prior to 2011 are highlighted by Sha'ban Yusuf, 'Al-shi'r wa-thawrat 25 yanayir: taqdim wa-namadhij', *Alif* 32 (2012), pp. 312–37: 312–14. Some novels now bear slogans like 'the novel that predicted the uprising' on their front covers, e.g. Khalid al-Khamisi's *Taksi* (2007) on the 2011 edition of its English translation and Muhammad Salmawi's *Ajandat al-farasha* (2011). However, the most well-known exposé of the rottenness of Egyptian society is Alaa al-Aswany's bestselling novel *'Imarat Ya'qubian* (2002), which was also turned into a blockbuster film (2006) and enjoyed huge reach and popularity.
2. Atiq Rahimi, 'Words as a Pledge', keynote address, St Malo, Edinburgh World Writers Conference, 20 May 2013, http://www.edinburghworldwritersconference.org/should-literature-be-political/rahimi-in-france-keynote-on-should-literature-be-political/.
3. Clearly, questions arise over the accuracy of terming the events of 2011 a 'revolution' and there are many who consider the struggle ongoing. For ease of refer-

ence, this chapter will use the term '2011 revolution' on the understanding that readers can interpret this in a more complex way as events continue to unfold.

4. The survey asked a scientifically randomised and weighted sample of two thousand Egyptians their opinions on a range of issues including culture, religion and politics. It was conducted by Mazen Hassan (Cairo University), Stephen Whitefield (Oxford University) and this author.

5. Walid El Hamamsy and Mounira Soliman, 'Popular Culture – a Site of Resistance', in Walid El Hamamsy and Mounira Soliman (eds), *Popular Culture in the Middle East and North Africa: A Postcolonial Outlook*, New York and London: Routledge, 2013, pp. 1–14: 13.

6. Elliott Colla, 'Revolution Bookshelf: *Revolution Is My Name*', *Jadaliyya* (3 July 2013), http://www.jadaliyya.com/pages/index/12588/revolution-bookshelf_revolution-is-my-name.

7. Elliott Colla, 'The Poetry of Revolt', *Jadaliyya* (31 January 2011), http://www.jadaliyya.com/pages/index/506/the-poetry-of-revolt.

8. Reem Saad, 'The Egyptian Revolution: A Triumph of Poetry', *American Ethnologist* 39:1 (February 2012), pp. 63–6: 65.

9. See Marie Duboc, 'Egyptian Leftist Intellectuals' Activism from the Margins: Overcoming the Mobilization/Demobilization Dichotomy', in Joel Beinin and Frederic Vairel (eds), *Social Movements, Mobilization and Contestation in the Middle East and North Africa*, Stanford: Stanford University Press, 2011, pp. 61–79.

10. See Peter Bürger, *Theory of the Avant-Garde*, Minneapolis: University of Minnesota Press, 1984.

11. Barbara Harlow, 'Resistance Literature Revisited: From Basra to Guantanamo', *Alif* 32 (2012), pp. 10–29: 12.

12. M. M. Badawi, *Modern Arabic Literature and the West*, London: Ithaca, 1985, pp. 23–4 and 98–100. Both essays referred to here ('Commitment in Contemporary Arabic Literature' and 'Convention and Revolt in Modern Arabic Poetry') were originally published in the early 1970s.

13. See a review by Jeanmarie Higgins, 'Poetic Portraits of a Revolution', *Theatre Journal* 65:1 (March 2013), pp. 117–19.

14. See the poet/artist's website at http://amiraha.com/qamos-al-thawra/.

15. Elisabeth Kendall, *Literature, Journalism and the Avant-garde: Intersection in Egypt*, New York and London: Routledge, 2006, pp. 163–76.

16. For a thorough discussion of the pros and cons of the prevalent tendency to categorise Egyptian writers into generations, see Yasmine Ramadan, 'The Emergence

of the Sixties Generation in Egypt and the Anxiety over Categorization', *Journal of Arabic Literature* 43 (2012), pp. 409–30.

17. Hoda Elsadda, *Gender, Nation, and the Arabic Novel*, Edinburgh and New York: Edinburgh University Press and Syracuse University Press, 2012, pp. 145–50; Sabry Hafez, 'Jamaliyyat al-riwaya al-jadida', *Alif* 21 (2001), pp. 184–246: 186–8.

18. Elsadda, *Gender, Nation, and the Arabic Novel*, pp. 149–51.

19. Rania Khallaf, 'Change, Not Reform', *Al-Ahram Weekly* 755 (11–17 August 2005), http://weekly.ahram.org.eg/2005/755/cu5.htm.

20. Sahar El Mougy, 'The Future of the Novel', keynote address, Cairo, Edinburgh World Writers Conference, 1 July 2013, http://www.edinburghworldwritersconference.org/the-future-of-the-novel/el-mougy-in-egypt-keynote-on-the-future-of-the-novel/.

21. El Hamamsy and Soliman, *Popular Culture*, p. 13.

22. See http://www.tahrirdocuments.org/category/culture-2.

23. Ken Seigneurie, 'Discourses of the 2011 Arab Revolutions', *Journal of Arabic Literature* 43 (2012), pp. 484–509: 491–2. Seigneurie writes that the secular discourse of the 1950s and 1960s gave way to a more sectarian thrust from the 1970s.

24. Richard Jacquemond, '*The Yacoubian Building* and Its Sisters: Reflections on Readership and Written Culture in Modern Egypt', in Walid El Hamamsy and Mounira Soliman (eds), *Popular Culture in the Middle East and North Africa*, New York and London, 2013, pp. 144–61: 149.

25. For a discussion of how the name of Nasser has been invoked to support anti-Brotherhood and pro-military rhetoric, see Amr Adli, 'The Problematic Continuity of Nasserism', *Jadaliyya* (31 March 2014), http://www.jadaliyya.com/pages/index/17135/the-problematic-continuity-of-nasserism.

26. El Hamamsy and Soliman, *Popular Culture*, p. 13.

27. Lila Abu-Lughod, 'Living the "Revolution" in an Egyptian Village', *American Ethnologist* 39:1 (February 2012), pp. 21–5: 21.

28. Charles Hirschkind, 'Beyond Secular and Religious', *American Ethnologist* 39:1 (February 2012), pp. 49–53: 49. In his concluding paragraph, Hirschkind acknowledges that the secular–religious divide has subsequently spread.

29. A useful brief synopsis of contemporary culture in Islamist circles can be found in Sonali Pahwa and Jessica Winegar, 'Culture, State and Revolution', *Middle East Research and Information Report* 263 (August 2012), http://www.merip.org/mer/mer263/culture-state-revolution.

30. Samia Mehrez (ed.), *Translating Egypt's Revolution: The Language of Tahrir*, Cairo and New York: AUC Press, 2012, p. 20.

31. Muhammad Shu'ayr, 'Inqilab ikhwanji washik 'ala al-thaqafa al-misriyya', *Al-Akhbar* 1659 (14 March 2012), http://www.al-akhbar.com/node/45451.

32. Elliott Colla draws attention to one fine example: Muna Prince's literary memoir *Ism-i Thawra* (Cairo, 2012). Colla's analysis suggests that literary works can and should capture revolution in progress and therefore that, while they may date quickly, they maintain artistic integrity and value. Colla, 'Revolution Bookshelf'.

33. Significantly, pro-Brotherhood protestors also descended on the Ministry to defend it from occupation by the intellectual elite.

34. The call was publicised on several blogs. The full text can be read on Marcia Lynx Qualey's Arabic Literature (in English) blog: http://arablit.wordpress. com/2013/06/06/international-call-for-action-from-egyptian-centre-of-the-international-theatre-institute/.

35. Elliott Colla, 'Revolution on Ice', *Jadaliyya* (6 January 2014), http://www. jadaliyya.com/pages/index/15874/revolution-on-ice.

36. Youssef Rakha, 'The Terrors of Democracy', The Sultan's Seal blog, 23 August 2013, http://yrakha.com/2013/08/23/the-terrors-of-democracy/.

37. Significantly, al-Aswany ends the article by warning of two potential dangers: the return to power of either the military (which he considers unrealistic) or the Mubarak regime (which he considers possible). Alaa al-Aswany, 'Mulahazat sariha 'ala mashhad ra'i'', *Al-Safir* (9 July 2013), http://www.assafir.com/ Article/314557.

38. These have been well mapped by Samia Mehrez, *Egypt's Culture Wars: Politics and Practice*, New York and London: Routledge, 2008. See in particular Kindle locs 293–359.

39. See Talcott Parsons, *The Social System*, London: Routledge & Kegan Paul, 1952; Claude Lévi-Strauss, *The Savage Mind*, London: Weidenfeld & Nicolson, 1966.

40. This description is drawn from Youssef Rakha's intellectually rigorous (and highly entertaining) rant against patronising and simplistic approaches by some Westerners to Arabic fiction. In it he points out that popular novels (such as al-Aswany's *The Yacoubian Building*) that apparently resonate with Western critics do not require of the novelist 'anything more sophisticated than goody-goody repulsion at systematic injustice'. Youssef Rakha, 'In Extremis: Literature and Revolution in Contemporary Cairo', *The Kenyon Review* 34:3 (Summer 2012), pp. 151–66: 156, 163.

41. Theodor Adorno and Max Horkheimer, *The Dialectic of the Enlightenment*, New York: Continuum, [1947] 1972; Mahmud Amin al-ʿAlim and ʿAbd al-ʿAzim Anis, *Fi al-Thaqafa al-Missriyya*, Cairo: Dar al-Thaqafa al-Jadida, [1955] 1989); Ghali Shukri, *Al-ʿAnqaʾ al-jadida: siraʿ al-ajyal fi al-adab al-muʿasir*, Beirut: Dar al-Taliʿa, 1977.

42. See Marina Stagh, *The Limits of Freedom of Speech: Prose Literature and Prose Writers in Egypt under Nasser and Sadat*, Stockholm: Almquist & Wiksell International, 1993; Yves Gonzalez-Quijano, *Les gens du livre: Edition et champ intellectuel dans l'Egypte républicaine*, Paris: CNRS Edition, 1998.

43. Bill Moyers, television interview with Chinua Achebe, *Bill Moyers World of Ideas*, USA, Public Broadcasting Service (PBS), Episode 114, 29 September 1988, http://teacherweb.com/CA/StaggHighSchool/Bott/IntervwTranscript.pdf.

44. Fredric Jameson, 'Reification and Utopia in Mass Culture', *Social Text* 1 (Winter 1979), pp. 130–48; Janice Radway, *Reading the Romance: Women, Patriarchy and Popular Literature*, Chapell Hill and London: University of North Carolina Press, 1991.

45. Louis Althusser, 'Ideology and Ideological State Apparatuses', in L. Althusser (ed.), *Lenin and Philosophy and Other Essays*, London: New Left Books, 1971, pp. 121–76; John B. Thompson, *Studies in the Theory of Ideology*, Cambridge: Polity, 1984.

46. Stuart Hall, 'Encoding/decoding', in Stuart Hall et al. (eds), *Culture, Media, Language: Working Papers in Cultural Studies, 1972–79*, London: Hutchinson, 1980, pp. 128–38.

47. Raymond Williams, *Marxism and Literature*, Oxford: Oxford University Press, 1977; E. P. Thompson, *The Poverty of Theory and Other Essays*, London: Merlin, 1978.

48. Moyers, television interview with Chinua Achebe.

49. Pahwa and Winegar, 'Culture, State and Revolution'.

50. Amanda Lohrey, 'Can Literature Affect Political Change?', keynote address, Melbourne, Edinburgh World Writers Conference, 23 August 2013, http://www.edinburghworldwritersconference.org/should-literature-be-political/lohrey-in-australia-keynote-on-should-literature-be-political/.

51. Jacques Derrida, *Writing and Difference*, London: Routledge & Kegan Paul, [1967] 1978; Michel Foucault, *Power/Knowledge: Selected Interviews and Other Writings, 1972–1977*, Brighton: Harvester, 1980.

52. Glenn Jordan and Chris Weedon, *Cultural Politics: Class, Gender, Race and the Postmodern World*, Oxford: Blackwell, 1994.

53. Seigneurie, 'Discourses of the 2011 Arab Revolutions', pp. 485, 501.

54. Italo Calvino, 'Right and Wrong Political Uses of Literature', in Dennis Walder (ed.), *Literature in the Modern World: Critical Essays and Documents*, New York: Oxford University Press, [1990] 2004, pp. 114–16.

55. Lawrence Venuti, *The Translator's Invisibility: A History of Translation*, New York and London: Routledge, 1995; Mona Baker, *Translation and Conflict: A Narrative Account*, New York and London: Routledge, 2006.

56. Mehrez, *Translating Egypt's Revolution*, pp. 1–20.

57. The survey covered a variety of governorates (including Cairo) and was designed to represent upper and lower Egypt and the urban–rural divide. The sampling procedure was a combination of multistage cluster random sampling and systematic random sampling. Quotas were set for certain demographic features to match population demographics. More precise details of the survey methodology and further analysis can be found in Mazen Hassan, Elisabeth Kendall and Stephen Whitefield, 'Media, Cultural Consumption and Normative Support for Democracy in Post-revolutionary Egypt' (forthcoming article, 2015).

58. For practical reasons, the survey questions distinguished between literary genres but not between the different content within each genre. This could be a useful refinement in future research. However, it is worth remembering that post-structuralist approaches demonstrate that the meanings a consumer takes from a literary work are in any case not inherent in that work's content; rather, meaning is a product of the cultural formation of the consumer long before the act of consumption.

59. Jacquemond, '*The Yacoubian Building* and Its Sisters', pp. 146–7.

60. Tamim Al-Barghouti, 'Poetry and politics', keynote address, Cairo, Edinburgh World Writers Conference, 7 September 2013, http://www.edinburghworldwritersconference.org/should-literature-be-political/al-barghouti-in-egypt-keynote-on-should-literature-be-political/.

61. Youssef Rakha, 'The Heavenly Jeep', The Sultan's Seal blog, 2 April 2013, http://yrakha.com/2013/04/02/the-heavenly-jeep/.

Notes on the Contributors

Roger Allen is Emeritus Professor of Arabic and Comparative Literature, University of Pennsylvania.

Marilyn Booth is Khaled bin Abdullah Al Saud Professor of the Study of the Contemporary Arab World, University of Oxford.

Miriam Cooke is Braxton Craven Professor of Arab Cultures, Duke University.

Sabry Hafez is Distinguished Professor of Comparative Literature, University of Qatar, and Professor Emeritus of Modern Arabic and Comparative Literature, SOAS, University of London.

Derek Hopwood is Emeritus Fellow in Modern Middle Eastern Studies, St Antony's College, Oxford.

Abdul-Nabi Isstaif is Professor of Comparative Literature, Modern Criticism and Translation, University of Damascus.

Elisabeth Kendall is a Senior Research Fellow, Pembroke College, Oxford.

Hilary Kilpatrick is an independent scholar.

Mohamed Mahmoud is an independent scholar.

Robin Ostle is Emeritus Research Fellow in Modern Arabic, St John's College, Oxford.

Paul Starkey is Emeritus Professor in the Department of Arabic, Durham University.

Index

Note: page numbers in **bold** indicate illustrations